European Pensions & Global Finance

European Pensions & Global Finance

GORDON L. CLARK

OXFORD
UNIVERSITY PRESS

OXFORD
UNIVERSITY PRESS

Great Clarendon Street, Oxford OX2 6DP

Oxford University Press is a department of the University of Oxford.
It furthers the University's objective of excellence in research, scholarship,
and education by publishing worldwide in

Oxford New York

Auckland Bangkok Buenos Aires Cape Town Chennai
Dar es Salaam Delhi Hong Kong Istanbul Karachi Kolkata
Kuala Lumpur Madrid Melbourne Mexico City Mumbai Nairobi
São Paulo Shanghai Taipei Tokyo Toronto

Oxford is a registered trade mark of Oxford University Press
in the UK and in certain other countries

Published in the United States
by Oxford University Press Inc., New York

© Gordon L. Clark, 2003

The moral rights of the authors have been asserted
Database right Oxford University Press (maker)

First published 2003

British Library Cataloguing in Publication Data

Data available

Library of Congress Cataloging in Publication Data
Clark, Gordon L.
European pensions & global finance / Gordon L. Clark.
p. cm.
Includes bibliographical references and index.
1. Pension trusts—Europe—Case studies. 2. Retirement income—Europe—Case
studies. 3. Old age pensions—Europe—Finance—Case studies. 4. Social security—
Europe—Finance—Case studies. 5. International finance. I. Title.
HD7105.45 .E85 C55 2003 332.67'314—dc21 2002030360
ISBN 0-19-925363-3 (hbk.)
ISBN 0-19-925364-1 (pbk.)

1 3 5 7 9 10 8 6 4 2

Typeset by Newgen Imaging Systems (P) Ltd., Chennai, India
Printed in Great Britain
on acid-free paper by
Biddles Ltd., Guildford and King's Lynn

....

ABOUT THE AUTHOR

Gordon L. Clark is the Halford Mackinder Professor of Geography, Fellow of the Saïd Business School, and Faculty Associate of the Institute of Ageing at the University of Oxford, and is Fellow of St Peter's College, Oxford. He is a member of the Panel of Academic Experts of the UK National Association of Pension Funds and a Governor of the Pensions Policy Institute.

For Peter and Shirley

CONTENTS

LIST OF FIGURES

LIST OF TABLES

LIST OF ABBREVIATIONS

ASB	Accounting Standards Board (UK)
BEPG	Broad Economic Policy Guidelines (European Council)
CAPM	Capital Asset Pricing Model
CoE	Council of Europe
DB Plans	Defined Benefit or Final Salary (Pension) Plans
DC Plans	Defined Contribution or Accumulation (Pension) Plans
EC	European Commission
ECB	European Central Bank
ECJ	European Court of Justice (Luxembourg)
EFRP	European Federation for Retirement Provision (Brussels)
EMU	Economic and Monetary Union
ERISA	Employee Retirement Income Security Act (1974) (US federal statute)
ESRC	Economic and Social Research Council (UK)
ETIs	Economically Targeted Investments
EU	European Union
FASB	Financial Accounting Standards Board (US)
GDP	Gross Domestic Product
IASB	International Accounting Standards Board (or Committee as it was)
IFS	Institute of Fiscal Studies (an ESRC sponsored research institute at the University College, London)
ILO	International Labour Organisation
IMF	International Monetary Fund
IOSCO	International Organisation of Securities Commissions
MPT	Modern Portfolio Theory
NAPF	National Association of Pension Funds (UK)
OECD	Organisation for Economic Cooperation and Development (Paris)
PAYG	Pay-As-You-Go (a method of current funding of social security)
PBGC	Pension Benefit Guaranty Corporation (US)
SEC	Securities Exchange Commission (US)
UK	United Kingdom
US	United States of America

PREFACE

This book is about European pensions, using the phrase to refer to the various national social security and retirement income systems. For a European audience accustomed to believing that social security is a public institution with many complementary social functions, the looming pensions crisis is a most problematic phenomenon—it is an economic question, a demographic issue, and a crisis of confidence in the inherited social and political institutions. The introduction of the Euro, the slow integration of European and global financial markets, the forecast unfunded costs of paying for the retirement of the baby boom generation, and the budgetary constraints imposed by the Maastricht Treaty have conspired to undercut the legitimacy of a most important institution. As we shall see, however, this issue is not shared in the same way by France, Germany, the Netherlands and the United Kingdom (for example). In fact, one goal of the book is to show and account for the various ways in which these countries have responded to the pensions funding crisis. Nevertheless, just as the United Kingdom and the United States of America share many distinctive institutions and regulatory traditions so too do many of the leading countries of western Europe. Social solidarity, equitable incomes policies, and the sharing of power in public and private institutions are important commitments in many European countries.

For an Anglo-American audience accustomed to limited state-sponsored social security benefits, public and private supplementary pensions are very important beneficial institutions in their own right. Whereas continental European pension systems are typically comprehensive and universal benefit systems with high rates of income replacement upon retirement, these are not the basic principles underpinning the Anglo-American pension systems. Outside of mandatory social security, only about half of the working populations of the

United Kingdom and the United States of America are covered by supplementary pensions. Moreover, the nature and likely value of the supplementary pension benefits vary enormously by industry, occupation, and employer. There are exceptions, like Australia. In the main, a high income-replacement rate is hardly ever an official government policy except in a most abstract or idealized sense. Most importantly, the Anglo-American pension funds are important financial institutions in their own right, operating via the global financial services industry at the very centre of the traded regional, national, and international economies. This is hardly a new observation, although told in a variety of ways witness Michael Clowes' *The Money Flood*, Hawley and Williams' *The Rise of Fiduciary Capitalism* and my own *Pension Fund Capitalism*. Pension funds drive stock markets, just as they have been important in driving economic innovation and the knowledge economy via venture capital investment in regions such as the Silicon Valley and the Rt128 Boston.

In large part, this book is also about the intersection of, and rivalry between, the European pension systems and the global financial industry located in London and New York. For many financial analysts, the European pensions crisis is simply an issue of institutional obsolescence. Whereas the state-sponsored pay-as-you-go (PAYG) was once an appropriate 'solution' to post-war retirement income provision, it is now neither viable in its own right nor is it plausible against the better alternative: Anglo-American public and private pension institutions. Therefore, it is claimed, the proper issue is one of managing the transition to a version of the Anglo-American model rather than remaining committed to the past. There are also many financial analysts who believe European countries are obsessively nationalistic. It is claimed that Europe protects relatively inefficient financial institutions from the harsh light cast by global financial competition; the claimed failure of continental European countries to adopt the Anglo-American pension systems is another instance of economic nationalism (and a willingness to make citizens inside and outside of Europe pay the costs of inefficiency). It is clear that the political economy of globalization is, in part, about the contested powers of nation-states in relation to the enormous leverage of the Anglo-American financial institutions.

I do not think the proper response of the European nations to the looming demographic and pensions funding crisis is to jettison the past. Just because the Anglo-American economies have quite different systems of retirement income provision combining funded and unfunded elements does not mean that continental Europe should simply copy the alternative model. There are many aspects of continental European pension and retirement income systems that deserve our respect. Comparing, for example, current retirees' incomes across Europe in relation to the United Kingdom and the United States of America is surely enough to remind the reader that there is little virtue in the gross inequalities of income and old age poverty. History and geography remain essential ingredients in any comprehensive understanding of the contemporary responses to the problems of funding the retirement of the baby-boom generation. Furthermore, it would be quite misleading to imagine that continental European systems have not adapted and accommodated elements of the Anglo-American model. One goal of the book is to demonstrate that the past is not necessarily the future. There are many instances of European policy response and innovation, combining the past (e.g., a commitment to social solidarity) with the future (global finance and capitalism).

This brings us to an important juncture—where the book fits in terms of topic, discipline, and audience. While I have made every effort to take account of the history and distinctive status of the national retirement income systems, it should be clear from the outset that this book is neither about that history nor is it about the deeply entrenched social and political alliances that sustain such systems. There are remarkably good histories available, and there is a veritable mountain of material on comparative welfare policy and its institutional incarnations. Throughout, I rely upon and refer to that material. But on many of these issues, I willingly defer to my more knowledgeable colleagues and friends. By contrast, I believe the book has much to add to our contemporary understanding of the role and status of European pension systems in relation to the financial imperatives driving globalization. In this sense, the book is an economic geography and political economy of the changing pension systems; in flux are whole systems of social organization and their economic and territorial structure. Here, I develop related insights drawing upon the methods of these two branches of the social sciences.

My interest here is in the scale of economic life, especially the nation-state relative to the global economy. I aim to show that whatever the significance of a bottom-up approach, we should also be concerned about the penetration of global finance down into the national systems of finance and corporate and institutional governance. Most obviously, the book is organized so as to facilitate this process of geographic and political analysis and argument. We begin with separate statements about the issues and methodology (Chapter 1), the pensions crisis and points of tension (Chapter 2). This leads on to separate chapters on French social solidarity and the challenges posed by global finance (Chapter 3), the transformation of large German firms, their pension systems and co-determination in relation to global financial imperatives (Chapters 4 and 5), the governance of Dutch pension funds and their place in the European market for financial services (Chapter 6), and then the role that London plays in the global flow of funds and management of investments (Chapter 7). The last chapter brings these threads together (Chapter 8).

A book such as this has immediate disciplinary and cross-disciplinary audiences. As it is about economic geography and political economy, it fits with the burgeoning and linked research fields of finance, globalization, and systems of institutional governance. I hope it will allow those concerned about European welfare to better understand what is currently 'in play', what has changed over the past decade, and what may be the shape of things to come. Even so, I do not intend to broker a rapprochement between the global finance and continental European traditions. Indeed, I recognize that my argument about European pensions and the intersection between national pension systems and global finance may be quite controversial for some. I have been fortunate to receive many critical and perceptive comments on my arguments, even if some critics have accused me of an Anglo-American bias and an unwillingness to consider deeply rooted and justly held national sentiments. I concede that my arguments and interpretations take sides in the debate over the future of European pensions, recognizing that I take seriously the challenge posed by global finance, its institutions and its imperatives.

However, I do not mean to imply or suggest that global finance is the proper solution to the demographic and pensions funding crisis, nor do I mean to suggest that the imperatives driving accommodation (at least) or convergence (at the limit) in pension systems are themselves unproblematic and virtuous. But I do mean to suggest that the global finance option should be taken seriously and I do mean to suggest that many continental European pension systems will find it very difficult to provide beneficiaries the level and value of benefits promised to successive generations over the last fifty years. No one gains by remaining silent on these issues, just as a broad as well as a deep understanding of the relevant issues enriches public debate. In fact, silence is worse than ignorance; silence is the enemy of knowledge and policy making. If globalization and European integration gathers pace we may be at the start of an era of national and European reimagination. What we have inherited, what was built over the past fifty years, and what can be learnt from others has been jumbled together into a cauldron of change. This is one future of the European economic political life.

One point of argument and terminology should be noted. Throughout, I refer to country-specific institutions of social security, and whole blocks of countries like continental Europe and the Anglo-American world. As suggested in the chapters on France, Germany, and the Netherlands, there are distinctive elements in each just as there are significant differences between the United Kingdom and the United States of America. Where appropriate, I take the reader into the detail of each country's institutions. And yet, the book is less about each country's social welfare institutions than it is about the interaction between these institutions, whole nation-states, and the forces of global finance. In general, I tend to use interchangeably and across countries terms such as social security, social insurance, and social welfare blurring differences and eliding distinctions. Likewise, I refer to the Anglo-American model, neo-liberalism, and market imperatives in a similar vein. Even so, I hope the book remains sensitive to the distinctive traditions of each country.

ACKNOWLEDGEMENTS

Three different research grants helped take the project from preliminary thoughts to fruition. Especially important was an Economic and Social Research Council (L215 26 2026) grant held with Professor Adam Tickell from the University of Bristol. Our participation in the ESRC Future Governance programme managed by Professor Edward Page at LSE was vital in securing the core components of the research. Also important was support through a European Union (SOE1-CT98-11114; Project 053) grant on corporate governance and finance managed by Professors William Lazonick and Mary O'Sullivan at INSEAD (Fontainbleau). Finally, my own European Union (HPSE-1999-CT-00035) grant on European competitiveness and regional economic development provided resources for on-going conversation with Paul Tracey and Helen Lawton Smith about comparative studies and the future of Europe.

Initial support for the project was provided by the AIG Financial Products Corp. Robert Hirst, Kris Mansson, and Joe Cassano encouraged me to travel throughout Europe learning firsthand from all kinds of industry, company, and government respondents about the challenges facing European pensions and retirement income systems. Also early in the project, I benefited from many conversations with Joel Chernoff then the London correspondent for *Pensions & Investments*. Joel (now in San Francisco) and Mike Clowes (the Executive Editor in New York) have been always welcoming and encouraging sources for contacts and information. Likewise, Fennell Bentson at *Investments & Pensions Europe* was an important reference point for information while sharing networks and contacts. Not least of all has been the institutional support of the University of Oxford. The University provided me with sabbatical leave at a crucial juncture in the project, and then provided sabbatical leave for the completion of the book.

At this point, I would like to recognize the help provided by Chris Verhaegen from the European Federation for Retirement Provision in Brussels. She was generous with her time as well as her own contacts and thoughts about the issues involving the European Union and its member states. In this regard, also significant were the advice and comments from the European Commission staff (Brussels) in the economics and finance directorate, the competition directorate, the employment and social affairs directorate, the single market director-ate, and the taxation directorate. Following on from these contacts, I am especially pleased to acknowledge the help of Minister Yannis Pottaki, and staff at the Council of Europe (Strasbourg). At the OECD, Monika Quiesser and Peter Scherer (social policy), André Laboul and Juan Yermo (insurance and pensions), and Allan Fels, Bernard Phillips, and the staff of the competition policy group all provided willing commentary and helpful ideas.

I have conducted many formal and less formal interviews for the project, involving over one hundred different people. The issues cov-ered in these interviews and related methodological issues are noted in the Appendix. I would like to recognize, moreover, the help of a number of key individuals who opened the doors so to speak to their own networks and contacts. Especially important was Beat Hotz-Hart's introduction to Werner Nussbaum in Switzerland. Werner proved to be an especially enthusiastic guide to the Swiss pension industry and its various institutions. Likewise, Harry Wolf and Karl Stiefferman in Germany, Robert Boyer in France, Karel Lannoo in Belgium, Chris Verhaegen and Sean Kelly for the Netherlands, and Pierre-Marie Valenne in Luxembourg gave freely of their own advice and invaluable contacts. In the United Kingdom, I was pleased to have the help of the National Association of Pension Funds and, in particular, the initial interest and support of David Hart and John Rogers.

I have also benefited from talking to many industry respondents. Gareth Derbyshire, Alan Rubenstein (London), and Peter Koenig (Frankfurt) from Morgan Stanley Dean Witter have been an interested and encouraging audience. Also Mike Orszag and Roger Urwin from Watson Wyatt, and Don Ezra and John Gillies at Frank Russell helped with comments and advice. Likewise, I have benefited greatly from the comments of email correspondents on my web posted papers, espe-cially from those networks managed by Mike Orszag (pensions@ yahoogroups.com) and Wayne Marr (ssrn.com). All these venues pro-vided commentary and discussion helping me to refine the points at issue. Most importantly, at a crucial juncture in the writing phase of the project I had the benefit of detailed comments and advice from Ronald Dore and Noel Whiteside. They offered challenging but supportive comments on the entire project. Likewise, I received useful comments on the completed manuscript from Sir Howard Davies, Robert Fenge, Ben Fischer, and Alicia Munnell. This kind of generous help should be underestimated in terms of its academic value even if I have not been able to do justice to all their insights and misgivings.

Closer to home, I should thank Jane Battersby, Dan Mansfield, Zoe Morrison, Chloe Flutter, Dariusz Wojcik, Isla Wright, and Merridy Wilson for their willing and able research assistance as well as for their perspicuous intellectual intervention in some of the crucial arguments made during the writing-up process. Less directly but no less importantly, I would like to thank Esther Howard and David Merrill, Michelle Lowe and Neil Wrigley, Linda and Nigel Thrift, and Adam Tickell for their friendship and my Oxford colleagues at the School of Geography and the Environment (Colin Clarke and Andrew Goudie), the Saïd Business School (Anthony Hopwood and Colin Mayer), and the Institute for Ageing (Sarah Harper) for their encouragement. Not least in my thoughts, I should thank Jan Burke for her dedicated assistance in making possible the research process that underpins the book. She was truly inspirational in setting-up interviews, making and sustaining contacts, and transcribing what has become a veritable library of sources and interviews. She took garbled commentary and made it into a coherent argument. For all that, and many other instances of support, my thanks go to her.

Whatever the particular interests, goals, and objectives of the various sponsoring institutions and helpful informants and colleagues, the opinions expressed in this book are mine entirely. I have no personal stake or interest in any of the firms, institutions, and government organizations interviewed or analysed. I stand by accepted national and international social science codes of research practice, and recognize that the status of the so-called 'independent' research on the 'sell-side' of the finance industry is subject to justifiable doubts about its integrity. I do have a long-term interest in the stability and growth of global finance since my family and I are future beneficiaries of employer-sponsored retirement funds: one a US defined contribution fund (TIAA/CREF) and the other a UK defined benefit fund (USS). However, nothing I say in this book will affect either the performance of those funds or indeed the future value of promised benefits. Indeed, I am very uncertain about the value and longevity of those retirement benefits.

I should also acknowledge the following publishers for permission to republish revised versions of papers that first appeared in scholarly journals. Specifically, Taylor and Francis for Gordon L. Clark 'European pensions and global finance: continuity or convergence?' in *New Political Economy* (2002) 7: 67–91 http://www.tandf.co.uk; Pion Limited, London for Gordon L. Clark 'Requiem for a national ideal? Social solidarity, the crisis of French social security and the role of global financial markets' in *Environment and Planning A* (2001) 33: 2003–24 and Gordon L. Clark and Paul Bennett 'The Dutch model of sector-wide supplementary pensions: fund governance, finance and European competition policy' in *Environment and Planning A* (2001) 33: 27–48; Clark University for Gordon L. Clark, Daniel Mansfield, and Adam Tickell 'Emergent frameworks in global finance: accounting standards and German supplementary pensions' in *Economic Geography* (2001) 77: 250–71; the Royal Geographical Society for Gordon L. Clark, Daniel Mansfield, and Adam Tickell 'Global finance and the German model: German corporations, market incentives, and the management of employer-sponsored pension institutions' in *Transactions*, Institute of British Geographers (2002) NS 27: 91–110; and Oxford University Press for Gordon L. Clark 'London's Place in the World of Finance: A Supply-side Approach' in *Journal of Economic Geography* (2002) 2.

Finally, I would like to thank, once again, Shirley and Peter for their commitment, for encouraging and supporting my travel and pre-occupation with the project in all its manifestations and all its venues! With all my love…

Oxford, September 2002   Gordon L. Clark

1

Introduction: The Nation-State in the Twenty-First Century

There was a time, not so long ago, when the nation-state represented the boundaries of social life. From post-war reconstruction and the long drawn-out cold war to the remarkable revolutions in Eastern Europe and the former Soviet Union about a decade ago, the nation-state was the most important unit of geopolitics and social life. Indeed, for the baby boom generation having been brought up according to this logic and apparent necessity, the fragility of the nation-state during the nineteenth and early twentieth centuries seems inconceivable. One's opportunities and life chances are derived from and then inscribed upon the territory of nations. With so much of the twentieth century focused upon national politics, culture and society, it is an essential reference point in understanding people's aspirations and prospects. Who would reasonably think otherwise?

At the core of the western nation-state have been two more or less significant institutions: the social contract, representing a formal or informal agreement amongst classes and interest groups regarding the distribution of income and opportunities, and the social welfare system, representing the aspirations and expectations of many citizens regarding their long-term welfare including their likely retirement incomes. For those responsible for the funding and management of state-sponsored social security, these two institutions are intimately connected. Consider the comments made by Reynaud (2000: 1) from the International Labour Organization (ILO). Whatever the nature of pension systems, 'modern societies' have relied upon 'various forms of consultation, negotiation, and public debate' to make decisions about the tension between long-term resources and expenditures and hence the value of social security benefits. Furthermore, a comparative analysis of social security systems must be sensitive to the fact that they 'are the product of the societies concerned and inevitably reflect a series of specific characteristics, especially concerning the relationship between the State and society, political traditions, industrial relations, structure of the economy, and perceptions of justice and equality' (Reynaud 2000: 8).

The idea of the social contract is widely debated in western societies. For many Europeans, the social contract is as much a fact as it is an ideal. But for many Anglo-Americans the ideal has given way to claims of individual autonomy and separate benefit. Anglo-American societies are, by any recent account, liberal rather than social democratic. The social contract is a theoretical instrument rather than a lived reality (as exemplified by Rawls 1971). By contrast, continental European citizens hold to its principles even if the middle classes and those on the margins of society increasingly doubt its functional value. Like national social security systems, we might suppose that national social contracts are the product of history and geography; representing the accumulated circumstances of each and every country, mediated by economic and political events but nonetheless resolved according to citizens' aspirations regarding their rights and entitlements. Hence, whatever the differences between nation-states regarding the funding and value of social security benefits, those differences are deeply embedded in the distinctive traditions of these countries. Therefore, to 'reform' European social security would be to 'reform' the very structure and organization of each society—a daunting prospect.

Social security systems are very complex, are highly regulated, and are increasingly the dominant component of western governments' budgets. Not only are there considerable differences between countries in terms of the current funding and value of social-security benefits, some systems are inclusive (bringing together a wide range of social welfare functions including unemployment, sickness, and disability benefits) while other systems are exclusive (distinguishing long-term retirement income from other forms of assistance, which may or may not be provided by the nation-state). Witness Gillion *et al.*'s (2000) compendium on social security and its variants. Accounting for these differences is a basic responsibility of the disciplines of social administration, sociology, and political science. Indeed, some of the most important contributions to the field of comparative studies have been made by those concerned to understand the differences between systems while accounting for their roots in common western social traditions. See the survey edited by Clasen (1999), the seminal contributions by Esping-Andersen (1990, 1999), and the recent most remarkable empirical analysis of these systems by Goodin *et al.* (1999).

Some social analysts, and many political interests, would like to hold history constant. What we have inherited from the past, the social and political institutions that developed alongside the welfare state and national social-security systems, ought to go forward into the future as they came from the past. By this account, these institutions represent the achievements of the twentieth-century progressive struggles for greater equity and justice. By this account, the benefits of these institutions are properly about to be realized with the retirement of the baby boom generation. During the course of this research project, and in conversation with continental European Social Democrats, these views were expressed often and with great force. Further, the difference between systems were often idealized to the point where protecting inherited difference was designated as the object of political struggle; to be sustained in the face of Anglo-American claims to the contrary. For many, difference is the legitimate result of systematic territorial political processes; the separate circumstances of nation-states mediated through the political process. In this sense, it may be argued that nation-state 'solutions' to social welfare problems are at the proper geographical scale at which to negotiate peoples' well-being.[1]

Deeply embedded in this argument is an 'organic' conception of the relationship between people and their nation-state—an intimate and finely textured connection between people, their territory, and institutional forms. It is an idea that links culture and consciousness, language and subjectivity to certain places being invoked, more often than not, as the bedrock of nationhood. This idea, of course, has a long history stretching back over the past millennium; see, for example, Simon Schama's (1996) argument regarding European national identity and the landscape. At the same time, it can be found in the various national social movements of the twentieth century. While it is tempting to suppose that it is an idea related to the 'extremes' of communism and fascism, it is also invoked time and time again by those seeking to hold the forces of change at bay; witness, for example, British anxieties about the proper relationship between Britain and Europe. Ontologically, however, this is difficult to accept. Notwithstanding the development of different cultures and institutions, I wonder about the existence of profoundly different 'national' psychologies—in any event, material life is a powerful driving force providing an important means of explaining European differentiation.

Given the enormous global competitive pressures being brought to bear upon European institutions of retirement income, I am sympathetic to claims in favour of national solutions to justice and equity. My disagreement with those who advocate the inviolability of 'national' solutions to retirement income problems, is a disagreement about the reality of the national institutional capacity and responsibility. In a stronger vein, there are others who suppose that presumptions in favour of national solutions are a 'primitive' conception of the role of the nation-state in Europe. As Weiler (2000: 1) notes, over the past 25 years or so national elites have sought to fashion an economically and politically integrated European Union (EU), giving up national sovereignty over a wide range of issues including economic and monetary policy making. Has the time passed for national social contracts and national systems of social security?

SOLIDARITY IN THE TWENTY-FIRST CENTURY

As noted above, Esping-Andersen's (1990) path-breaking study underpins much of the current research on European social welfare. And yet if we reread his conclusions one is struck by the fact that he believed that what was inherited from the post-war era of social welfare institution building was in flux. More than a decade ago he noted that 'ours is an epoch in which it is almost universally agreed that a profound realignment, if not revolution, is under way in our economy and society' (Esping-Andersen 1990: 222). From that observation he goes on to sketch the various ways in which the social institutions of the industrial revolution were being remade by the imperatives driving 'the post-industrial society.' He returns to this theme in his latest book (Esping-Andersen 1999) arguing that one crucial institution—the household—is particularly significant in this on-going transformation linking gender and the family with work and the changing nature of the welfare state.

In his earlier book, Esping-Andersen reminded readers that the welfare state is a corollary of the industrial development, structuring and organizing the economy as the latter provides a framework for the welfare state itself. To illustrate, he used examples from Sweden, Germany, and the United States of America. He sought to demonstrate that the particular design of the welfare state provides social agents scope for action while limiting options and opportunities, thereby structuring the responses to economic change. He documented this point by noting that the Swedish welfare state provided incentives for the growing female labour force participation and their employment. In the German case, by contrast, he argued that the welfare state was a means of income maintenance for those in the workforce, but also a system of exclusion for those outside the workforce. And in the US case, he suggested that the mosaic of institutions, governments, and policies that are the 'welfare state' have prompted the growth of a dual economy characterized by a distinct separation between those in the core of the economy (with high salaries and benefits) and those in the non-core of the economy (with poor conditions of work and wages).

Ten years on from his (1990) analysis there can be little doubt about his clear-sighted understanding of the imperatives and incentives embedded in the different welfare state systems. Even if he now voices unease about the scope of those arguments, it could be argued that he underestimated the success of the US model during the 1990s and discounts its successes (in terms of employment creation) now. While no doubt correct in arguing that the US economy has become a dual economy in terms of the value and benefits of employment, the rate of growth in employment during the 1990s far surpassed the rate of growth of employment in continental Europe. Furthermore, high rates of female participation in the workforce combined with higher rates of female employment have contributed enormously to the growth of the household income. Of course, household income is different from the average workers' income. These measures ignore the increasingly adverse distribution of income in the US economy. The success of the US model has been accompanied by a rapidly increasing wage and salary inequality, especially if we consider the segmentation of jobs according to the value of wage-related benefits including the provision of retirement income.

Writing at the end of the 1980s, Esping-Andersen was unclear as to the likely trajectory of the various models surveyed in his book. In conclusion, he argued that welfare-state capitalism may be 'heading towards three diverse post-industrial' welfare-state models. This idea of a persistent diversity was taken-up through the 1990s by social science analysts and scholars concerned to show that social institutions like the welfare state and social security are deeply embedded in the history and geography of nations. Expressions of this intellectual agenda can be found across the social sciences including economics, geography, political science, and sociology.[2] Ideas like path dependence and embeddedness provide a ready language of theory and argument (see Crouch and Streeck 1997). On the other hand, he also indicated that unexpected events might prompt rapprochement between systems. It has become increasingly difficult to sustain exclusive definitions of the various types of welfare states, such has been the pace of mutual incremental adjustment within and between systems. Nevertheless, it should be noted that the relatively poor performance of many continental economies in terms of the unemployment, employment growth, rates of labour force participation (especially amongst women and younger people), and average real income growth compared to the United States of America and the United Kingdom has put enormous pressure on the largest continental European countries to reform further (see Chapter 2).

In this context, there can be little doubt that the Anglo-American model of economy, finance, and the welfare state poses a serious threat to the perceived integrity of continental European traditions.[3] At one level, it might be argued that this threat is also ideological as it is about real circumstances and institutions. Even if this were to be the case, there can be little doubt that the virtues of the Anglo-American model have become essential weapons used by the European elites in their arguments in favour of institutional reform and greater capital market and labour market flexibility. Indeed, it could also be argued that the relative performance of the continental European economies during the 1990s provided economic policy makers in key European, French, and German institutions, the means of legitimizing the centralization of economic policy making and the increasing scrutiny of nation-state decision-making (as evidenced by the status and significance of the Stability and Growth Pact ratified by the Amsterdam Treaty; for a critical assessment see Hine 2001).

If these appear to be issues of national and European politics and policy-making, a decade after Esping-Andersen's initial study numerous reports have been written documenting the development of post-industrialization and all that entails for the fragmentation of the continental European welfare states. For example, Supiot's (2001) report on employment law, collective bargaining, and solidarity is premised on the assumption that post-industrialization represents a profound challenge to the inherited institutions of the twentieth century. Most importantly, the high rates of labour turnover, the outsourcing of functions otherwise held internal to large organizations, the degradation of apprenticeships and training systems, and moves towards greater flexibility of wages and salaries are taken to be indicative of the increasing decentralization and dis-intermediation of national social norms and customs. Even the much vaunted 35 hour week introduced by the French Socialist government to redistribute employed time through the creation of more jobs, can be interpreted as a supply-side policy aimed at increasing the plant and firm levels flexibility so as to encourage labour productivity (Flutter 2001).

All these issues are widely debated among the various institutions that make up the EU and beyond. The nature and consequences of these changes for the integrity of the national welfare state systems is a vital test of social science theory and practice. Here, I do not intend to adjudicate between those who argue that the effects of post-industrialization and dis-intermediation have been exaggerated against those who suggest that the integrity of nation-state welfare systems is being undercut from within and without. My view tends towards the latter camp as opposed to the former: like Esping-Andersen and others, I believe that the accelerating changes in the nature, structure, and organization of social formation and work have raised serious doubts about the long-term future of institutions designed in the middle twentieth century to cope with the immediate effects of post-war reconstruction. As we shall see, these issues have been given a greater urgency by the demographic ageing of European populations, and the need to reform in some fashion or another the formula and value of promised retirement benefits. The future of nation-state social security has become a crucial part of the argument about the nature and pro-spects for European economic growth and integration; ideas such as institutional persistence often appear as rear-guard actions designed to check the political forces of nation-state dis-intermediation and European centralization.

These issues dominate Supiot's (2001) report, and include the declining status of collective institutions such as the unions, joint boards of management, and forums of consultation and collective negotiation. These institutions continue to claim our respect for their historic roles in the industry and society; we should be wary of any argument to the effect that these collective institutions have been discounted in the same way as similar organizations in the Anglo-American world. On the other hand, there is an increasing unease about their isolation from important sources of innovation and eco-nomic development in continental Europe. Furthermore, their histor-ical association with particular industry segments, firms, and systems of management appear to be at odds with the imperatives driving the so-called 'new' industries and organizations. Accommodation can be made. Indeed, Supiot's report is all about remaking these collective institutions in ways that are consistent with the changing nature and organization of work. However, to the extent to which rapprochement has been slow, uneven, or insignificant than the combination of economic change and demographic change, the financial imperatives accompanying both threaten these institutions and their continuing status in European societies. This is a vital theme that runs through the entire book.

To illustrate, the post-war model of economic development based on a national framework for accumulation and political representation has been challenged by the emergence of local and regional economies capitalizing upon their own particular advantages while reaching out into the global economy (Cooke and Morgan 1998). This much is apparent in what are termed regional clusters of innovation, centres of economic change that concentrate in one place or set of related places the forces of economic development. One often-quoted instance is the Third Italy; a model of economic growth that is more often than not built around networks of small firms with very particular modes of organization and management running parallel (at best) or in direct conflict (at worst) with the dominant nation-state systems of accumulation and regulation. Such clusters of innovation tend to be based on intensive transactions and communications either at the local level, or similar extensive systems that bypass nations reaching out to the global economy. In this respect, formal, well regulated, and hierarchical nation-state systems of economy and society appear to be at odds with the new model of economic growth. This realization dominated the Lisbon Declaration (2000) about European job creation and industrial and geographical patterns of economic development.

At the same time, the geographical scope of European firms and their related organizations is broadening and deepening. The nation-state is no longer the boundary limiting market size and potential. Pan-European, international, and indeed global market opportunities beckon those firms capable of responding. Equally, competition from elsewhere in Europe and from the rest of the world threatens those firms, industries, and institutional relationships that are unable to respond. Inevitably, as mergers and acquisitions have accelerated industry competition and the emergence of larger and larger firms capable of operating across the world, these same firms have begun to question the efficacy of inherited domestic institutions. In this respect, the issue of solidarity looms large: to whom do such corporations owe their allegiance? To what extent are the past arrangements of power sharing, collective deliberation, and negotiation consistent with the geographical scope of action now available to corporate executives? In this book, Chapters 4 and 5 are devoted to this question focusing upon large German corporations and their changing relationships with global finance, shareholders, and workers.

In effect, we must recognize a world in which social solidarity is increasingly at odds with the nation-state. Solidarity may be found within a firm and between its stakeholders, solidarity may be found within a region as opposed to the nation, and solidarity may be found amongst individuals as opposed to the nation. For those knowledgeable of southern Mediterranean countries, this kind of downscaling or dis-intermediation of social solidarity will not be surprising. For many years, the building blocks of southern Europe have been the family and community rather than the national systems of economic and social solidarity. National institutions have held an uneasy and oftentimes barely recognized status in many regions of the south.[4] What we imagine to be an organic and integrated nation-state able to manage the economy and social solidarity in favour of the long-term welfare of its citizens is open to question.

SOVEREIGNTY AND MONETARY UNION

Writing before the tidal wave of commentary on demographic ageing and the funding of social security, Esping-Andersen (1990) recognized that the nation-state as the embodiment of social welfare was under threat. More than a decade later, in the midst of global economic crisis and ongoing political debate about the integrity of national social-security institutions, there are increasing tensions between the older and younger citizens. As the baby boom looks forward to retirement, the younger workers are alarmed by the long-term economic and tax burdens of promised benefits. Furthermore, even if many citizens support the inherited social-security institutions these same citizens have lost faith in the capacity of these institutions to deliver long-term retirement income. Not surprisingly, middle-class defection in the form of the consumption of related insurance and financial products has come out into the open. In making these observations, I am simply recording the obvious—we go into detail about these propositions in the following chapters (see Chapter 3 on the French system). My point is entirely straightforward: more than at any other time since the Second World War, nation-state social solidarity is fragile and highly contested.

If the coherence and integrity of nation-state social-security institutions are under attack from within, at the other end of the spectrum the evolving single-market and European Monetary Union (EMU) have also undercut the capacity of the nation-state to sustain 'national' welfare solutions. By deliberately conceding 'authority' to the EU and ultimately the European Commission (EC) over matters such as budget deficits and surpluses and the value of national currencies, nation-states have also given up claims of autonomy with respect to the funding and structure of their social-security institutions. National fiscal policy initiatives are increasingly set within previously agreed European parameters particularly the Maastricht Treaty and the consequent Stability and Growth Pact. The major European nations have exchanged sovereignty for leverage in the bargaining process over the shape and structure of the evolving European economy. In doing so, however, they have had to accept an external scrutiny of their actions against these parameters. If, as Reynaud (2000) suggests, social-security institutions 'are the product of the societies concerned' this seems an increasingly doubtful claim about European nation-state sovereignty.

As originally conceived, the Stability and Growth Pact was a means of managing member states' governmental budgets, consistent with the monetary union and ultimately the introduction of the Euro in 1999. In its Resolution, the EC explicitly linked 'budgetary discipline' to the economic and monetary union, and more generally associated 'sound government finances' with price stability, sustainable economic growth, and employment creation. In doing so, the Pact provided that member states should deal with the 'normal cyclical fluctuations by keeping the government deficit within the reference value of three per cent of the GDP' (Amsterdam, 27th June 1997; 97/C 236/01). The Resolution also set out seven itemized obligations of member states with respect to the stability and budgetary policy, including an obligation to take 'corrective budgetary action' in circumstances where excessive deficits may arise or be forecast. Similarly, with respect to the Commission the Resolution set out five itemized obligations consistent with ensuring 'the strict timely, and effective functioning of the ... Pact'. To sustain the Pact, the Resolution of the European Council made 'sound government finances' an explicit member state treaty obligation.

The penalties to be imposed upon member states that failed to adhere to their obligations under the Stability and Growth Pact were rather abstract, given the recurrent tensions between member states and the EC over these issues. Not surprisingly, the abstract nature of sanctions dominates academic discussions about the plausibility of the Growth Pact as an instrument of policy making (Eichengreen 1997). See also Beetsma and Uhlig (1999) on the economic issues as well as the policy issues from a variety of competing perspectives. As well, the implications of the Pact's golden rule for public investment have been extensively discussed. And again, not withstanding recognition of the political importance of the resolution, doubts have been raised about its plausibility as an economic rule of policy making (Balassone and Franco 2000). In any event, until recently the Pact operated in rather benign circumstances; its integrity and, by implication, the integrity of the Euro has been closely scrutinised by global financial markets in the early years of the first decade of the twenty-first century as recession threatens nations' budgetary circumstances.

Despite the doubts about the structure of the Stability Pact, it is a significant public process of scrutiny and accountability (Forder 2001). So, for example, in its opinion on the German stability programme for the period 1999–2003, the Council focused upon the medium-term budgetary position and the plausibility of an assumed annual growth rate of 2.5 per cent over the programme period (C 098, 6/4/2000). As the Council focused upon the gross debt ratio, it also focused upon the structure of German government spending and the necessity for reforms in the financing and administration of pension and health care systems. In a subsequent published review, the Council further recommended that the German government undertake reforms so as to 'render the labour market more flexible'. The Council again identified the forecast long-term debt associated with the 'ageing of the German population' (C 374/3, 28/12/2000). These themes are repeated in the Council's assessment of the French stability programme (C 111, 18/4/2000). Although, at that time, there was a more favourable budgetary situation compared to the German situation, the Council focused upon 'the problem of relatively high rate government expenditure' and its impacts upon economic efficiency. In a detailed assessment of France, the Council also emphasized the problems of financing pensions and retirement income.

The Stability Pact is one element of a larger and more comprehensive programme of economic integration and policy coordination (Portes 2001).[5] For example, at the Lisbon meeting of the European Council in

2000, the Broad Economic Policy Guidelines (BEPG) were adopted that focused on particular policies whose aim has been to promote economic growth and job creation. In this context, it might be argued that the overwhelming thrust of this initiative has been to sustain the efficiency of European product markets, capital markets, and labour markets. When linked to an overarching commitment to innovation and technological change, consistent with the new economy or what the EU would term the 'knowledge-based society', the BEPG process like the Stability Pact has been a process of setting targets, of monitoring progress towards targets, and their public scrutiny. Again and again, assessments by the EC of the performance of member states and their governments with respect to the BEPG return to the issue of the enhancing of the 'quality and sustainability of public finances'. And not surprisingly the EC identifies long-term pension and social security liabilities as a basic impediment standing in the way of achieving that goal. See especially the European Commission (EC) (2001a) report on the implementation of the BEPG and the related recommendations of the EC (2001b) for the coming year.

Many factors have sustained the drive towards policy coordination amongst member states, including the complex relations between the French and German leaders (Dyson and Featherstone 1999). 'Sound' monetary policies focused upon stabilizing government expenditure both with respect to the cyclical fluctuations and the long-term obligations have by many accounts undercut the viability of the European social model. A most important element has surely been the relative performance of the Euro in relation to the goals of European monetary integration. In Figure 1.1, the relative value of the Euro is set against the UK pound, the US dollar and a number of other currencies over the last five years. Until recently, it is apparent that the value of the Euro appears driven by long-term discounting against the two Anglo-American currencies. How and why this is the case are the subjects of extensive debate and argument in academic, policy, and financial market circles.[6] At this point, it is not my intention to offer an original or profound observation about the ultimate causes and consequences of the value of the Euro. However, it should be noted that many commentators suggest that the Euro's value is symptomatic of a more general valuation of Europe's economic flexibility, relative opportunities, and future prospects. Perhaps paradoxically, any increase in the value of the Euro (c.f. US dollar) may only add to Europe's problems of *global* competitiveness.

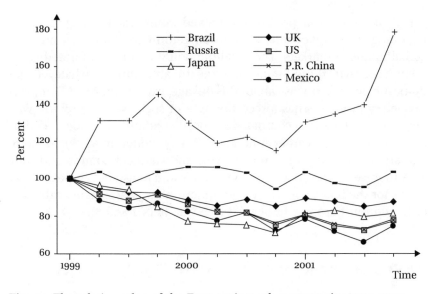

Fig. 1.1. The relative value of the Euro against other currencies, 1999–2002.

In this context, the views of the European Central Bank (ECB) assume considerable importance; see the September 26th, 2001, comments of Willem Duisenberg in Gothenburg (Sweden) on the new world of advanced communications and globalization.[7] Beginning with the entirely obvious and uncontested remarks about the demographic ageing of Europe (developed further in Chapter 2), he went on to associate the long-term financial burdens of the Pay-As-You-Go (PAYG) social security systems that dominate continental Europe with the management of governments' budgets and fiscal options. He suggested that 'debt financing' is not an option, and that any delay in pension reform will inevitably 'require higher risk premia on new debt'. He might also have said that the risk premia implied by existing pension obligations is such that the value of the Euro is, in part, a cost attributed by financial markets against the economic growth potential of Europe. Of course, it is more complicated than this—any one who pretends that there is such a simple and singular explanation behind currency values ignores the less than fundamental aspects of market-based herd behaviour (witness the boom, bubble, and bust of the new economy foretold by Shiller 2000 amongst others). Even so, there can be little doubt about the shared consensus amongst European policy makers that the management of government spending and debt requires a fundamental reform of European pension systems.

Left unexplored at present are related points made by Duisenberg regarding the implications of pension reform for European and the global financial markets. There is little doubt amongst informed commentators that these issues are inextricably linked; whatever the domestic political unease about this linkage, expert control of European budgetary processes has forced the pace of social security reform well beyond the slogans accompanying social solidarity and social democracy (Dyson and Featherstone 1999). Barely hidden in all this rhetoric and argument about reform is the role and status of London and New York in the emerging new world of finance and pensions. These are vital topics for the book, and in the end underpin our assessment of the role of London in Europe and beyond (see Chapters 7 and 8).

REFORM (PARAMETRIC AND STRUCTURAL)

In the mid-1990s, the UK House of Commons convened hearings on the prospects for European social security and the necessity for reform. At that time, policy analysts inside and outside of Parliament identified the continental European pension liabilities as likely future enormous burdens upon the citizens of each country and possibly Europe in general. Indeed, coming after the failure of the European exchange rate mechanism (ERM) and cautious assessment of the prospects for a European monetary union (EMU) these looming liabilities were said to be 'unsustainable' and a threat to the UK economic integrity.[8] Reform was needed and needed urgently. And yet little confidence was placed on the likelihood of reform. This view dominates the Anglo-American literature on continental European pensions and social security. If there is one thing that unites the disparate and often competing perspectives on the consequences of demographic ageing it is a pessimistic attitude regarding the prospects for reform of the continental European social-security systems.[9]

But what does reform actually mean? There are surprisingly more answers than there are obvious means of adjudicating between the competing conceptions of what is properly understood as reform (Lindbeck 2000). At the outset, we should take care not to repeat the common Anglo-American perceptions that the largest continental European countries have not reformed their social-security systems. This idea had common currency through much of the 1990s and was especially prevalent towards the end of the 1990s. It is repeated with attendant dismay and resignation even now not withstanding the evidence of a slow but steady accumulation of so-called 'parametric' reforms to countries' benefit systems (compare Barker 2001 with Mantel 2001a). Indeed, keeping up with the steady flow of 'reforms' country by country, year by year, and institution by institution is an enormous task best done by the pan-European law firms, financial houses, and think tanks whose functions and resources are such that either by virtue of their business or by virtue of their consultations and negotiations it is their responsibility to keep up with the changes to social-security eligibility, scope of benefits, and value of benefits.[10]

To illustrate, consider two Scandinavian examples. As documented by Mantel and Bowers (1999: 52–53), through the 1990s three different pieces of reform legislation cut Finnish pension benefits, changed their indexation arrangements, ensured that the basic pension benefit was means tested, introduced graduated increases in contribution rates, extended the official retirement age, lowered the level of early-retirement benefits, and provided for the gradual introduction of private sector pension schemes. During the 1990s, similar significant and wide-ranging reforms were introduced in Sweden—nominally the ideal reference point for those analysts committed to the social welfare state. In 1998, the Swedish reforms linked pension benefits to lifetime earnings and average life expectancy, introduced a defined contribution system across the entire economy, discounted retirement benefits for early retirement, and introduced a partially-funded pension scheme aimed at accumulating pension assets for investment in *anticipation* of long-term social security liabilities. In fact, by virtue of the scope of these reforms Scandinavian social security and pensions now look much more like the social-security systems of the Anglo-American world than Esping-Andersen's (1990) conservative welfare state (Finland) or socialist welfare state (Sweden).

What of France and Germany? Here, for all the political debate about reform, reform has been less about the redesign of whole systems and more about the long-term discounting of inherited and prospective liabilities. In the German case, as in the French case, numerous reports and inquiries have sought to accommodate competing and diverse political perspectives on the proper nature of social security and social solidarity. As governments have come and gone, reform has been placed on and off the agenda and the need for reform 'redefined' as political pressures are brought to bear within and between parties. Even so, reforms introduced in Germany have included lowering the target income replacement rate from 70 to 64 per cent over 30 years, adjusting the reference wage to the gross wage bill, shifting benefit indexation from wages to prices, increasing the retirement age, encouraging corporate pension retirement schemes, and most recently the introduction of the so-called Riester individual pension accounts.[11] Likewise in France, many changes have been made to contribution rates, the terms needed to work to obtain maximum benefits, the discounting of early-retirement pensions, and the encouragement of private voluntary employer-sponsored savings schemes (Palier 2002).

Reform means many different things and can be usefully distinguished as being either parametric or structural. Assuming that the cost of a PAYG social security system is the product of the old-age dependency ratio and the financial cost ratio (Gillion *et al.* 2000: 128), many of the reforms noted above and particularly reforms in France and Germany should be thought to address the parameters of the PAYG systems. For example, reforms that discourage early retirement aim to affect the old-age dependency ratio just as reforms that discount the expected value of the pension aim to affect the financial ratio. These kinds of reforms seek to discount the long-term expected liabilities associated with such systems. There have been many attempts at estimating continental European social security liabilities; these estimates dominate expert commentary on the integrity and sustainability of such systems over the next 25–50 years. With few exceptions, expert commentaries suggest that the continental European PAYG social security systems are unsustainable without significant parametric reform (see e.g. EcoFin 2001).

There are, of course, other versions of reform. For example, the OECD (2000: 46) suggested that reform ought to mean introducing 'modern' pension schemes characterized by 'comprehensive coverage, sustainable financing, and a mix of public and private components.' This term 'is used in opposition to systems that are over-reliant on a single pillar (usually a large pay-as-you-go (PAYG) public pension) and in contrast to less developed arrangements—often composed of many uncoordinated elements and often with large gaps in coverage.' In this respect, the parametric reform of the PAYG social-security is deemed inadequate because such systems are deemed financially unsustainable and over-reliant on just one means of providing long-term retirement income. By this account, the French system of retirement income is less a 'modern' pension system than the German system, the latter being a combination of social insurance, employer-sponsored pension schemes, and individual pension and savings accounts. Of course, the contrast drawn here between France and Germany is a contrast about the nature of recently introduced and codified arrangements rather than a distinction based upon well-developed complementary pension systems.

If mixed systems combining public and private arrangements are the most desirable systems does this mean that the Anglo-American model is the most desirable model for continental Europe? There are a variety of arguments and examples used for and against this model. For example, many contend that the Anglo-American model combines income inequalities with minimum state-provided pension benefits and less than adequate coverage by employer-sponsored pension plans. Added to these problems are, of course, very low rates of individual savings particularly amongst those most at risk to low lifetime earnings and inadequate or poor coverage and participation in employer-sponsored pensions. At issue here are questions of intragenerational equity, the long-run level and value of total retirement incomes, and the relative virtues of competing pension institutions. These issues were brought into sharp relief with the Enron scandal— the use of defined contribution (DC) schemes in the place of defined benefit (DB) schemes, the use of stock-based company pension, and the concentration of risk by virtue of policies designed to encourage employees to hold their stock (Mitchell and Utkus 2002). The consequences of this scandal for US pensions policy remain to be resolved.[12]

By contrast, the Dutch and Swiss pension systems are often held to be better models of modern pension systems. They combine universal coverage, high income-replacement rates, and modest income redistribution with a three-tiered system of pension benefit and funding. The Dutch system is the subject of Chapter six of this book. It is, however, like the Swiss system a pension and retirement income funding model deeply immersed in national, European, and global financial markets. For many European social democrats, dependence upon financial markets is anathema to the principles underlying the PAYG social security: in particular, the ideal that the nation-state is the insurer of last resort of people's lifetime incomes and welfare.

Still there are those who advocate convergence to the Anglo-American model. Not withstanding apparent income inequalities and the prospects of expanding income inequality amongst pensioners as the baby boom generation retires over the coming 25 years, there remain advocates of the Anglo-American model who stress the enormous economic and financial benefits of funded pension systems. Indeed, just as projected social-security liabilities are a crucial reference point in the debate about the future of European pensions, the volume of pension fund assets against gross domestic product are an equally important reference point in this debate. Table 1.1 provides a country-by-country summary of pension assets against GDP. There, as is well recognized, it is apparent that the United Kingdom and the United States of America have enormous stored wealth in pension fund assets just like the Netherlands and Switzerland on the continent. When combined with data on dependency ratios, more often than not the point accompanying such tables of pension assets is that pre-funding provides a remarkable means of economic growth and trans-formation missing in those economies where growth potential is based upon inherited productive capital and human capital. By this logic, pension fund capitalism is equally a regime of capital accumulation and a regime of retirement income provision (Clark 2000).

Hence, amongst the strongest advocates of the Anglo-American model there is a presumption that the reform of nation-state social security is a matter of financial restructuring just as it may be a means of securing long-term retirement income. The recent debate in

Table 1.1. European population (millions) and dependency ratios*, value of current pension assets ($bn) as a per cent of the GDP, 2000

Country	Population	Dependency ratio	Value of pension assets	Pension assets/GDP
Austria	8.1	23.0	28.0	12
Belgium	10.2	26.2	29.7	11
Denmark	5.4	22.4	186.0	100
Finland	5.2	22.4	52.0	36
France	59.2	24.6	82.0	5
Germany	82.3	23.5	288.0	13
Ireland	3.8	16.8	49.0	43
Italy	57.6	27.0	275.0	22
Netherlands	15.9	20.9	695.0	162
Norway	4.5	23.1	43.3	24
Portugal	10.0	23.0	12.0	10
Spain	39.5	23.2	32.0	5
Sweden	8.9	26.6	308.0	112
Switzerland	7.1	22.4	318.0	111
UK	59.5	24.6	1403.0	91

* Population aged 65+ as a proportion of population aged 15–64.

Source: European Commission (2001d: 12), and *Investment & Pensions Europe* (June 2001: 71) based on data supplied by the European Federation for Retirement Provision (ERPF) and Population Concern.

Europe about economic growth potential and job creation have had to come to terms with the connection between the financial structure of Anglo-American economies, the nature and rate of economic innovation in these economies during the 1990s, and the means by which the new economy or post-industrialization has been facilitated by many institutions otherwise designated as retirement income institutions. Consequently, a vital topic of debate within the EU and amongst member states has been the extent to which the reform of social security is also a question of reform of financial intermediation and financial markets. In this context, the competition between financial systems has been given a geographical reference, represented by the competition between London, Frankfurt, and Paris. At issue is the following question: if social-security is to be reformed according to financial imperatives, what role will continental European financial institutions play given the global hegemony of London and New York? This question is addressed in each and every chapter of the book.

LOOKING FORWARD

Ultimately, this book brings together the tensions and imperatives accompanying European demography and social security with the tensions and imperatives accompanying global financial integration. My aim is to make explicit their intersection even if it is difficult to offer a ready recipe that would resolve these tensions in favour of the long-term income and welfare of European citizens.

To sustain my argument, I first review in detail the literature related to demographic ageing and the funding crisis of the European PAYG social-security systems that will accompany the baby boom generation through their retirement years. In Chapter 2, I also make explicit the connection between these issues and recent discussion in the EC about the necessity for the pan-European reform of member states' regulation of pension and insurance. In that respect, I show that when considering the prospects for European economic development the EC believes that funding retirement has a clear and obvious connection with the financing of future economic development. This is the backdrop for subsequent analyses of the circumstances in France (Chapter 3), Germany (Chapters 4 and 5), Netherlands (Chapter 6), and ultimately the United Kingdom (Chapter 7).

Clearly, my approach to European pensions is selective: I have chosen a small group of EU countries out of a much larger set of countries inside and outside of the current EU membership. This does not mean that those countries not chosen are in any way less interesting, complicated, and contentious. In point of fact Greece, to take just one example, is remarkable for the complexity of its pension system, the looming problems related to the PAYG social security, and the political issues concerning entitlement and early retirement. See Featherstone *et al.* (2001) for a synopsis of the issues and politics of Greek pensions in the context of European monetary integration. This example, with significant variations on the issues and themes related to different countries and their inherited institutions could be repeated for Finland, Sweden, and many other cases. I chose France for its reliance upon social security and its commitment to social solidarity, Germany for its size and significance for the EU and the global economy, and the Netherlands for its place in between continental Europe and the Anglo-American world. Whether I have used the right examples, and whether I have provided sufficient material to sustain my case remains to be seen.

My analysis of the French situation emphasizes the PAYG social security system both in abstract and in reality. Here, I introduce the reader to the theoretical rudiments necessary to explain the significance of demographic and economic growth for funding future retirement benefits. Also, I explain how and why the current French predicament is a predicament of governance. In doing so, I also note that the recent debate about the reform of the French system has included an assessment of the potential benefits of pre-funding a portion of the long-term social-security obligations. At issue, in this respect, is the extent to which pre-funding may be a means of anticipating future obligations through the investment of such assets in global financial markets. Even if the French economy is a large economy by European standards, there may be considerable benefits in diversifying the risks associated with future national and European rates of economic growth. But, of course, to do so requires a close scrutiny of French governance practices as well as the capacity of the French financial industry to adequately manage and invest such assets. Not far away figuratively and geographically is the role of London.

The two chapters on Germany have different emphasis. Here, my interest is less about reform or otherwise of national social insurance than it is about the status of corporate-sponsored private retirement income institutions. Looking forward, during the first decades of the twenty-first century, these institutions may be vital mechanisms for absorbing some of the funding problems associated with the social insurance programme. However, we must recognize that these institutions are more often than not associated with large employers in manufacturing industries. I show that, in the first instance (Chapter 4), these firms have become particularly attuned to Anglo-American accounting standards as regards their financial reporting practices. This has put into play the integrity and funding of inherited corporate pension obligations. In the second instance (Chapter 5), I show that many of the same corporations have learnt a great deal about the management of pension assets and liabilities from their Anglo-American colleagues and competitors. In effect, the large German corporations are increasingly Anglo-American in terms of their financial reporting practices and management practices, even if they would appear to be German in the sense that their domestic relationships remain embedded within the German system of corporate governance. Recognizing the penetration of Anglo-American financial reporting practices in the German model of corporate governance allows us to better understand the increasing importance of financial markets for continental European retirement income plan sponsors.

In this context, the Dutch model looms large. It combines state-sponsored social security with an almost universal coverage of the working population by employer-sponsored supplementary pension plans and voluntary savings plans. It is a model that the other continental European countries might wish to emulate. The Dutch model has the advantage of retaining a significant social-security element in retirees' total retirement income. Also, many employer-sponsored supplementary pension plans socialize risks associated with long-term retirement income. Therefore, those committed to social justice have reason to support the Dutch model even if it reproduces the wage and salary income inequality through the benefit structure of many pension plans. But the Dutch model is more than a tripartite system of responsibility. It is also a financial industry, with many overlapping and intersecting financial functions and institutions contributing to the investment and management of pension fund assets and liabilities. Understanding its place in the European single market is an important goal of the chapter. There are significant implications, in this respect, for London and New York and the global financial industry at large.

This brings us then to the penultimate chapter of the book devoted to the place of London in the European and global financial industry. It is my contention that a debate about the reform of European social-security and retirement income systems is as much a debate about the increasing significance of Anglo-American financial institutions in domestic financial markets as it is a debate about retirees' future incomes. Almost always hidden in debate about reform is concern to buttress and if possible expand the competitive status of the national financial champions against the power and significance of London and New York. Ultimately, the entire book comes to ground in London because it is so important for the mobilization and transfer of European financial assets into the world at large. In my opinion, the London-based Anglo-American financial industry is likely to dominate the production of financial products relevant to the provision of long-term retirement income. This is one of the driving forces behind member states' social-security and pension reforms. Whether or not my opinion about the future role of London will be realized is open for debate. Nevertheless, European policy makers are preoccupied with reforms that might in some way or another make this prospect less likely.

Finally, I should state the obvious: like many other analysts' of national social-security programmes I believe that the continental European countries face a very difficult future.[13] If they rely upon unfunded PAYG social security for their citizens' retirement income not only do they face an unenviable squeeze upon their governmental budgets, they also face the prospect of much lower real working and retirement incomes compared to those countries with funded or partially funded tripartite retirement income systems. On the other hand, as recent events have shown, funded systems that rely upon the global financial market performance carry with them significant and uninsurable risks. The past is not the future. Workers' interests are not always the same as employers' interests and the interests of financial institutions. Just as the performance of the fund management companies is uncertain over time, so too are the potential benefits for future retirees of funded retirement income schemes. The trouble is, just at the moment, as globalization proceeds apace, neither system seems capable of guaranteeing retirement incomes in a comprehensive manner. The judgements that must be made are judgements about which type of system carries the least risks and which type of system is more able to spread these risks away from those least able to carry them. Such judgements must be informed by principles of social justice (Barr 2002).

NOTES

1. A claim along these lines is made philosophically by Miller (2000) amongst others.
2. See for example the edited collections of Clark *et al.* (2000), Crouch and Streeck (1997), Hall and Soskice (2001), and Hollingsworth and Boyer (1997) as well as the argument of Whitley (1999).
3. Consider, for example, the comment made by Martin Wolf (2000: 25) in the *Financial Times*: 'in the sweep of history, all successful economies will continue to become more "American". Information becomes ever freer; interventionist states are relaxing the reins; markets and contracts substitute for relationships and hierarchies; formal regulation replaces nods and winks; and welfare states are cut back'. While he doubts that the American model can be or should be copied entirely, he is also in no doubt about the significance of the model for contemporary public policy.
4. This point has been made by many scholars over the years. Nation building is fraught with many long-simmering regional rivalries and loyalties. A useful treatment of these issues related to the Italian experience can be found in Dickie (1996).
5. Some commentators draw the implications of this process far wider than I do here, invoking the neo-liberal 'free market' project initiated and inspired by Thatcher and Reagan. See, for example, Peck and Tickell (2001: 1–2) on neo-liberalism defining it as a process of 'rationalisation for globalization and state "reform"' combining 'market deference with vigorous anti-collectivism' and 'aggressive forms of state downsizing, austerity financing, and public-service "reform"'. This connection is also made in Dyson and Featherstone's (1999) conclusion to their book on the Maastricht Treaty and beyond. In making reference to this issue I do so as a gesture of commonality rather than a central theoretical reference point that will appear throughout the book. There are many other connections to be made between European pensions and global finance before driving home the connection in the stratosphere of theory and discourse.
6. Witness recent reports on Euroland macroeconomic and monetary conditions (European Central Bank 2001), and commentaries on the process of policy making in Europe (Heikensten and Ernhagen 2000) amongst many other sources.
7. Compare the comments of his counterpart at the US Federal Reserve. Greenspan (2000) suggested that communication technologies integrating the world are not new, referencing the laying of the trans-Atlantic cable in the late nineteenth century. He also noted that the international exposure of many advanced industrial economies is still less than it was a century ago.
8. There was a danger, according to the Social Security Committee, that 'if the United Kingdom joined a single currency British taxpayers could be called upon to help finance the PAYG pension obligations of other EMU members, or suffer the consequences of being tied to interest rates on the single currency that were forced up by the market pressures of financing certain countries' inherited pension commitments' (House of Commons 1996: 1). In debate, the Chair of the House of Commons committee, Frank Field, emphasized that the concern over European pension liabilities was a bi-partisan matter, shared by Euro-sceptics and pro-European advocates. See his comments on the First Report from the Social Security Committee of Session 1996–97 (House of Commons 1996: col 195). Subsequently, the issue has been raised in the House on occasion mostly in relation to arguments between the parties about domestic pension policy. See, for instance, the exchange between a conservative MP and the Prime Minister about the tax on pension fund dividends (House of Commons 2000: col 34). Most importantly, pensions debate in the Commons has focused upon the inadequacy of UK state-provided retirement

benefits, the inability of the Labour Government to re-establish the link between pension benefits and paid wages (abolished by Thatcher), and the poverty that will likely affect many retirees over the coming years (House of Commons 2000: cols 674–6).

9. A more recent expression of this sentiment is to be found in the widely-cited manifesto by leading academics against the Euro (from the perspective of the United Kingdom). Therein Lascelles *et al.* (2001: 50–51) summarized the progress or lack thereof in continental pension reform, emphasizing France and Germany. They suggested that if the United Kingdom were to join the EMU, the continental pensions burden would become a United Kingdom burden and would have to be paid for by British taxpayers. The implied threat is tax harmonization, presumably at higher continental tax rates. They then return to the House of Commons report of 1996 to underline their concern. Their analysis is neither systematic nor compelling. In fact, compared to many other issues dealt with at length in their report, the pension issues are skated over rather than analysed in depth.

10. See, for example, reports undertaken by Merrill Lynch, CS First Boston, and the OECD explained in more detail in Chapter 2.

11. For a review and assessment see Bonin (2001). See also Fenge (2001) for a theoretical treatment of related issues concerning the efficiency costs of any transition from an unfunded PAYG system to a system of funded pensions and individual savings accounts.

12. There was considerable political posturing involving House Republicans and Senate Democrats over the proper response to Enron, culminating with the passage of the Sarbanes-Oxley bill in mid-2002. In debate, further doubts were raised about the value and significance of defined contribution schemes in relation to the traditional (but declining) defined benefit schemes in the post-September 11th world of poor equity market performance. See, for instance, Orszag's (2002) commentary on the House version of the pension 'reform' bill, the GAO report on low-income workers' low rates of participation in DC schemes (US Government 2001), and the evidence that most 401(k) participants are passive (even captive) participants in their company schemes (see Choi *et al.* 2001).

13. We should recognize, of course, that there is some debate about the viability of Anglo-American social security systems in relation to the question of ageing and the retirement of the baby-boom generation. These issues are discussed in Munnell (2002) and Aaron and Shoven (1999). For many Europeans, however, the potential problems associated with the funding of the US system seem minor and of little relative significance. The recent report of the US Board of Trustees (2002) provided a remarkable measure of difference between systems and prospects: whereas the Europeans are concerned about low rates of economic growth and the consequent increasing levels of pension liabilities, the US system has benefited from higher rates of economic growth and productivity over the 1990s, pushing into the future the expected shortfalls in social security funds.

2

Overview: Demography and Pension Funding

A most problematic issue facing western countries is the looming retirement of the baby boom generation over the first twenty-five years of the twenty-first century. While an issue of profound social and political importance it is, inevitably, also an issue of enormous economic significance. This has been widely recognized by many academic, policy, and industry commentators.[1] Not surprisingly, there has been an increasing stream of research devoted to demographic trends and their economic, political, and social implications; witness the leading research undertaken and published by the OECD and its staff (Leibfritz *et al.* 1995) on behalf of member countries. In this chapter, I comment upon and make reference to this and other related research, emphasizing its significance as well as the interaction between European demographic trends and global finance. In doing so, this chapter amplifies the recent comparative research on European pension systems including an analysis of the causes and consequences of early retirement for the fiscal health of the European social security systems.

To illustrate the significance of demography, the Charpin (1999) report to the French government summarized the problems in paying for forecast social security liabilities. Assuming current trends remain constant, by 2040 there could be 7 retirees for every 10 workers (compared to 4 retirees for every 10 workers during the 1990s). In effect, those working will have to carry nearly twice the burden of those not working compared to the current generation of working people. In terms of expected financial commitments, it was estimated that by 2040 retirement benefits could account for more than 18 per cent of

French gross domestic product (GDP) compared to the current (2000) rate of approximately 12 per cent of French GDP. As we shall see, this would be a very large burden on the French economy compared to the UK and the US economies (but not Germany or Italy). Furthermore, it was estimated that the accumulated deficit of the social security system could be as much as FF700 billion if unemployment were to average 6 per cent over the first 40 years of the twenty-first century. Given the relatively weak performance of the French economy in terms of employment growth over the last few decades, more difficult scenarios can be reasonably forecast. The reform of French labour markets, capital markets, and retirement systems are argued, in some quarters, to be the only viable options (Gardiner 1999).

The near-term future of France is shared to varying degrees by other large continental European countries. By contrast, the Anglo-American world appears less concerned about demography and its implications for public finance. For the United States of America and the United Kingdom, more often than not concerned about the proper balance between government and private provision of retirement income, the proclaimed benefits of market provision rather than the threats posed by demography have been at the core of public discussion. In the United States of America, debate about privatizing social security is as much a continuing debate about the importance of individual auton-omy as it is a debate about optimal long-term pension financing and investment performance (see Aaron and Shoven 1999; Diamond 2000). In the United Kingdom, the limited benefit value of state-provided social security is augmented for some by individual savings and employer-provided supplementary pensions (Budd and Campbell 1998). As in many other countries, public pension obligations are not fully funded in the United States of America or the United Kingdom. Even so, the discounting of future social security liabilities combined with the importance of the private funded sector has rendered debate about demographic trends less significant when compared to continental Europe.

For continental Europe, the demographic time bomb has pre-cipitated a crisis of confidence in the national systems of social welfare, finance, and corporate governance (Bonoli 2000). Many commentators question whether continental Europe has the political will and eco-nomic resources to resolve the crisis in favour of future generations. Fealty to the inherited models of intergenerational social solidarity may be impossibly expensive, while capitulation to the Anglo-American model of economy and society would seem to imply acceptance of individual levels of risk and inequality at odds with continental traditions (Bonoli *et al.* 2000). Pressures for the reform of European pension and retirement income systems are (internally and externally) significant and insistent. However, as the German case shows, reform is always heavily contested being subject to shifting political alliances and the entrenched interests of organized constituencies (Mantel and Bergheim 2000). The way forward is strewn with many obstacles. Indeed, some commentators deny the need for reform, arguing instead for the prospects of increased rates of real economic growth (Dupont and Sterdyniak 2000). Others cling to the principles of social solidarity, arguing that reform must reconcile new models of retirement financing with past commitments to social solidarity. Yet others see the adoption of the Anglo-American model as the solution to both adverse European demography and lagging economic performance— critical issues for this chapter and book but nonetheless widely disputed (see Borsch-Supan 2000a; Breyer 2001; Orszag and Stiglitz 1999; and Taverne 2000).

This chapter is about the contested world of European pensions, and the tensions between continuity (with the past) and convergence (with respect to the Anglo-American model). One goal of the chapter is to show how and why European pensions is an important topic for the social sciences. In doing so, I argue that resolution of seemingly adverse European demographic trends and imperatives may be found in EU policies designed to foster the development of the 'new economy' over the twenty-first century. A second goal of the chapter is to show that the principles of social solidarity remain very important in the European debate over national systems of retirement income and finance. A third goal of the chapter is to articulate the connection between the demographic crisis and global financial markets. Official solutions to the crisis may involve the dismantling of nation-specific systems of finance and retirement income in the favour of financial capitalism. To put it plainly, Deutschland AG may have to be 'reformed' and 'restructured' according to Anglo-American terms and conditions (see Nöcker 2000).[2] Finally, I raise questions about the proper role of markets in relation to social solidarity in regulating the provision of retirement income, noting the very different conceptions of risk allocation and risk management.

With respect to continental European inherited PAYG social security systems, I suggest that these systems are not economically sustainable: if demographic trends persist and if the real value of retirement benefits are to be kept to past standards, demographic imbalances, the costs of early retirement, and the underfunding of social security in combination imply a higher long-term real rate of growth at odds with past macro-economic performance. Demography and finance look likely to overwhelm the inherited social welfare systems of European nation states. I also argue that the Anglo-American model poses a serious alternative to the past, offering a model of pension funding and economic development that has many desirable features given the growth of the new economy over the 1990s. But, of course, the Anglo-American model brings with it market risks and income inequalities at odds with the post-war continental European social welfare traditions. Indeed, for some commentators, the Anglo-American model itself may not be politically sustainable over the long term if existing and growing income inequalities are amplified through future retirement incomes (Mantel 2001b). Even so, it should also be recognized that European solutions to the demographic crisis that in effect discount the future value of pension benefits might also be destructive of social solidarity within and between the generations. Solutions to the demographic crisis must come to terms with global finance.

DEMOGRAPHIC TRENDS AND THE DEMOGRAPHIC CRISIS

Not everyone believes that the European demographic trends are, or need be, a demographic crisis.[3] It could be argued that the forecast demographic transformation is an opportunity for economic development and growth; concomitant changing consumption patterns may represent opportunities for product innovation and product development. New markets, new sectors, and new types of customers are plausible consequences of any demographic transition. It is also arguable that demographic ageing need not translate into lower rates of economic growth. Long-term higher rates of technological innovation could sustain increased labour productivity, changing current cost and benefit calculations about the possible effects of demographic ageing. Furthermore, it is possible that much higher rates of female labour force participation combined with higher rates of immigration to Europe could make a substantial difference to forecast dependency ratios, matching the past, and forecast a beneficial labour market profile of the US economy (Ermisch 1995).

Given the immigration patterns during the 1990s, however, few analysts believe that higher rates of net migration to Europe are plausible. There are many social and political barriers to increased immigration that make this a most unlikely scenario (see Aranda-Hassel and Duval-Kieffer 2001; Krueger 2000).[4] At the same time, the current low rates of labour force participation are an expression of the relatively low rates of economic growth. Any increase in future labour force participation rates (and hence more viable dependency ratios) would also require sustained higher levels of employment growth. Demographic transformation will result in changing consumption patterns and the demand for consumer products. But this need not increase the rate of economic growth. Furthermore, it is questionable whether technological innovation could make a big difference to current trends in European labour productivity. To suppose that this is a realistic possibility implies European labour markets and capital markets as flexible as their UK and US counterparts. Still, whatever my doubts about the plausibility of these related arguments, there remains an important issue to be confronted: how and why these trends may be a demographic crisis rather than simply an economic transition to be paid for by higher labour productivity and economic growth.

To explain, consider the basic data. In Table 2.1 known and forecast dependency ratios for major European economies and the United States of America are presented. Comparing country-by-country over the period 1990–2030, it is apparent that forecast elderly dependency ratios will likely double or, in some cases, increase by more than 150 per cent. So, for example, the French elderly dependency ratio will double, the German elderly dependency ratio will increase from about 20 to nearly 50 per cent as will the Italian and Swiss dependency ratio. There are some slight variations amongst European economies. Notice, however, that both the United Kingdom and the United States of America will be less affected by demographic ageing than most European countries. Taking the story further with respect to the expected total dependency ratio (during 1990–2030), this data is viewed with alarm by European political leaders. If past patterns remain the same, the economic burden of dependency for those working in 2030 could be quite unlike anything experienced by similar cohorts during the nineteenth and twentieth centuries.

At this point in the story, we could go further and compare country-by-country demographic profiles. Given the fact that these profiles are well known (see e.g. Hokenson et al. 2001), in this chapter I simply refer the reader to Figure 2.1. In Figure 2.1, the actual and forecast age

Table 2.1. The dependency ratios for European economies and the United States of America, selected years 1960–2030

Country	Elderly dependency ratio[1]						Total dependency ratio[2]					
	1960	1990	2000	2010	2020	2030	1960	1990	2000	2010	2020	2030
France	18.8	20.8	23.6	24.6	32.3	39.1	61.3	51.1	52.8	51.2	59.6	67.9
Germany	16.0	21.7	23.8	30.3	35.4	49.2	47.4	45.3	46.7	50.0	57.3	75.1
Italy	13.3	21.6	26.5	31.2	37.5	48.3	47.9	45.5	47.8	51.5	58.8	72.7
Netherlands	14.7	19.1	20.8	24.2	33.9	45.1	63.9	44.5	47.7	47.5	58.1	73.2
Spain	12.7	19.8	23.5	25.9	30.7	41.0	55.1	49.3	45.3	46.9	52.7	64.8
Sweden	17.8	27.6	26.9	29.1	35.6	39.4	51.8	55.3	57.9	58.5	65.1	70.4
Switzerland	15.5	22.0	23.6	29.4	37.8	48.6	51.5	46.1	49.6	53.7	62.4	77.0
United Kingdom	17.9	24.0	24.4	25.8	31.2	38.7	53.7	52.9	54.0	52.3	58.3	68.0
OECD Europe	15.3	20.6	22.1	24.7	30.8	39.2	57.9	50.9	50.4	50.6	57.1	67.4
United States of America	15.4	19.1	19.0	20.4	27.6	36.8	67.4	51.7	52.0	50.5	57.4	68.0

[1] Population aged 65 and over as a per cent of the working age population.
[2] Population aged 0–14 and 65 and over as a per cent of the working age population.

Source: OECD (1997: 102) *Ageing in OECD Countries: A Critical Policy Challenge.*

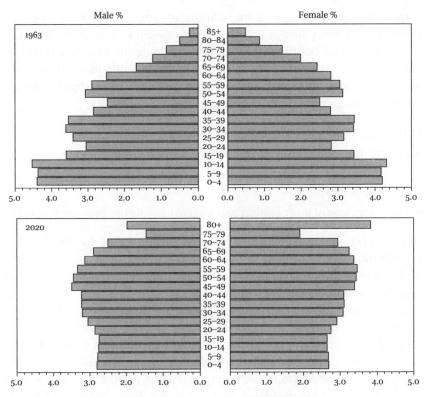

Fig. 2.1. The French demographic structure, 1963 and 2020.

Source: United Nations, Sex and Age Distribution of the World Population the 1996 Revision.

distribution of the French population (male and female) is given for 1962 and 2020. Two observations can be made that summarize a great deal of post-war French and European history. Obviously the impact of the post-war baby boom generation was apparent in the early 1960s, being the dominant age cohort for each subsequent date. By 2020, the baby boom generation will have transformed conventional expectations of normal pyramid-shaped age distributions—comparing 1962 with 2020, the proportion and absolute numbers of older people (older than 65 years) will dominate the social and political landscape of France. After the baby boom generation, subsequent generations have been smaller and smaller. There are real prospects of an absolute decline in the French population by the mid-century, despite the contribution made by past immigration and the propensity of French people to stay at home in larger numbers than virtually any other developed country.

In summary terms, and in relation to advanced economies, the demographic story brings together a set of empirical claims about the future European population dynamics by academic analysts, financial service firms, and policy think tanks. In brief, four related processes appear to drive observed and forecast patterns of European demography through to the mid-century:

- The ageing of the baby boom generation
- Longer life expectancy of those aged 65 and over
- Declining age-specific fertility rates, and smaller cohorts of childbearing women
- Low past rates of immigration and forecast low future immigration rates.

The combined effect of these processes will result in much older populations living through to their late 80s, consuming their own and national retirement savings as well as unprecedented levels of related health care and disability benefits.

If sustained, these trends will represent significant economic costs to European economies. Accentuating these trends, however, are overlapping economic and social policies and expectations that add additional burdens to the so-called simple demographic effects. Assuming little can be done about demography (not withstanding the recent Bundesregierung Deutschland 2001 report on demography and immigration), the added burdens of current social policy and expectations are the focus of considerable research and political debate (see, e.g. Gruber and Wise 1999; OECD 1998a). These additional burdens would seem to include at least the following:

- The displacement of older workers through industrial and economic restructuring
- Incentives for early retirement, particularly for those aged 55 and over
- Relatively low rates of female labour force participation
- Penalties (reduced benefits and the like) on part-time work by retired persons
- Benefit levels (often) only weakly related to contribution rates.

So, for example, early retirement at high rates of income replacement brings forward in time the onset of adverse demographic trends. Put slightly differently, this kind of labour market policy raises, sooner than later, the required real rate of economic growth necessary to accommodate forecast demographic trends.

Population dynamics and economic policy are important aspects of the demographic crisis. But another crucial issue has to do with the financing of retirement and, in particular, the costs of retirement of the baby boom generation through to 2040 and beyond. In Table 2.2 the projected public pension liabilities of major European economies are summarized and compared. Notice that underlying these projections are complex assumptions made about the demography, economic growth, pension benefit values, and levels. As recognized in the previous chapter, it is difficult to ascertain, at this point in time, the reliability of such projections (European Commission 2000d, 2001d). Even so, these cost projections are the basis of current policy debate and financial market calculations. The gross differences between continental Europe and the Anglo-American world are stark and profound. In many cases, high levels of current public sector expenditure on social security pensions for European countries may nearly double by the year 2040. By contrast, not only are the current Anglo-American public pension expenditures quite small compared to most European economies, these expenditures are predicted to remain small through to 2040. At issue, is the nature of the European pension obligations and the methods by which they are to be funded compared to the Anglo-American world (Clark 2000).

Table 2.2. The European public pension expenditures, per cent GDP for 2000 and 2040

Country	2000	2040
Austria	14.5	18.3
Belgium	10.0	13.7
Denmark	10.5	14.0
Finland	11.3	16.0
France	12.1	15.8
Germany	11.8	16.6
Greece	12.6	23.8
Ireland	4.6	8.3
Italy	13.8	15.7
Luxembourg	7.4	9.5
Netherlands	7.9	14.1
Portugal	9.8	13.8
Spain	9.4	16.0
Sweden	9.0	11.4
UK	5.5	5.0
EU	10.4	13.6

Source: EC (2001d: 22).

The European demographic crisis is arguably the combination of common population dynamics, overlapping and reinforcing social policies, and the nature and financing of public sector sponsored social security. Even if the Anglo-American economies share ageing of the baby boom generation, for Europe these demographic trends have become a demographic crisis by virtue of the inherited institutional structure and obligations of the national welfare states (Ploug and Kvist 1996). In fact, the apparent differences between Europe and the Anglo-American world with respect to the significance of demographic trends are the differences driven by basic choices made many years ago about the role and significance of the unfunded public sector social security in relation to the private funded systems of retirement provision. For Europe, leaving out many subtleties and country-specific institutions, following the lead provided by the EC (2000d) it can be observed that:

1. Many countries rely heavily upon unfunded PAYG systems of social security, depending upon social solidarity between generations to pay for the promised benefits.

2. In most continental European countries, the public pension goal is to replace a large portion of final worked income rather than provide a basic minimum benefit.

3. While most countries require individual contributions to social security, such contributions are often actuarially inadequate in relation to the actual benefit.

4. Embedded within many countries' contribution formula are other important social goals such as income redistribution post-employment.

5. In many countries, public sector pensions have been used as a means of regulating the supply of labour, thereby providing younger citizens employment opportunities.

6. Few continental European countries encourage the private provision of retirement income, though those that do tend to require funded systems as opposed to partially or unfunded systems.

SOCIAL SOLIDARITY AND THE MARKET

Much has been written about the principles and practice of social solidarity. In this chapter, it is not my intention to review the relevant political philosophy or the political institutions underpinning this concept in France and its various expressions throughout continental Europe (see Chapter 3). Needless to say, it is familiar to Anglo-American audiences even if it represents a muted echo of past ideals rather than a strong thread underpinning current policies and politics (Esping-Andersen 1990). The idea of social solidarity was important in the United Kingdom at the end of the Second World War; witness the preamble to the Beveridge report on social welfare. But it is plain that the discounting of social security benefits coupled with the growth of private funded retirement income arrangements over the last 40 years has effectively neutered the concept. Even so, the search for viable solutions to the demographic crisis in countries such as France, Germany, and Italy is informed by an historic commitment to the ideal, albeit obvious that it is perceived by many to be an enormous burden on future generations.

The fact that the observed demographic trends are a continental European demographic crisis rather than a transition shared amongst all advanced economies has undercut the viability of past commitments and institutions. In fact, in leading policy think tanks there is a presumption against the PAYG systems of retirement income in favour of the Anglo-American model. Debate about the future of European pension systems often revolves around the tensions between continuity with the past (ideal conceptions of social solidarity and social security) and convergence to some form of the Anglo-American model (with all that it implies about the role and status of markets). At the same time, a debate about the proposed national 'solutions' to the European demographic crisis almost always reference the imperatives driving global economic integration. It is at the intersection between the European nation-specific systems of retirement income (built upon principles of social solidarity) and the forces driving the global integration of financial markets (built on principles of market competition) that the resolution of the European demographic crisis is debated.

Nevertheless, there are many commentators in France and Germany (for example) who are very uneasy about the role and status attributed to 'external' financial markets given what may otherwise be properly thought to be a purely 'internal' national political debate. To illustrate the significance of these issues, consider the following four questions that touch upon the future of the European national retirement systems.

(1) *Can solidarity between generations be maintained by increasing the long-term rate of national economic growth thereby avoiding the*

necessity of discounting the value of retirement benefits and discounting the future welfare of younger generations of workers? Many analysts believe that the answer to this question is simply no. Others are more circumspect, calibrating the various options including the beneficial consequences of possible higher levels of productivity (Visco 2001). In all countries, considerable analytical effort has been devoted to clarifying the prospects for social security under a variety of macro-economic scenarios. Assuming unchanged benefit formula and entitlements, unpublished simulations by the French government think tanks suggest that if social security obligations are to be met the needed annual real rate of growth would have to be in the order of 3–4 per cent through to 2050. While there are circumstances in which such forecasts may be plausible, such forecasts are significantly above the long-term post-war trend-line (1.9 per cent for 1990–2000 and the predicted 2.1 per cent for the period 2000–2005; European Commission 2001d). Recognizing the adverse French macro-economic circumstances through the 1980s and much of the 1990s it would seem difficult to justify any argument in favour of the consistently higher annual rates of growth. A significant global recession would increase subsequent needed yearly rates of economic growth.[5] For this scenario to work, higher real rates of economic growth would have to be cumulative (see generally Aaron 1966 and Samuelson 1958).

One way to cope with macro-economic limits would be to 'reform' social security benefit formula and entitlements thereby decreasing the needed annual real rate of economic growth. In a number of countries, parametric reform gathered momentum through the 1990s involving right-of-centre and left-of-centre governments. For example, in France moves were made to increase the needed number of years ('terms') worked for maximum pension benefit. Likewise, benefits to be paid at early retirement have been recalculated to better reflect actuarial circumstances and entitlements. And most importantly, future retirees face the prospect of having increases in retirement benefits linked to the rate of price inflation as opposed to the rate of real wage growth in the economy. In effect, these adjustments will make it more difficult for French workers to attain maximum retirement benefits, while discounting the future real value of those paid benefits as people age through retirement. More comprehensive 'reforms' entailing funded employer-sponsored pensions, however, have been stymied by political conflict inside and outside of the Chamber of Deputies, being deeply implicated, as well, in the Presidential elections (Mantel and Thomsen 1999).

(2) *Could reform of European financial systems be the means by which the value and scope of public pension entitlements are maintained and the rate of economic growth sustained at a level consistent with expected standards of living?* In Germany, where commentators have raised the prospect of a tax revolt by younger workers, it has been argued that 'reform' would be best placed at the level of capital markets rather than in systems of public retirement income (Mantel and Bergheim 2000). This argument has been driven by the remarkable growth of Anglo-American economies over the 1980s and 1990s, and the related significance attributed to neo-liberal and efficiency-oriented capital market regulatory regimes. It has been argued that a crucial element in any solution to funding public pension entitlements must be in the wealth that is locked-up in untraded financial institutions and relationships. We consider this issue in more detail in the next section, noting the connection made by the EC between finance, the new economy, and demography. At this point, however, it should be recognized that any related 'reform' of the German financial system would involve the institutions that underpin Deutschland AG. Whereas some Anglo-American commentators argue that these internal relationships have been essential to the success of the German model of stakeholder representation and economic growth (Hall and Soskice 2001), it can be asserted that these relationships now limit the market potential of large German firms, the welfare of their employees, and the potential value of benefits paid retirees (see Chapter 4).

The adoption of Anglo-American financial models and regulatory practices could have far-ranging implications for German corporate governance and existing pension entitlements. For example, consider the connection between corporate finance and the corporate-sponsored supplementary pensions. For many years, large German firms sponsored supplementary pensions for their workers 'funding' those commitments via the much discussed book reserve system. Basically this system of pension funding subsidized the firms' cost of capital; pension funding was intermingled with corporate treasuries providing the financial resources for new technology, training, and investment (Koenig and van der Lende 1999). However, in the Anglo-American world not only are internal financial subsidies at odds with shareholder value, the restructuring of the industrial structure and corporate form have been essential tools driving local and global competitiveness. As the federal German government has introduced tax incentives to encourage employers (amongst others) to provide supplementary pensions, accelerating financial reform has been accompanied by an increasing global interest in the financial value of large German firms. Inevitably, inherited systems of corporate pension financing are at risk to the introduction of Anglo-American accounting and financial practices (see Chapter 5).

(3) *Could accepted principles of social solidarity be sustained if Anglo-American models of supplementary pensions were introduced in Europe in the near future?* A number of smaller European countries have made significant moves over the past 20 years towards systems of pension and retirement income that combine the public sector and private sector contributions. In Switzerland, for example, in the mid-1980s the federal government introduced a mandatory supplementary private pension system aimed at sustaining social goals of income replacement and income equality. Likewise, in the Netherlands the government-regulated private system of fully funded supplementary pensions has been required to contribute an increasing proportion of the ideal 70 per cent income replacement rule characteristic of the social-security system (Blomsma and Jansweijer 1997). As the costs of public social security have risen, the Dutch government has looked to the private sector to make up shortfalls in the government fiscal capacity. Even so, social solidarity remains the core principle driving the organization and funding of supplementary pensions. Contribution rates and final retirement income are based, in part, upon a commitment to equality.

Therefore, the question posed immediately above could be answered in the affirmative. But notice that any affirmative answer presupposes a mandatory universal participation in highly regulated mixed public and private pension and retirement income systems. In this respect, the Dutch model is widely appreciated in continental Europe and draws considerable regard from the French and German commentators. An important feature of the Dutch model is its comprehensive nature. Although firmly embedded in systems of collective bargaining, any defection by individuals and firms is closely regulated by the government (see Chapter 6). Likewise in France, it could be contended that their system of unfunded but jointly-managed complementary pensions is worth emulating even if it is subject to widespread employer dissatisfaction and problems of sustaining equitable income replacement. By contrast, the Anglo-American (but not Australian) supplementary pension systems barely cover half the working population, have highly variable contribution rates and pension benefit values, and utilize tax incentives that reward the middle-class participants in employer-sponsored pension funds as opposed to the lower-paid workers with volatile employment histories (Davis 1995). Social solidarity requires modes of private organization that can accommodate all kinds of workers (and employment histories) according to diverse and shared social aspirations (Esping-Andersen 1999).

(4) *Can workers be protected from the risks of the market if some combination of public and private retirement income provision is deemed necessary and inevitable?* For many, the market is the enemy of equitable and predictable retirement income. Indeed, the French, German, and Italian retirement income systems being based upon the PAYG social security are direct responses to the failure of the funded and under-funded private systems of the interwar years. By this logic, social solidarity between the generations is thought to be a means of mutual insurance, evening-out the long-term fluctuations in economic welfare by the transfer of current earned income to retirees. The problem, however, with intergenerational mutual insurance is that it only works if there is a reasonable balance between earned income and entitlements (see Chapter 3). Otherwise, the state is the insurer of last resort. This may have been possible in the past, but it presumes a robustness of national public finance at odds with recent experience, and a nation-state financial capacity at odds with the enormous growth of global financial market resources. To assume the state can even out intergenerational earned income and entitlements invokes the ideal of a Keynesian nation-state, a point of reference now widely disputed by academics and policy makers. The market may be the only mechanism for balancing intergenerational accounts. But to return to the market as an essential pillar underpinning the flow of retirement income is to return a debate that dominated much of the twentieth century—the proper allocation of risk between the civil institutions, the state, and the market.

In the Anglo-American world, this debate has been resolved in favour of the market. Variable rates of participation in employer-sponsored schemes combined with variable rates of contributions reflect the labour and capital market imperatives. The maintenance and investment of pension assets relies heavily upon traded securities and assumes, more often than not, a growing and stable (in the long term) economic system. Furthermore, the apparent shift from the DB to DC pension plans, the increasing use of cash balance plans and the re-emergence of individual retirement accounts separate from sponsoring organizations are all aspects of much the same phenomenon: the reallocation of risk from institutions to individuals and their families. Given that many Anglo-American social security systems typically provide minimum benefits according to the principles of need or welfare, the supplementary pensions may be thought to add a necessary but uneven and volatile component to individual's total retirement income. It seems impossible to reinsure such risks; neither markets nor states seem capable of assuming the task (Allen and Gale 1995).

EUROPEAN AND GLOBAL FINANCIAL MARKET INTEGRATION

Having moved from social solidarity to financial markets, we need to better understand the structure and organization of these markets in relation to European initiatives designed to promote economic development. As I hope to show, proffered solutions to the demographic crisis are increasingly connected to the 'reform' of the European financial markets and the prospects for building a distinctly European new economy. Most importantly, the relatively poor performance of continental European economies during the 1990s compared to the United States of America, and to a lesser extent the United Kingdom, has prompted national and European policy makers to reconsider the role and status of financial markets. The Anglo-American pension fund capitalism provides an important reference point for those driving the process of European financial market integration (especially considering the fact that forecast increases in long-term labour productivity associated with the 'new economy' have prompted the US government to discount further the likely timing and costs associated with the funding of social security pensions; see the Annual Report of the Social Security system referenced as US Board of Trustees (2002).

We can treat markets as universal institutions, dominated by commonly understood exchange relations, economic transactions, and competitive advantage and disadvantage. These are the rudiments of any economic theory of market capitalism. We would be shortsighted in underplaying these types of imperatives. But we should also be conscious of the fact that market formation is a deliberate process, just as market agents may pursue various strategies intended to affect and take advantage of the design process. So, for example, the process of European financial market integration has been very much affected by these design considerations—many countries have been reluctant to embrace financial integration without first protecting or enhancing the competitiveness of national champions in relation to potential Anglo-American rivals. At the same time, for many years the economic geography of European finance has been thought properly national by virtue of the difficulty faced by consumers in assessing the integrity and value of financial products offered by vendors located outside of their home jurisdictions (Chapter 6).

As we noted above, there is a close connection between the national financial systems and corporate governance (Hopt *et al.* 1999). In Germany, financial markets have been kept regional and national by overlapping and reinforcing institutions and regulatory practices. Long-term untraded financial relationships between regional banks and local firms, the presumption in favour of corporate insiders as opposed to outsiders, and the internal retention and sharing amongst the stake-holders of corporate income have all contributed to a distinctive system of finance (Dore 2000). Similarly, the regulation of pension assets and liabilities including quantitative limits on asset allocation as well as strictly enforced year-to-year asset-liability matching has narrowed the available scope for financial markets and their intermediaries. This general point can also be made, of course, with respect to the other continental European countries including France. European financial integration promises to breakdown these preferential relationships and regulations in favour of a single market for financial products and services. This may mean competition between financial institutions whatever their national origins, and it may also mean cross-border flows of capital and financial products (including retirement products) (De Ryck 1999).

If integration were simply a matter of taking the single market to its logical conclusion, the pace of integration would be slow over the coming decade. However, the EC has sought to accelerate financial market integration. The introduction of the Euro, the discounting of its value against the US dollar, and the relatively lower economic perform-ance of continental Europe with respect to the United States of America have all given greater urgency to financial integration. Fur-thermore, and underscored by repeated observations from the EC, continental Europe seems to have missed most of the labour pro-ductivity effects of the US new economy (for an assessment of the evidence see Basu *et al.* 2001). To summarize, this can be shown in the following simple ways (Figure 2.2), referencing economic indicators from the OECD's Economic Outlook:

1. The real GDP growth in the United States of America accelerated in the 1990s, whereas continental Europe experienced a significant recession in the early 1990s, and the rates of economic growth at the

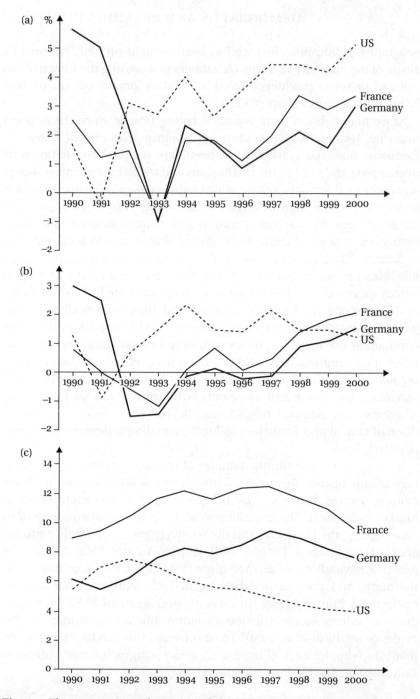

Fig. 2.2. The economic performance of the United States of America and two major European economies, 1990–2000. (a) Real GDP growth; (b) Employment growth; (c) Unemployment rate.

Source: OECD, *Economic Outlook*, December 2000.

end of the decade were about half that of the United States of America.

2. The growth in US employment varied between one and three per cent per year whereas continental Europe experienced negative rates of growth in employment over the balance of the 1990s (not withstanding higher rates of employment growth just at the end of the decade).[6]

3. The US unemployment declined throughout the 1990s, being less than half the unemployment rate of the major continental European economies by 2000 (not withstanding a modest and slow decline in European unemployment over the decade).

Many commentators, Anglo-American and continental European, attribute the remarkable performance of the US economy in the 1990s to the emergence of the new economy.[7] According to optimistic views of the matter, the new economy has brought forth a virtuous cycle of technological innovation, labour productivity, and economic growth (Jorgenson 2001; Jorgenson and Strioh 2000). Less optimistically, it is arguable that the new economy prompted a remarkable speculative bubble and bust in the United States of America and in global financial markets now being unwound through devaluation, liquidation, and bankruptcy (as predicted by Shiller 2000). Even so, the new economy is believed to be a distinctive way of organizing human capital and of financing economic innovation (see Florida 2002; Saxenian 1994; Teece 2000). The driving force behind the new economy has been located with small, often unlisted companies located in distinct regional clusters of innovation like the Silicon Valley and Rt. 128/495 Boston—centres of human and financial capital. The new economy has been financed by venture capital (from the initial stages of start-up to maturation) and ultimately traded securities markets (through initial public offerings). Large multinational firms have come late to this mode of organization, though with substantial resources to play the 'catch-up' game.

It is hardly necessary to recount the logic and dynamics of the new economy.[8] There are now many sources of information on the new economy, including contributions to Clark *et al.* (2000). But it is important to emphasize that the European policy makers have come to believe that the exclusion of continental Europe from this phenomenon is indicative of the following: (1) The shallowness and relative inefficiency of European capital markets, (2) the lack of transparency, knowledge, and information of European investment decision-making, and (3) the lack of sufficient risk capital, and (4) the lack of market intermediaries skilled at valuing the costs and benefits of financial risks. The EC has recognized that the new economy is as much a financial phenomenon as it is about the application of electronic technology to production, consumption, and distribution. By this analysis continental Europe lacks the necessary financial infrastructure needed to sustain innovation and economic development (and hence the costs of social security and social insurance).[9]

But often ignored in this story of financial risk and technological innovation is the social organization of the new economy (Teece 2000). Whereas large firms of the old economy manage human resources according to the standard rules of functional capacity and authority, firms in the new economy sought to open up hierarchies and devolve line management. As a consequence, the standard categories of seniority and responsibility have been overtaken by individual initiative even at the risk of undercutting the conventional models of the organization of work. This is most apparent where compensation is involved. Many new economy firms have deliberately discounted current income (wages and benefits) in favour of promised future income (stock options and the like). Shorn of the protection of being employed in large firms, and highly attuned to market fluctuations in their net worth, the promise of the new economy has been immediate reward for individual risk taking. In this world, there is less concern with, or commitment to, social solidarity; the socialization of risk would seem to be anathema to the motive forces driving the new economy (Thrift 2001). These are important lessons for corporate structure and compensation, now being reproduced in Europe's largest firms (Chapter 5).

After almost a decade of debate, the EC (2000b) produced a proposed directive covering the investment and management of European private retirement systems, only for it to languish in the European Parliament (11th October, 2000; revised June 2001).[10] The Directive allowed for the development of funded private pension systems, even if it did not match the flexibility and robustness of the Anglo-American regulatory systems. It also provided the means by which the European economic growth and financial integration would benefit from the expansion of private pensions, while relying upon their development to supplement national social security systems. In a speech made just before the launch of the proposal, the EC Commissioner Bolkestein (23rd September 2000) noted the pressing need for European financial integration referencing the 'knowledge-based and dynamic economy of the next decade'. He also noted the vital importance of the forthcoming directive for the supervision of private pension funds. In sum, he managed to connect one with the other, intimating that financial integration and pension fund regulation would contribute to the long-term global competitiveness of the European single market. Pensions and European capital market integration are closely connected; witness the Lamfalussy report on strengthening the pan-European securities' markets regulation.

In the Anglo-American world, funded pension plans depend upon the financial services industry for the management and investment of pension assets. Much has been written about the structure and organization of this industry (see Blake 1995; Davis 1995; Davis and Steil 2001). The market for financial services has driven down the costs of asset management, while new products and new investment regimes have expanded the available options open to pension funds and their plan sponsors. For the most part, the regulatory and statutory regimes are permissive rather than definitive sustaining the autonomy of agents' decision-making according to the inherited trust law conceptions of fiduciary duty (Langbein 1995, 1997). It is arguable that this kind of organizational structure contributed directly to the remarkable performance of Anglo-American financial markets over the 1990s, and the double-digit performance of pension funds throughout much of that time. The EC's directive sought to emulate this umbrella; considerable attention was paid to the prospects of integrating the national custodial traditions with the more expansive Anglo-American prudent man rule (Brydon 2000; De Ryck 1999).

Social security remains the bedrock underpinning continental European retirement income. But even here proposals have been floated for the advance funding of the PAYG social security liabilities (Leinert and Esche 2000). This is particularly apparent in France, where the Charpin (1999) report raised the prospect of establishing a central reserve fund in anticipation of the looming demographic crisis. Advocates of this approach include Bismans and Docquier (1996) and Aglietta (2000). Essentially three arguments may be made on its behalf. If the long-term real rate of French economic growth is about 2 per cent per annum, the available evidence suggests that the rate of return on invested assets (US equities) over the past fifty years has been about 6 per cent per annum (Clark 2000). Therefore, the advance funding of liabilities and the investment of social security assets could make a significant cumulative difference to the national fiscal capacity compared to the PAYG system (Modigliani et al. 2001). Also, a central

reserve fund that was invested according to international best practice may be more cost efficient than the administration of social
security (Whitehouse 2000). A central reserve fund could significantly enhance national savings through global equity markets while
reducing net costs (Pesando 1992), and may even provide the needed
investment in technology, regional clusters, and the new economy
(Maarek 2000).

While there are important advocates for such a strategy, there are
also many critics who are disturbed about the idea that the funding of
social security should be shifted from social solidarity and state guarantees to the vagaries of the international financial markets. The stock
market bust in the wake of the TMT bubble has reinforced anxieties.[11]
If one function of social security is to provide a guaranteed core value
of retirement income, it is supposed that the state is the proper institution to indemnify that guarantee. However, for Aglietta and others
the state now appears to be too weak to sustain such a guarantee.
Furthermore, the size and influence of global finance promises rewards
far beyond the capacity of the nation-state and Europe to deliver—a
point made by many Anglo-American commentators including Schie-
ber *et al.* (2000). Therefore, perhaps the only alternative may be to
harness the global financial services industry on behalf of the objectives
of the social partners. To continue along the current path will require
discounting the value of social security and an increase in the rate of
tacit defection from the institutions of national social solidarity (see
Chapters 3 and 8).

The French debate over the possible advantages of a central reserve
fund is unresolved. It should be noted, moreover, that there are aspects
of the proposal that may fit uneasily with the Anglo-American model of
pension fund finance that it is presumed to emulate. Most notably, any
central reserve fund would remain embedded within the existing
relationships between the social partners and the state. Not only would
the goals and objectives of such a fund be subject to the national
interest, it is likely that the management of the investment process
would also be subject to these relationships. While joint trusteeship is a
familiar mode of pension fund management in the Anglo-American
world, it is apparent that there are advantages in separating the interests of plan sponsors from the management of the pension fund itself.
This is as true in the public sector pension funds as also in the private
sector pension funds. In the Anglo-American world, the governance
and investment performance of pension funds and their service providers relies heavily upon principles such as fiduciary duty. Reasonable

doubts may be raised about the investment potential of any fund that was required to satisfy such a multiplicity of constituencies and goals (Clark 2000).

Perhaps less appreciated in the debate over the virtues (and otherwise) of a central reserve fund is the extent to which its management would have to rely upon the institutions and centres of global finance. At issue here is the extent to which the formation of national reserve funds would allow London and, to a lesser extent, Wall Street to reinforce their dominance over Paris and Frankfurt as centres of finance (see Chapter 7). Over the 1990s, London reinforced its pre-eminence as the leading centre of international finance, being one of just a few essential switching-points in the enormous and growing flows of financial assets and liabilities around the world. Not only have their European rivals failed to make inroads into London's share of global finance, London has attracted talented continental European financial managers. The most advanced financial services and the most reputable financial service companies are located in London. Inevitably, given the potential size of a central reserve fund, such a financial institution would rely heavily upon the expertise of London-based global firms. Deeply implicated in such a possibility are intensive political and economic rivalries between the European nation-states. The EU-sponsored European financial integration combined with new institutions for funding European retirement income may become centred upon London at the expense of Frankfurt and Paris. At issue, then, is the future of London in Europe and the global financial markets (noted in Beaverstock *et al.* 2001).

CONCLUSIONS

For those that celebrate the achievements of the European welfare state, and for those that celebrate the continuing role that the social partners play in mediating market imperatives, the national systems of retirement income are indicative of distinctive and valued traditions of social justice and social protection. Many are wary of proffered 'solutions' to the looming demographic crisis; it would seem easier if national systems could be kept intact and adjustment made through macro-economic policy and/or government budgets. Otherwise, there is a sense in which social solidarity may be sacrificed in order to achieve financial objectives which may, or may not, contribute to adequate and secure retirement incomes. This point was made by the EC Commissioner for Employment and Social Affairs in the following manner: 'Reforms cannot happen overnight. Pensions must be not only economically sustainable but also socially sustainable' (Diamanto-poulou 2000: 1). And under the heading 'Guiding principles and objectives for pension reforms' the related EC (2000c: 13) commun-ication noted that '[n]ational choices and priorities... remain the responsibility of Member States'.

There are, clearly, deeply entrenched political interests concerned about the continuing viability of European systems of social security (see Mantel and Bowers 1999). Likewise, amongst academics there are many who suppose that continuity with the past is an essential ingre-dient in any understanding of the processes of economic development and spatial economic differentiation (Krugman 1991). Notions such as path dependence, lock-in, and sunk costs are often invoked to help explain regional and national differences in economic innovation and performance (see Clark *et al.* 2000). Therefore, on a variety of counts, the idea that European systems of retirement income could or should converge upon the Anglo-American model as suggested by commen-tators in the media, goes against the grain of those committed to the integrity of the past. I do not wish to suggest that such commitments are empty gestures of theory or nostalgia. Simply, it is obvious that the past has enormous analytical and political significance in con-temporary discussions about the future of European pensions.

If the forthcoming retirement of the baby boom generation was simply a matter of reorganizing budget priorities, it is doubtful that so much research and commentary effort would have been expended on the topic of European pensions. As I have tried to show in this chapter and in Chapter 1, European demographic trends are more than evidence of an on-going demographic transition. Demography represents a crisis for Europe for the following reasons. Most obviously, demographic ageing is pronounced in continental Europe compared to the Anglo-American countries. Furthermore, the accumulated public policies and circumstances favouring early retirement appear likely to bring forward in time the onset of the financial problems inherent in the PAYG social security. And it seems quite unlikely that the cumulative long-term rates of real economic growth will be sufficient to cover the looming financial obligations. The problem with European demography is that it is simultaneously an issue of ageing, economics, and finance, set against the advantages of the Anglo-American funded retirement systems and the related structure of the global financial markets.

For many European commentators, funding the retirement of the baby boom generation threatens the fiscal capacity of governments and threatens the economic growth potential of Europe's largest economies. In some quarters, these threats also represent long-term threats to the political and social integrity of distinctive national traditions. By this logic, continuity with the past is hardly a recipe for the future: by honouring social solidarity and inherited pension entitlements, the long-term economic integrity of the whole European project must be questioned. On the other hand, it is hard to imagine that continental Europe will suddenly simply overturn past commitments and institutions by adopting the Anglo-American model. Rather, the most likely scenarios are either *accommodation* or *incremental convergence* to selected elements of the Anglo-American model. It seems inevitable that forecast social security obligations will be discounted by changing rules relating to maximum benefits and maintenance of the real value of paid pensions. Furthermore, as recent events have shown, even France and Germany have moved to encourage the private provision of supplementary retirement income and may even institute policies designed to accumulate pension assets and invest them in the global economy (as in the Dutch model; see Chapter 6).

But notice that I have also argued that proffered pension reforms could have significant implications for the financial structure of the continental European economies. This is most obvious when considering the intimate connection between German corporate-sponsored supplementary pensions and the German model of long-term untraded financial relationships and corporate governance (Chapters 4 and 5). There are many pressures on the German model given the development of international accounting regimes and the performance of Anglo-American financial markets. Pension funding is not the only issue driving the restructuring of German financial, economic, and industrial relationships in relation to global competitors. As in so many aspects of the collision between the German and the Anglo-American models, the problem of funding public and private pension obligations has put in play the costs and benefits of non-market relationships. While German commentators look favourably upon the social market, believing that the proper order is social solidarity and then market imperatives, global finance threatens to reorder this logic such that market imperatives dominate the possible organization of social relationships.

It is tempting, therefore, to see Anglo-American financial markets as the enemy of continental European society. There is an often-voiced fear of those concerned to protect past commitments and entitlements. Moreover, given the interests of London-based financial service firms in fostering solutions to the demographic crisis consistent with their competency in global financial markets, political conflict occasioned by attempts at pension reform has seen the fracturing of the post-war consensus. Indeed, the rhetoric of reform is deeply affected by a most general conflict between the (Anglo-American) market and (European) society as it is affected by conflicts between local interests (Clark 2001). In this respect, European pensions and global finance are deeply entwined with domestic and European politics.

However, the Anglo-American financial markets may be more than the enemy of social solidarity. The rise of the new economy and the remarkable macro-economic performance of the United States of America and, to a lesser extent, the United Kingdom economies in the 1990s has brought into question the long-term economic potential of continental Europe. The funding of the PAYG social security systems relies heavily upon the real rate of economic growth. Furthermore, there is a significant gap between the long-term European rate of economic growth and the long-term risk-adjusted rate of return available in international financial markets. Recognition of these facts of economic life has prompted economic policy makers to reconsider the efficacy of national and European economic policies and institutions (Diamantopoulou 2001). If continental European pension systems are to retain their commitment to social solidarity, corporate and industrial restructuring consistent with the success of the US economy in the 1990s may be the future price paid for sheltering European citizens' retirement income from the market.

NOTES

1. See respectively Disney (2000), World Bank (1994), and Mantel (2000).
2. Other opinions have been expressed in the *Financial Times*. In an article devoted to the prospects for Europe in the context of an apparent accelerating decline in the US economy, Tony Barber (2001: 20) suggested that some European policy makers are optimistic about the prospects for a distinctively European growth trajectory. He noted that an Italian member of the European Central Bank's executive board used the following analogy to illustrate the gathering strength of Europe with respect to the United States of America. It goes as follows: 'Europe is like a long distance runner with a pocket full of stones. It has thrown away one stone—or obstacle to growth—after another. It has introduced a single internal market, launched the Euro, practiced greater budgetary discipline and abolished barriers to competition.... The Continent has gradually gained speed and is now overtaking a flagging US'.
3. Demography and its various components including migration have been staple topics of geography and related sciences for many years. Much of the related work on Europe has stressed patterns of migration, focusing upon urban and regional dimensions within countries as well as comparison across countries (see Fassman and Munz 1992; Rees and Kupiszewski 1999). At the same time there is an important tradition of country-specific studies, integrating demography with economic and social change. Clearly, there are distinct European local, regional, and national population trends that foreshadow the retirement of the baby boom generation and deserve further scrutiny

and analysis (Coleman 1996). See also studies such as Berentsen (1999) on demography and German east–west unification, Clout (1994) comparing changing demography across western Europe, and Winchester (1993) on France.

4. See also the EC (2001c) report on employment trends, noting that although geographical mobility remains low (by international standards) it is growing. At the same time, during the last couple of years of the 1990s, there was evidence of significant 'labour and skill shortages' in some regions and sectors.

5. In an IMF (2001) report on the performance of the French economy, it was noted that the economy appeared very vulnerable to a global cyclical slow down. While applauding recent labour market initiatives, the IMF was critical of limited steps towards structural reform especially in areas sensitive to demographic trends such as pensions, health care, and overall budgetary priorities.

6. See again the EC (2001c) report on employment trends. Therein, the Commission noted that employment growth over the period 1995–2000 was significant albeit concentrated in regions and sectors associated with the burgeoning 'knowledge economy'. The report manages to imply that the growth of employment is sustainable over the coming decade, eliding the difference between the structural and cyclical factors contributing to recent employment growth.

7. Witness, for example, the comments made by Diamantopoulou (2001) in introducing the EC (2001c) report on employment. She suggests that promotion of the 'knowledge economy' is the only way that Europe can sustain economic growth and employment opportunities for all.

8. This argument (and the argument in some sections of the European Commission) about the superior economic performance of the Anglo-American system over the 1990s is about the rates of innovation and growth over this period as reflected in labour market variables such as employment and unemployment. Like Baumol (2002), I believe that the rate of product and process innovation drives long-term economic growth, and that the financing of innovation is a crucial ingredient in this process. In this respect, while the TMT stock market bust may have significant consequences for consumer demand and corporate investment, it is arguable that the long-term growth of US productivity will remain significantly above its' comparable European reference point (Berndt 2002).

9. This idea was also developed in an IMF (2000) report on Germany, and its 'readiness for the "new economy"'. While much of the report was devoted to information technology and German industry, the report also suggested that the apparent lack of risk financing through equities and venture capital were significant barriers to the development of the sector in Germany and Europe. It was also suggested that the 'current bias towards retained profits' amongst German corporations tended to trap investment resources, starving the venture capital sector of motivation and resources.

10. The proposal was debated in the European Parliament and substantially revised in the light of concerns about the consequences of an accelerated pan-European level-playing field in financial services. However, thereafter, it ran into considerable opposition, being blocked before final acceptance and approval. Once again private firms are mobilizing around a court challenge to member countries' discriminatory practices directed towards pan-European funded pension systems. See the related 'model' framework provided by the European Federation for Retirement Provision (2000). Given the goals of this project, it is not possible to look indepth into the complex and evolving debate in the EU over the nature and prospects of the EU pensions proposal.

11. Furthermore, there has been a flurry of empirical research about the 'disappearing' equity premium most notably Fama and French (2002), Pastor and Stambaugh (2001), and Wang (2001). It remains to be seen whether the equity premium in the US and other global markets will continue within the long-term band of 2–4% (see Claus and Thomas 2001, Dimson et al. 2002, and the commentary provided by Engelen 2002). The argument presented in this book is not meant to idealise the Anglo-American system so much as understand the apparent tensions between European pensions and global finance.

Requiem for a French Ideal

French retirement income depends upon a set of related institutions commonly known as the PAYG social security.[1] In general, the objectives of French social security are three-fold: (1) universal coverage, (2) benefits related to earnings supplemented where necessary by government contributions, and (3) a high income-replacement ratio between 50–70 per cent of average worked incomes. Although a compromise solution to pressing problems immediately after 1945, a system stitched together with pre-existing occupational pension institutions, for some it has become an ideal form of state guaranteed income security. To illustrate, many commentators distinguish between social security schemes that provide flat rate minimum retirement benefits as opposed to earnings related benefits; this distinction is often articulated by comparison between the United Kingdom, and France and Germany (Budd and Campbell 1998). Referenced or implied is a distinction between Beveridge and Bismarck—the principals personifying the history of twentieth-century western welfare states (Lannoo 1996).

Whatever its virtues, the future of the French social security system is heavily contested. Like many PAYG systems, it faces a demographic crisis (the pending retirement of the baby boom generation) as well as a financial crisis (the payment of promised benefits and obligations). There is a huge literature devoted to the topic and to France in particular; see Chapter 2 for an extensive review and analysis.[2] Though incremental reforms over the past decade have discounted the future costs of social security, many commentators believe that European social security systems are not viable compared to Anglo-American mixed public and funded private systems (Brahs 2001). Yet, hidden in the debate over the French 'crisis' is a presumption that this is in some way new or unanticipated. In fact, government reports over the past 30 years or so have raised concerns about the difficulties of paying future social security liabilities. Here, I contend that at the time of its design and implementation reasonable doubts could have been raised about its long-term financial viability. This does not mean that French social security was destined to fail. In point of fact, higher than anticipated fertility rates during the 1950s first sustained but then ultimately undercut the intergenerational balance needed to sustain social security as a self-reproducing system of taxes and payments. If social security is understood as a financial accounting system it is very vulnerable to national demography.

However, social security is more than a financial and demographic accounting system. Given the uncertainties involved in estimating future liabilities, social solidarity between the generations can be seen as an essential ingredient in any PAYG social security system.[3] Indeed, it is argued here that social solidarity is a necessary political instrument or bridging mechanism between current costs and future benefit expectations. It is suggested that the institutions of social solidarity effectively 'managed' reasonable doubts about the robustness of French social security for many years. I also suggest that *economic circumstances* and *intra-generational transfers* by those with a special place in French policy making have compromised the vitality of social solidarity as a means of 'balancing' intergenerational interests (see also Boldrin *et al.* 1999). The state as the custodian of social solidarity has undercut the financial and political legitimacy of the ideal. One response has been defection by the middle class from the ideal. Being unable to opt out, they have become significant consumers of quoted and unquoted equities, savings, and retail investment products designed to augment or protect their long-term welfare against the discounting of promised social security benefits.

Basically, three sets of arguments are made in this chapter. In the first instance, the focus is upon demography. We begin with the classic formula that underpins the funding of social security systems owed to analysts such as Samuelson (1958) and Aaron (1966). We then move on to demographic accounting to show how and why such pension systems are vulnerable to demographic imbalances. In abstract, this analysis could be thought to be like generational accounting as developed by Auerbach *et al.* (1999). But, as we shall see, the logic used here is simpler and more direct. In the second instance, the focus is upon a social solidarity. Social solidarity can be understood to be a national ideal concerning the proper organization of society *and* a means of mutually insuring the welfare of related generations. Third, the likelihood of defection by younger workers is discussed in the context of the globalization of finance and industry. Whereas French social security was conceived in reaction to the market uncertainties of the first half of the twentieth century, global financial markets may be a necessary element in any solution to the financial burdens that threaten the welfare of younger workers and retirees over the coming decades.

In making these arguments, the chapter uses analytical logic rather than a detailed historical exposition of French political and economic debate. Given the available commentaries on contemporary French public policy, it is unnecessary to reproduce those details (see Friot 1999; Mantel and Thomson 2000). Also, understanding the looming crisis of French social security requires an appreciation of the basic economic and demographic building blocks as well as the historical evolution and political debate about reform. Unlike many Anglo-American commentators, I remain sympathetic and supportive of the ideal of social solidarity. Even so, recognition of ideals such as social solidarity should not blind us to the emerging faults of these institutions. Defection is not just evidence of middle class self-interest; it is also evidence of the failure of national institutions in the context of changing European economic (Supiot 2001) and social conditions (Crouch 1999).

DEMOGRAPHIC AND ECONOMIC PRINCIPLES

Let us begin with the simplest of cost-accounting identities provided by Gillion *et al.* (2000: 128) amongst others. See also Disney (2000), Hassler and Lindbeck (1998), and the EC (2001d) for similar cost-accounting logic. Assuming a PAYG system without the accumulation of assets beyond that necessary to pay for immediate liabilities, it can be shown that the current cost (time t) of a PAYG social system is the product of the dependency and benefit ratios.

That is:

$$\text{PAYG}(t) = P(t)/A(t)^*AP(t)/AIW(t) \tag{3.1}$$

Ignoring for the moment the young, infirm, and unemployed, the dependency ratio can be defined as the number of pensioners $P(t)$

divided by the number of active workers $A(t)$. Also, by ignoring the systematic variations in pension entitlements, the cost of living and productivity growth, the benefit ratio can be defined as the average pension value $AP(t)$ divided by the average amount of insured wages or earned income $AIW(t)$. Assuming constant pension values and insured wages, an increase in the dependency ratio from time t to time $t+1$ will directly increase the total cost at time $t+1$ of the country's social security system.

To understand the logic of this system, imagine that society wished to reduce future expected pension costs. The age at which retirees were eligible for a state pension could be increased so that in time $t+1$, P was smaller relative to A. Deferring eligibility may discount costs if, for example, in the mean time A were to increase in greater numbers than the numbers of deferred beneficiaries, and the life expectancy of retirees were to remain constant. Alternatively, society could reduce the future value of the paid pension. This could be achieved in a number of ways. By reducing the income replacement rate; by breaking the nexus between the pension and future wages by indexing pensions to prices; and by distinguishing between the hourly wage rate and total compensation, thereby limiting the reference wage when setting the pension. All these options have been contemplated or introduced by the European governments over the past 10 years. For example, the UK government shifted from wage to price indexation thereby discounting long-term pension liabilities (a policy adopted by the French government during the early 1990s; see Zanni 2001).

Consider other possibilities. Imagine society were to reduce the age at which retirees were eligible for a state pension while keeping constant the paid pension. Some active contributors A would join the ranks of the pensioners P bringing forward in time the cost of their retirement. If those pensioners were to live longer, the costs of their pensions would increase in proportion to their total (early + middle + late) years of retirement. In this regard, Lynes (1967: 13) noted that in the early 1960s nearly 50 per cent of French workers retired at the conventional age of retirement (65 years). When asked about their preferred age of retirement, however, over 80 per cent of workers would have retired by age 60. Revisiting the issue nearly twenty years later, Lynes (1985: 13) observed that the majority of French workers had retired by 60 years of age and very few remained in work through to 65. In the meantime, the rules allowing early retirees to draw social security pensions had been relaxed—by that time, the numbers of pensioners P had increased faster than the number of active workers or tax contributors A. Notice that *net* immigration could play a significant role in these circumstances by adding to the total stock of active contributors. Also, policy makers might impose limits on the long-term pension eligibility of guest workers.

There are a variety of advantages to the PAYG social security. For one, PAYG retirees share with current workers the earned income of the economy. They may also share in the fruits of economic growth to the extent to which higher labour productivity is rewarded with higher wages. Equally important, in practice PAYG systems protect the consumption expenditures of retirees, being maintained at levels consistent with past habits and tastes. In doing so, the elderly may avoid the poverty so often associated with old age and retirement, a point of contrast often introduced to distinguish continental pension systems from the Anglo-American world. Furthermore, and unlike contribution-based social insurance programmes, in practice PAYG systems tend not to penalize workers with variable employment histories and incomes. While the value of the social security pension entitlement may be linked to the average worker's earned income, it need not rely upon the workers' accumulated lifetime earnings. If caps are imposed on pension benefit entitle-ments and if minimum benefit levels are guaranteed then the PAYG social security can help achieve the social democratic goals of income equity and redistribution (see Diamond 1977; Goodin *et al.* 1999).

The PAYG systems are, however, national systems characterized by hard borders: citizenship is a common qualification for entitlement (van Amersfoort 1999). At the same time, while net immigration may benefit 'local' dependency ratios, such systems penalize interjurisdictional labour mobility and economic integration (Aranda-Hassel and Duval-Kieffer 2001). For individuals subject to the system-specific rules regarding vesting periods, minimum terms of work, and measures of average income, the sustained episodes of 'outside' employment can translate into limited long-term benefits. As these systems rely upon earned wage income, reflecting local employment contracts and the norms of employment relationships, they are often insensitive to corporate compensation systems tied to global as opposed to local career paths. Furthermore, being tied to local earned wages these systems rely upon commodity trading systems that (hopefully) localize the benefits of exchange between countries while widely distributing any costs of such trading regimes. Inevitably, the social security pension income is very sensitive to the economic performance of the 'sponsoring' country. Presumably, the larger the national economy the more diversified the pensioners' long-term income risks. But equally important, these systems ignore finance: not only the dividend income from stock ownership but also the risk-adjusted rate of return on globally invested assets (Aglietta 2000; Boyer 1996).[4]

INTERGENERATIONAL SOCIAL SOLIDARITY

It is tempting to suppose that the PAYG social security is simply a demographic and economic system of intergenerational taxes and income transfers. For critics of such systems, the demographic imbalances combined with the expected financial liabilities are sufficient to justify counter-arguments in favour of the Anglo-American funded public and private systems. However, it should be understood that the PAYG social security is also a social institution. This is most obviously the case in France, as indicated by the complex array of jointly managed government and non-government organizations that administer social security. But it is also a social institution in another most important sense: it is a system of mutual obligation and entitlement. As each generation works to support their children, they earn a claim to their own retirement income in the future by virtue of the obligation passed to their children. Binding each generation together in this system of mutual obligation and entitlement is the concept and practice of social solidarity. Implied is a moral order (compare Keyfitz 1976 who disputes this idea).

Perhaps the easiest way to explain social solidarity is to invoke Durkheim's [1893] (1984) treatise on the division of labour. In doing so, I do not mean to suggest that Durkheim is the only appropriate reference point or necessarily the most up-to-date source relevant to contemporary French political debate. Rather, it provides an accessible source for an ideal that has evolved and developed over the twentieth century through institutions such as the post-1945 French welfare state (Jones 1999). According to Durkheim, prior to the industrial revolution social solidarity was imposed by 'rigid social controls in uniform belief'. Whatever the mode of economic organization prior to the industrial revolution, Durkheim characterized modern society by the division of labour, capital accumulation through firms and corporations, and economic growth through the medium of exchange. For Durkheim social solidarity derives, in an organic fashion, from the complementarities between individuals, their mutual dependence and reciprocal relationships, and a form of collective consciousness (modernity).

Essentially, social solidarity is a response to the anonymity of market exchange relationships.

If social solidarity is the product of modern society it is also an important functional component of modern society, binding together disparate individuals with (at times) antagonistic and competing interests. Indeed, social solidarity within a generation may be thought to be functionally necessary for economic growth just as social solidarity may be necessary for the reproduction of society from generation to generation. This notion is rarely discussed in Anglo-American social science. In many respects, rational choice theory and the prospects for cooperation dominate the space in which social solidarity might be fully elaborated and discussed. Crudely speaking, it could be thought analogous to social capital if defined as the social resources of society such as authority, trust, and customs and norms—the untraded components of social life that enable individual action. Coleman (1990: 300) noted that social capital stands inbetween individual agents, thereby providing the resources for social life and identity set against the stripped-down view of autonomous and rational economic agents that dominates much of the Anglo-American social theory and policy expectations.

Social security as an intergenerational obligation and entitlement could be also thought of as an insurance contract, 'a bond or note, an exchange of money now for money later' (Arrow 1984: 78). As workers support their children, they effectively purchase a claim to retirement income at a specified date in the future. In doing so, the state sustains the exchange of income between generations *and* guarantees the redemption of the bond in the future. Left unspecified, except in an abstract manner, is the net present value of future retirement income. Historically, the commitment made by the French social security system was to pay future retirement benefits in accordance with the future level of earned income. This would have maintained the relative value of retirement income (workers compared to retirees). It would also have factored some portion of the wage and salary benefits of productivity growth into retirees' income now and in the future. In this respect, Arrow noted that insurance is also a promise of future benefits contingent upon certain circumstances. If so, the future real value of the PAYG social security is contingent upon (1) the growth in labour productivity, (2) the distribution of its value between capital and labour, and (3) the continuity of commitment.

Current workers as future retirees have a variety of interests. They have an interest in retirees spending their income, thereby contributing to the level of current employment (the numbers of workers who bear the burden of contributions to the PAYG system) and future economic growth (the driving force behind their expected retirement income). They also have an interest in the state's efficient and cost-effective administration of the PAYG system as they have an interest in the commitment of the state to future economic growth. As the state indemnifies the bond, workers have an interest in the state's long-term solvency. As the state is responsible for ensuring the future value of the PAYG social security, workers rely upon it for ensuring that conditions (1), (2) and (3) are met at the time of their retirement. Most importantly, workers have an interest in the continuity of commitment—making possible the redemption of the retirement income bond in the future.

How are such interests protected? How is the PAYG social security to be regulated? There are a variety of possible answers. One obvious means of regulation is to invoke the ideal of social solidarity: mutual obligations and entitlements. But, as Durkheim indicated, this is insufficient for a variety of reasons not least of which is the possibility of spontaneous revision time and time again of the terms and conditions of mutual obligation and entitlement. For Durkheim the regulatory institution underpinning social solidarity over the long term is the contract. This can be thought to be a limited, legally defined set of rules governing discrete exchange relations. This would be consistent with much of the Anglo-American social theory, specifically rational choice theory (Coleman 1992). More importantly, Durkheim suggested that the contract is actually a commonly accepted moral order, a set of customs and norms that express the ideal of social solidarity and underpins the execution of the law of contract in specific cases. By this logic, social solidarity is constituted in the first instance by social norms like trust and reciprocity where trust refers to 'long-terms relations, a sharing of goals and expectations, and the suppression of short-term self-seeking' (see Deakin *et al.* 1997: 108–109 for related reasoning).

Being a moral order, social solidarity as a social contract may 'regulate' intergenerational obligations and entitlements by reference to moral sentiments like fairness, equity, and mutual regard. The exploitation of one generation by another would be properly ruled 'inequitable' given the accepted principles of fairness. Likewise, the distribution of obligations and entitlements between successive generations would have to meet the standards of fairness consistent with the reproduction of the whole society and the institution of the PAYG social security. Inevitably, the administration of such a system, being based upon codified rules and regulations regarding contributions and entitlements, would have to be consistent with the principles of social solidarity. In this sense, the state is both the *custodian* of social solidarity and the *regulator* of the social contract binding the generations together. These functions place the state at the very centre of society, being the instrument of its reproduction from generation to generation. These roles are not entirely unproblematic, given the abstractness of the underlying principles. Nevertheless, it should be apparent that the PAYG social security is premised upon a distinctive language of association and representation (Clark 2001).

THE FINANCIAL INTEGRITY OF SOCIAL SECURITY

In previous sections, we set out the economic and political logic underpinning the PAYG social security, and its French incarnation. Here, we evaluate the performance of this institution from its inception in 1947 through to the present day. In doing so, we concentrate on the integrity of the institution rather than its particular administrative and benefit formula. Much has been written about the latter; understanding the status and significance of the institution in French political life also requires a better appreciation of the former issue. Integrity is defined here as the long-term coherence of the institution relative to its initial goals and objectives. Integrity can also have a more explicit social meaning, referring to the degree to which the population at large accepts it as legitimate. In these ways, integrity has both a formal institutional quality as well as a less formal political quality.

To evaluate the integrity of the institution, we consider economic and demographic patterns and trends related to the dependency ratio introduced in eqn 3.1. We also consider the evolution of contributions and benefits, again referencing the terms introduced in eqn 3.1. Perhaps more difficult is an assessment of the governance and regulation of social solidarity, focusing upon the administration of the institution as well as its cost efficiency. In the next section, we refer to the nature and organization of governance rather than precise figures on cost efficiency (which, in any event, are unavailable). We must take care not to idealize the institution of social security, treating it as if it was established only according to the economic and political principles noted above. These principles may justify such institutions. But it would be foolhardy to suggest they were the only issues taken into account when the institution was established. Thus, we must take care not to apply ex-post reasoning either in the form of now recognized economic and demographic trends or in the form of consistent and far-reaching behaviour attributed to successive generations of policy makers.

Demographic trends. In the years leading up to the Second World War, adverse demographic trends preoccupied French governments. It seemed inevitable that the total population would fall from about 42 (1938) to 34 million by 1985 (Scargill 1985: 5). For more than 30 years, falling fertility rates combined with the enormous losses of young men during the First World War had conspired to produce crude birth rates lower than crude death rates.[5] During and immediately after the Second World War, grants, tax allowances, and provisions against birth control were introduced to promote population growth through the family (pro-natalism). Even so, when French social security was established in 1945, only the most optimistic nationalist would have forecast the baby boom that, in conjunction with inward migration, contributed to the rapid growth of population through to the mid-1970s. By contrast, a risk adverse actuary might have reasonably predicted a stable or even declining population base. See Table 3.1 for a summary of French population growth by broad age categories.

The newly established social security system had to accommodate the interests of three generations at once. Those retirees who had borne the brunt of inflation prior to the Second World War and had seen the value of their entitlements extinguished during the Second World War claimed compensation from the new Republic. Those workers who had been employed or unemployed through the Great Depression and had fought during the Second World War claimed an entitlement to a just retirement. And those who were about to enter the labour market or were to stay in the labour market sought to protect pension rights and privileges while recognising the claims of social solidarity and universal coverage. Given the exhaustion of the previous fragmented and partially funded retirement schemes, there was no option but to institute a PAYG social security system. Remarkably, and against expectations, the baby boom transformed French demography and the economy. Indeed, rapid population growth gave financial legitimacy to French social security as social solidarity.

By the mid-1970s, however, the baby boom had petered out. Fertility rates returned to pre-1945 patterns, and government officials again became concerned with the prospects and consequences of a stable or declining population (witness the Sullerot 1978 Report).[6] If post-war

Table 3.1. The French population (millions) and percentage distribution by age category, selected years 1931–1995

Year	Total population	Age cohorts		
		0–14	15–64	>64
1931	41.2	22.9	67.6	9.3
1935	41.3	25.2	65.0	9.8
1945	37.4	21.0	67.0	12.0
1950	41.9	22.0	67.0	12.0
1961	45.9	26.0	62.0	14.0
1972	51.7	24.0	63.0	13.0
1982	54.2	21.0	64.0	14.0
1990	56.6	19.0	66.0	13.0
1995	57.8	17.0	66.0	15.0

Source: League of Nations, International Statistical Yearbook (1931, 1935) and United Nations, Year Book; supplemented by Hokenson *et al.* (2001).

economic growth driven, in part, by population growth had saved the fledgling social security system, by 1970 the ratio of pensioners $P(t)$ to active workers $A(t)$ had moved massively in favour of active workers. With a normal retirement age of 65 years, rapidly accumulating contributions, and the prospect of future high rates of economic growth it seemed that the gamble on social solidarity had paid-off; indeed, it seemed that demography could be ignored as the social security system gained greater responsibilities and administrative coherence. Although a widespread view, not all agreed. In fact, even then, reports were issued warning about the long-term pension obligations implied by the baby boom generation (see Lynes 1985 for further information).

Labour force participation trends. As noted earlier, retirement at 65 years of age was normal even if the retirement age was increasingly earlier (in their early 60s) in the 1960s. But as we also noted, the preferred age of retirement was identified as being around 55 years of age. By the early 1980s, many older-aged working people had realised their preferences. From the late 1960s to the late 1990s, the labour force participation rate for men aged 60–64 declined dramatically from around 70 to less than 15 per cent. Over much the same period, the labour force participation rate of men aged 55–59 also began to decline, accelerating immediately after lucrative benefit revisions were introduced in the early 1980s. Consistent with patterns of female labour force participation around the world, over the same period the labour force participation rate of French women aged 60–64 also declined significantly (although the participation rate of women aged 55–59 increased slightly over the same period) (see Blanchet and Péle 1999). It is now rare for French men and women over 60 years to be working and contributing to social security institutions. No other western advanced economy experienced such a dramatic long-term decline in older-aged male and female labour force participation rates (see Johnson 2000; Gruber and Wise 1999).

In effect, the fathers and mothers of the baby boom generation began retiring earlier than expected in the late 1970s and early 1980s. Not only did the stock of active workers A as contributors to the social security system grow more slowly than expected due to the reduced labour force participation rates, the stock of pensioners P grew more rapidly than expected much *before* the on-set of the retirement of the baby-boom generation. There are various explanations of the apparent precipitous decline in labour force participation rates after 1970. Some commentators have suggested that the generation that went to work immediately after World War Two could claim special consideration, having endured the privations of the war and the burdens of driving economic growth and development. At the same time, it has been suggested that the restructuring of the state-governed industrial economy begun during the 1970s, prompted employers to encourage early retirement as a means of improving economic efficiency. Most importantly, however, with the employment crisis of the late 1970s and 1980s, it has been observed that early retirement was a form of job rationing, protecting the jobs of younger workers and, in theory at least, providing opportunities for the baby boom generation entering the labour market (Lynes 1985).

To make this possible and thereby encourage voluntary retirement, retirement benefits had to be adjusted to an earlier retirement age and the formula between pensions $AP(t)$ and wages $AIW(t)$ relaxed. Blanchet and Péle (1998: 105) noted that over the ten-year period 1974–1984 the ratio of the average retirement benefit to the average wage increased from approximately 0.33–0.57. This was the result, no doubt, of many new retirees from the labour market on benefits more liberal than before and the introduction of supplements to existing benefits. By 1976, the entitlement of certain government and nationalized industry workers to full benefits at the age of 60 had been extended to manual workers. With the passage of pension reforms in 1981, and enacted in 1983, the official age of retirement with full benefits was set at 60 years for the *régime général*. Note that, consistent with the job rationing logic, those workers who took retirement at 60 were required to leave the industry in which they had been employed. These changes in the benefit/wage ratio were paid out of the accumulated reserves of the social security institutions administered by the various *caisses*. Social security contribution rates borne by current workers and their employers were then increased to offset, in part, the future claims on pension reserves.

Employment and unemployment trends. Having encouraged earlier retirement, and having funded larger numbers of unanticipated retirees at higher benefit levels, the integrity of the French social security system became even more dependent upon (1) the continued high rates of population growth, and (2) the high rates of economic and employment growth through the 1980s and 1990s. But as we noted above, population growth was already faltering as fertility rates returned to pre-1945 levels. At the same time, there was concern expressed about the prospects for economic growth and employment growth over the coming decades. These concerns were realized over the last couple of decades of the twentieth century: the French economy underperformed when compared to many of its peers, in particular, the United States of America and (to a lesser extent) the United Kingdom. Consequently, French social security was profoundly, and perhaps terminally, compromised by the next 20 years of increasingly adverse dependency and benefit ratios (to 2000).

In terms of the growth of the GDP, the French economy marginally underperformed to the US economy and even the UK economy during the 1980s, and markedly lost ground to both economies during 1990s. Most importantly, low and uneven rates of real GDP growth were reflected in very low and even negative rates of employment growth over both decades. Only towards the end of the 1990s did the French economy begin to show signs of significant and sustained increases in employment, to be dashed by the onset of the global recession. Accentuating these trends was the sustained and increasing, higher than the OECD average, rates of unemployment. See Figure 3.1 (and Figure 2.2). As we know, unemployment in France is both a long-term phenomenon and a highly geographically concentrated phenomenon. Those regions most affected by industrial restructuring during the 1970s became the regions most affected by long-term structural unemployment during the 1980s and 1990s (Flutter 2001). Reflecting these trends, the overall French labour force participation rates remained on average

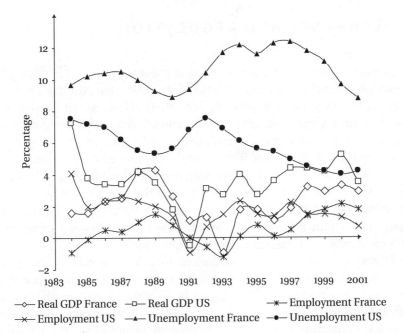

Fig. 3.1. Comparative economic performance of France and the USA, 1994–2001.

five percentage points less than the Anglo-American economies and at times almost 10 per cent less than these economies.

Basically, any chance of repaying the social security system for the opening of early-retirement in the 1970s was lost during the 1980s and 1990s through declining population and employment growth rates. Unfortunately, the costs associated with higher dependency and benefit ratios fell on a static working population. While accumulated reserves were initially important in funding retirement during this period, the prospect of current system-wide deficits prompted higher rates of contribution charged against workers and employers. Arguably, these higher costs then contributed to lower rates of employment growth and higher rates of unemployment. By this logic, Palier (2000: 121) has observed that 'the high level of contributions is seen to have an overall negative impact on the country's economic competitiveness and to be responsible for the high rate of unemployment. The argument is that social insurance contributions inhibit job creation, as they have a direct impact on the cost of low-skilled labour'. This was the legacy of twentieth-century French social security: it is in this context that the debate over the reform of the funding and the administration of social security institutions has taken place.

GOVERNANCE AND REGULATION

In previous sections, it was argued that the state is both the custodian of social solidarity and the regulator of its institutions (in this case, the institutions of social security). As we noted above, social solidarity is based upon intergenerational mutual obligation and entitlement. At the same time, the state must guard against 'over-consumption' by those who are retired, and 'over investment' by those currently working. In essence, the state's role is to promote mutual commitment and ensure that there is a long-term balance between the generations in terms of their current and future economic welfare. Ideally, this requires the state to be both a bystander and an adjudicator between competing intergenerational interests (Clark and Dear 1984).

There is, however, a temptation to idealize the role of the state, assuming that social security began as a coherent and comprehensive system and is accepted as legitimate by all citizens. In fact, the history of French social security tells a rather different story. Instead of a universal unitary system, French social security began as a combination of various new and old retirement income institutions. In the face of considerable opposition from certain segments of the population already covered by public and private pensions, the French government was forced to introduce a system marked by considerable complexity and variable accountability. Furthermore, the administration and financial management of the social security system was highly decentralized being based upon a large number of occupational, industrial, and regional jointly managed *caisses*. Consequently, the social partners have had a significant share of the state's custodial responsibilities; in the first couple of decades after 1947, the administration and financial management of social security was located with the *caisse* notwithstanding the fact that the state guaranteed its integrity.

In this section, two points are made. First, there was at first and there remains a considerable 'gap' between the ideal of social solidarity and the functional organization of the social security system. To make good on its custodial and regulatory responsibilities, the French government has had to fight to centralize control of the various functions and institutions of social security. Only in the last decade has the state accumulated sufficient powers to effectively manage the system, reflecting perhaps a common realization that its current financial problems and future liabilities threaten the integrity of the nation-state. The second point made here is that the coherence of the French social security system has been undercut by a series of unresolved conflicts over the functions of social security. Social solidarity has not been a robust or unambiguous overarching principle capable of resolving conflicting interests within and between the generations. To make these points, three observations are made about the governance and regulation of French social security.

Functional and organizational fragmentation. As many commentators have noted, the design and implementation of the post-war social security system was a contested and protracted process of accommodation. If originally conceived in terms similar to the UK Beveridge report, the agreed system combined three kinds of organizations that have coexisted in one form or another till today. At base were the state-sponsored institutions like the *régime général* (for private sector employees) and the *régimes spéciaux* (for civil servants and public employees). Also important were the administrative units responsible for supplementary benefits and provisions for those judged least well off. Added to the base were the so-called private voluntary occupational or industry arrangements known as *régimes complémentaires*. Local jointly managed funds or units (*caisses*) administered each institution. Lynes (1967: 22) noted that the *régime général* was administered by 16 regional *caisses*, the agricultural workers' scheme was administered by 86 local *caisses*, and the scheme for the self-employed was administered by 101 industry *caisses*. Over time, the complementary fund for salaried managers has become mandatory, and has been matched by other occupational funds, similarly jointly managed by nominated or elected employer and employee representatives.

At one level, the rules and regulations regarding coverage, minimum and maximum benefits, and contribution rates were the responsibility of the state. Likewise, the recognition of workers' membership and the jurisdiction of the various pension institutions and their *caisses* were established and administered by the French government. However, the *caisses* were initially responsible for collecting contributions, setting benefits, and distributing benefits in accordance with 'local' circumstances and national legislation. Embedded in this system were multiple and overlapping jurisdictions; over time, the resulting conflicts were to be resolved (as in the *régime général*) with reference to a formal top-down hierarchy of authority such as *the state, the scheme, the caisse*. In many cases, however, the claimed formal authority of the state was contested and disputed; the *caisses* also claimed considerable autonomy and administrative functions, legitimated by the representative nature of the boards and the local circumstances of individual participants and their special claims for justice. For more than three decades, the local *caisses* functioned as 'courts of appeal' and decision-makers rather than as economic and financial agents of the central state.

Even so, we should take care not to exaggerate the current autonomy of the various pension institutions and their *caisses*. In the 1980s and 1990s, the French state has successfully claimed greater powers of oversight, integration, and control than ever before. In part, centralization has had significant consequences for the relationship between the state and the *régimes complémentaires* (AGRIC and ARRCO). Even though these institutions can claim separate status with reference to employment and collective agreement law, the French state has increasingly regulated their funding protocols, their investment policies, and their status in relation to the *régime général* and *régimes spéciaux*. Now being compulsory, the private complementary pension arrangements have become integral to the whole pension benefit system, taking some of the responsibility for income replacement previously thought to be essentially the responsibility of the state. Indeed, one option for reform is to add greater responsibilities to these institutions, mimicking the funded sector-based pension plans in the Netherlands and the role of similar institutions in the United Kingdom and the United States of America.

Multiple responsibilities. With respect to intergenerational solidarity, the state, the pension institutions, and their *caisses* were to be joined together in their custodial and administrative responsibilities. In fact, overlapping and at times at odds with the ideal of social solidarity has been a broader conception of the role of the state. Reflecting the turmoil of the first 50 years of the century, the extensive version of social solidarity has been the welfare state—a proclaimed comprehensive system of benefits and entitlements combining pensions and retirement income with unemployment benefits, health care benefits, and social services. Whether this 'system' was ever as significant or as robust as claimed by many on the left is less important than the role of the ideal in justifying the accumulation of responsibilities of the social security system. In this respect, it is arguable that the roles and responsibilities of the various pension institutions and their *caisses* have been interpreted in ways *less* consistent with intergenerational social solidarity and in ways *more* consistent with intra-generational equity and social justice.

The economic crisis of the 1970s and 1980s added greater responsibilities to the pension system than is often recognized. In effect, it was required to implement an early-retirement scheme to protect the employment of younger workers and potential new entrants to the labour market. Legislative changes in the official retirement age, contribution rates, and benefit entitlements relative to work experience all contributed to an extensive reinterpretation of social security—from being a system of intergenerational mutual obligations and entitlements to being a system of intergenerational resource management and welfare. While many French workers preferred to retire earlier than expected, the connection between the contributions and benefits built-up over successive generations of workers was muted, as the system became (in effect) an increasingly onerous tax burden on the current workers. As the government sought to encourage industrial restructuring in the nationalized and non-nationalized sectors, the pension system and its administrative units were asked to absorb and rationalize the labour market consequences of industrial policy. Inevitably, the problems occasioned by these responsibilities reinforced centralized state authority just as they contributed to a (re-)interpretation of intergenerational social solidarity as an extensive welfare state.

One consequence of the multiple responsibilities assumed and imposed on the social security system has been a greater reliance upon the current tax revenue not just accumulated contributions and investment income for the payment of pension benefits. In this respect, it is arguable that the French system has become more a tax and transfer PAYG system than a *répartition* system (as originally intended). Another consequence has been the steady growth in social security contributions or taxes, adding a remarkable burden to the current wage costs. For 1996 it was estimated that the related non-wage labour cost burden was nearly 50 per cent of total labour costs in the manufacturing industry, being surpassed only by Italy and Austria amongst the developed western economies (Moss *et al.* 1997; UNICE 1998).[7] When considered in the light of related workplace rules and regulations, it is arguable that the crisis of social security has also become a crisis of the national welfare state (and vice versa).

Status of the social partners. As noted above, the social partners have had a significant long-term role in the administration and management of the social security institutions. The *caisses* are jointly managed institutions, drawing their board members from employer and employee groups. As such they are enmeshed within the centralized, national and regional French collective bargaining processes, thereby reflecting the inevitable tensions (structural and personal) that accompany such systems. Over time, however, the role of the social partners (especially unions) in these institutions has become increasingly problematic. In part, claims made against a continued role for unions in this system have been encouraged by the long-term decline of union representation in the French economy. Remarkably, union representation is the lowest amongst the western European nations—about 9 per cent (1997) against an average of about 35–40 per cent (Waddington and Hoffman 2001).[8] Such simple numbers hide the considerable diversity of institutional form and organization. Even so, few French workplaces (outside of the largest companies) have a quite limited contact with their union 'representatives'. In this context, there is a widespread belief that *caisse* membership may be the last remaining place of formal *répresentation* for the social partners even if their place in French society remains widely accepted.

It could be argued that the social security contributions and their promised benefits are deferred earned income, being part of the total negotiated hourly wage or negotiated salary. Consequently, these contributions are costs to the employer, whether borne entirely or shared in some manner (in selected industries and sectors) between the employer and employees. As such, these costs enter directly into the current per unit costs of production. Employers see solutions to current and future social security funding that involve increasing the rate of contributions as immediate threats to their short-term income and long-term investment. Not surprisingly, the French social security contributions have become a highly contested component of the current wage costs, being often identified as a problem if the French industry is to remain competitive with their European neighbours and international rivals. In this context, the jointly-managed *caisses* are identified by employer groups as having been 'captured' by 'unrepresentative' union interests, inimical to the immediate interests of employers in managing costs and the long-term interests of the French society in increasing employment. In response, in mid-2001 the principal employer group withdrew from participation in these institutions; the politics of social security 'reform' are as much about governance as cost accountability.

Where unions remain important is in the public services. Here, they have acted to limit the flow-on of pension 'reforms', disputing changes in early retirement provisions, increases in the number of years worked needed for maximum benefits, and the nature and value of supplementary pension benefits. At one level, the unions have held each government (left or right) hostage to their claims for differential treatment. At another level, however, the unions have acted on behalf of all the workers claiming to represent their interests and society's interests in an extensive interventionist state. Inevitably, as the union movement have sought to represent themselves as the 'true' custodians of social solidarity, the ideal of social solidarity has been 'rewritten' in terms consistent with the current distribution of income and entitlements and against the corrosive forces of globalization. In this sense, the ideal of social solidarity has been overtaken by political dispute about the proper nature of the state.[9]

DEFECTION IN A GLOBAL ECONOMY

On the basis of an opinion poll for Merrill Lynch, various observations can be made about the understanding of the French about their social security system (see Thomson 1999). Only about one quarter of the 1000 polled understood that the current social security system is a PAYG system, while nearly two-thirds of those polled believed that social security contributions are either partially or fully invested for the future. Many of those polled also believed that social security is currently in debt, while the vast majority of those polled expected it to run a deficit in the future. In essence, a significant majority believed that the social security system would be inadequate relative to their expected incomes, while a large majority believed they would have to make other private arrangements to supplement their expected retirement incomes.

Similar attitudes were reported in a study by Boeri *et al.* (2001b). They surveyed the attitudes of the French, German, Italian, and Spanish citizens about support for the welfare state, and their knowledge and commitment to publicly funded PAYG pensions. Using a sample of 1000 households from each country, they concluded that most respondents believed that social security will not provide the same high levels of retirement income in the future even if they underestimated the long-term expected PAYG pension liabilities (country by country). Boeri *et al.* also concluded that most citizens would not support increased contribution rates or taxation to support the welfare state even if many were ignorant about the current financial status of their respective national systems. Finally, and perhaps most importantly, they found that the support for public pension systems was closely related to age, education, and social status. The younger, better educated, middle class and professional households were most pessimistic about the future value of their retirement incomes and were most supportive of alternatives to current systems. Conversely, the older, less educated, lower status manual workers were stronger supporters of public pensions and the welfare state in general.

It should be observed, however, that the polling data do not imply that the majority of French citizens reject the principle of social solidarity. At present, and on average, they tend to 'balance' declining expectations against a more general commitment to the state as the custodian of social solidarity. Even so, few individuals apparently believe the state has been a perfect or an efficient means of delivering future retirement incomes. Also, given the enormous costs of the economic crises of the 1970s and 1980s for the funding of retirement pensions, it seems that older people have accepted the need to sacrifice expected incomes on behalf of the welfare of current and future generations. In this sense, social solidarity has provided a means of equitable relief, a balance between the interests of successive generations in the face of changing economic circumstances. This is, surely, a most appropriate reading of any social contract.[10] Nevertheless, it should also be recognized that many younger French citizens are very concerned about their long-term welfare and are even willing to consider (albeit in abstract) opting out.[11]

As Thomson (1999) noted, there is support for the private funded pensions. Also, there is popular support for the individual retirement accounts and the company-sponsored tax-preferred savings schemes (witness the support for the voluntary savings system PPESV introduced by the Jospin government in early 2001). And there is the widespread view that social security contributions are an uncomfortable cost burden on French enterprises and a 'tax' on workers' current real wages (Palier 2000). For these reasons, younger workers have sought the ways and means of defecting (albeit obliquely) from the institutions of social security. The increased household consumption of savings products, retirement insurance products, and equity financial products has been significant over the past five years. See Table 3.2 comparing 1995 to 1999. Most remarkable has been the growth in savings, equities, and pension-related assets. This is all evidence of *implicit* defection; those individuals who can afford to purchase such products do so while acting with the majority to limit increases in the public pension contribution rates. These trends in household savings have prompted new entrants to the domestic financial market and the consolidation of the French banking and financial institutions. Just as obvious are the growth of under-reported earned income and the flow of unaccounted cash to individual investment and savings accounts in jurisdictions like Luxembourg.

While younger French citizens have an interest in defection from the public pension system, they also have a strong interest in defection

Table 3.2. The financial assets of French households in nominal French francs (FF bn), 1995 and 1999

Category	1995	1999
Currency and saving deposits	4 490	5 346
Non-share securities	621	377
Loans	182	242
Quoted shares	496	1 374
Unquoted shares	1 829	6 434
Other equity	499	689
Mutual fund shares	1405	1 751
Insurance/pension reserves	2 285	3 997
Prepaid insurance premiums	338	415
Other	317	584
Total*	12 462	21 209

*Ignoring certain other minor categories.

Source: Banque-de-France, Paris (47-1421-DESM-SESOF).

from the national economy and those European economies dominated by unfunded pension systems.[12] Imagine that French workers are bond holders in the French and European economies—as is surely their status in that they hold at least an implicit (if not explicit) promise made by the state that society will repay their commitment to the welfare of younger generations (secured against the assets of the state; see above). As we have seen, the future value of their pension entitlement is a function of the rate of growth of population and the rate of growth of labour productivity (Boldrin *et al.* 1999). In effect, the value of their bond is a partial function of the benefit ratio and dependency ratio (eqn 3.1). If the Euro is a success, and if economic integration accelerates national growth will be even more closely correlated with continental Europe. Although closer correlation may promote economic growth and labour productivity, it may not translate into higher population growth. At the same time, by becoming even more dependent upon Europe, the French citizens will be even more dependent upon comprehensive solutions to similar public pension financial liabilities of Germany, Italy, and Spain.

In this respect, it is arguable that both the French state and its citizens are 'over-invested' in the expected growth of France and Europe. For individuals, one solution is obvious: diversify their savings and investments to other regions of the world via the investment strategies of private pension systems (as is common in the Anglo-American world) or the investment strategies of local finance and insurance companies. By doing so, the future value of their social security could be made dependent upon the relatively young and growing populations of the United States of America, China, and Latin America (but *not* Japan; see Oguchi and Hatta 2001 on the crisis of Japanese demography and pensions). Much the same argument can be made about the proper investment strategy of state-sponsored social security institutions. Perhaps the only way out of the long shadows cast by low demographic and economic growth is for the investment of social security contributions in a diversified portfolio of national and international demographic and economic growth futures (see Hokenson *et al.* 2001). Such a strategy would not violate the principles of national social solidarity, but would 'scale-up' its geographical contingency (Swyngedouw 2000). Nor would such a strategy violate traditional prudential concerns (Chemillier-Gendreau 2000), even if a different geography of risk were introduced into the flow of future income.[13] Those that advocate the development of a large state-managed central reserve fund have such an investment regime in mind.

If obvious in theory, there remain two obvious practical problems. One is the design of an appropriately diversified portfolio—what level of risk should be accepted given the maturity of the French population? Clearly a younger population, one with their lifetime ahead of them, are better able to absorb the higher risks over the long-term than an older population. In this respect, the younger French citizens should have a riskier investment portfolio than an investment portfolio that represented the population at large. A second problem has to do with the most appropriate organization of the investment process. We have noted above that the existing social security institutions combine various constituencies and objectives together under the rubric of joint-management and the representation of the social partners. For this kind of system to be effective in the wider world of investment management, the state would either play a stronger role overseeing the decision-making behaviour of these institutions and/or ensure that investment functions are provided by a competitive market for financial services. In this respect, the current policy of enhancing the competitiveness of 'national champions' may have to be jettisoned in favour of encouraging the entry of the most efficient and effective global investment managers.

Finally, it should be noted that the most obvious argument—that the state is the ultimate guarantor of the value of retirement income and the financial integrity of the social security system in general—would be difficult to sustain. If it was true fifty years ago, it is now quite implausible given the size and significance of the global financial markets (and the diversity of the demographic and economic growth prospects they represent). In this sense, the future value of French social security now depends upon these markets for realizing the promise of social solidarity even if we are unable to empirically assess the implied relative risk profile. Fifty years ago, of course, it was argued that social solidarity was the proper mechanism for insuring the welfare of successive generations of working peoples against the market. This is surely a most remarkable turn of events in the modern history of the state (Peck 2000).

CONCLUSIONS

In this chapter, I have traced the evolution of the French social security from its inception immediately after the Second World War till its current status and the future crisis. My approach to the topic has been analytical rather than historical. There are others more skilled and knowledgeable about the particular historical moments and circumstances of the French social security (see Whiteside 2000). In particular, I have tried to indicate how and why French social security has proved to be so fragile and yet, paradoxically, so robust. This has required the exposition of an analytical framework consistent with the seminal contributions of Samuelson (1958) and Aaron (1966), as well as the inclusion of concepts allied to the notion of social solidarity drawing upon Durkheim (1984).

As is well appreciated, the PAYG social security is heavily dependent upon demographic and economic growth (Keyfitz 1976). Immature systems characterized by the dominance of a younger working population may reap the benefits of demographic and economic growth while honouring their obligations to share current income with each generation as they come to retirement. On the other hand, mature systems dominated by older workers and retirees may be a burden on the working population and may, over the long term, drastically affect the income of future generations through 'over-consumption' and 'under-investment'. In this respect, the introduction of the PAYG system in France in 1947 was a gamble on an unlikely combination of increased demographic and economic growth; for the first 50 years of the twentieth century, the declining fertility rates promised successively smaller generations of French citizens. For a time, it is true, the gamble paid off. Now, however, the baby boom generation represents a double burden on the French social security: The sheer financial weight of paying for their retirement will be amplified by their failure to sustain a strong population growth (a recurrent French dilemma).

Tracing the implications of this argument, drawing upon demographic indicators and the uneven path of the French economy, has allowed us to better understand the limits of the PAYG systems. However, demography and economics are just two elements in a more complex social and political system of intergenerational social solidarity. While the PAYG social security makes a promise to each generation, such promises are contingent upon the need to balance the rather different interests of overlapping generations. In this respect, the promise of future retirement income is more akin to a bond rather than a property right. Insuring the long-term value of that bond is the role and responsibility of the state; it acts both as the custodian of social solidarity and the regulator of its social security institutions. However, as is apparent from the historical record, there are limits to state capacity just as the institutions of social security may be overtaken by other interests and objectives.

The future of the French social security (as inherited) is in doubt. The discounting of future benefits, and the apparent incentives for younger workers to defect from the social security system, suggest that social solidarity may not be able to hold the system together in the face of successively poorer retirees and overburdened workers. If the national system is to be 'saved', the demographic trends and the forecast lower than required rates of economic growth must be compensated for; global capital markets are one obvious way out for individuals and the population at large. Alternatively, governments may have to either encourage or at least remain neutral with respect to individual and employer attempts to fashion long-term retirement income strategies. Given the economic and financial integration of Europe, it seems unlikely that the French state will be able to deny individuals the opportunity to reach beyond Europe's borders to financial opportunities outside of historical commitments.

If, as I suggest, the global financial markets are a vital ingredient in any strategy to save French social security, there remain important questions about the governance and regulation of its institutions. A significant part of my argument concerned the complex array of agents, objectives, and interests that threaten to overwhelm the governance of the French social security. If these institutions are to enter the global financial markets there are reasonable doubts about their long-term efficacy (see generally Lindbeck 2000). There seems little doubt that London and the private institutions of the global financial markets will play more significant roles in 'managing' French expected pension benefits and liabilities. This goes against the grain of the efforts by the successive French governments to reform the local and European securities' markets in the hope of challenging the Anglo-American institutions and practices. Similarly, it goes against the grain of common commitments in favour of the role of the social partners in 'regulating' economic and financial decision-making.

In this respect, the 'reform' of French social security is as much a matter of discounting embedded political interests as it is a matter of discounting the future value of retirement income. Perhaps this is already well appreciated: attempts by the state to reform social security institutions according to financial accountability are widely perceived to be a threat to the powers of those social partners who have had long standing and significant roles in the administration and management of the system. In this respect, the principle of social solidarity has more work to do: it must legitimize the reform of the governance and regulation of social security in the interests of those who stand to benefit and those who stand to pay for the retirement of the baby boom and successive generations.

NOTES

1. French social security is more than a unitary institution sponsored by the state. At the base, there are pillar I institutions linked to complementary pillar II institutions, and combined in some cases with the employer-sponsored individual savings plans (pillar III). Certain occupations and government employees have their own jointly managed institutions, while the majority of private employees are members of the core institution known as the *régime général*. See Moss *et al.* (1997) for a detailed exposition.

2. There are, however, some who believe that solutions are at hand, which could be readily and easily implemented. See, for example, the study by Levy and Dore (1999: 270) where they suggested '[f]ortunately, policies can be specified that could help alleviate such an [demographic] imbalance, in particular those aimed at fostering higher employment and later retirement among cohorts aged 55–65'.

3. Strictly speaking, the French system is best thought of as a *répartition* system of intergenerational transfers (see Lynes 1967: Chapter 7). The conventional PAYG nomenclature obscures this feature of the French system, thereby encouraging some commentators to ignore the essential social commitment behind the intergenerational social solidarity. This chapter attempts to correct this possible confusion.

4. Thus, there is something odd about the EU proclaimed presumption in favour of national responsibility for pension and retirement income. See the recent Communication from the Commissioner responsible for the Employment and Social Policy Directorate (noted in Chapter 2). While no doubt consistent with past expectations regarding the site of regulation of relationships between the social partners, it would appear to be inconsistent with the evolution of European integration unless the Euro and related developments in capital markets make up the difference between the local and European economic performance.

5. In fact, of course, the question of population growth and decline has pre-occupied French political debate for more than a century. Whiteside (personal communication)

suggests it can be traced as far back as the 1872 defeat. These historical issues go far beyond the scope of this present chapter.

6. During 1975–95, the French population grew by only another 6 million. Whereas net immigration had played a significant role in driving the rate of population increase immediately after 1945, by the end of the 1990s the difference between in and out migration was negligible. In 1994, the crude birth rate was reported as 12.2 and the death rate was reported as 9.0. The EC (2001d) predicts that the French population will grow by about 5 per cent (compared with a UK growth rate of 4 per cent) during the period 2000–50.

7. The implications of such interjurisdictional differences in labour costs may be far-reaching. It is a commonplace observation that the competitiveness of firms depends upon 'local' cost structures including retirement benefits (Clark 1993a). Much of the relevant literature has focused upon interregional wage disparities, and the role of labour market processes including migration in balancing the local capital and labour markets (Martin 2001). As European economic integration develops, it is increasingly apparent that interregional wage dynamics will be closely related to national systems of the social wage. Indeed, the principal components of the social wage may overwhelm 'local' variations in wages, labour productivity, and supply, transforming the spatial scale of corporate location decisions from the region within the nation to the nation and Europe beyond.

8. Only Spain has a similarly low union density, being measured at about 15 per cent. By contrast, countries of similar economic size like the United Kingdom (30 per cent); Germany (33 per cent) and Italy (38 per cent) have a much higher albeit slowly declining rate of union representation.

9. See Béland (2001) for further discussion of the role and significance of French labour unions in 'pension reform'. He suggests that, by comparison, the US union movement has been effectively excluded from the debate over social security. This view surely discounts the important role of the US union movement in promoting the growth of private supplementary pensions (especially after 1949). Compare with Clark (1993, 2000).

10. Compare with Boeri et al. (2001) who find it hard to reconcile the fact that a significant number of respondents from all the surveyed countries would opt out of state-sponsored social security if they could, although they also support the principle of state provision of pensions.

11. The opt-out option is problematic. Those most vulnerable in the labour market would stay in the system, so as to protect their long-term income security. Those most successful in the labour market would leave to protect their long-term retirement incomes, and (hopefully) reap higher rates of return in money and capital markets. This is the often-observed problem of selection bias. A necessary but not sufficient condition for the success of the national répartition and PAYG systems is the mandatory participation of all citizens. There are strong grounds for denying individuals the right to opt out of such systems.

12. Here, I emphasize financial defection because it seems that significant out-migration from France to funded pension regimes such as the United Kingdom and the Netherlands is a most unlikely scenario. There are, of course, large numbers of younger French workers in southern England. Whether this is a permanent state of affairs remains to be seen. See Martin (2000) on European patterns of labour mobility compared to the United States of America.

13. This argument presumes segmented international capital markets, contributing a 'local' premium to global markets available to those investors willing to bear the appropriate risk. See Feldstein and Horioka (1980) for an early assessment of the significance of this phenomenon, Ross (2001) for arguments in favour of the continued regulatory differentiation between capital markets, and Wójcik (2001a) for an empirical assessment of its continuing significance for Europe. See also Christopherson (2001) for an analogous argument from the side of labour markets.

4

Global Finance and German Accounting Rules

The united Germany is at the heart of continental Europe, and is one of a handful of advanced western economies with firms that have a global reach and impact. By virtue of its market size, its prosperity, and its trading relationships with Europe and the world, Germany has become a major economic player in world affairs. For many commentators, the German 'social market' model is one to emulate, deemed a successful economic system with strong social democratic traditions; see Hutton (1995) comparing Germany to the United Kingdom. Described as the ideal type of a corporatist welfare state by Goodin *et al.* (1999), it is widely believed that Germany developed around reinforcing self-sustaining systems of social welfare and collective economic decision-making that have resulted in political stability and remarkable rates of long-term economic growth (Hall and Soskice 2001). Chapters 4 and 5 look at the plausibility of these claims, linking the presumed stability and persistence of the German model to pension funding and global finance.

Like France and Italy, Germany will be greatly affected by the ageing of its population and the underfunding of social insurance and related retirement benefits. It is clear that the current contribution rates are inadequate in the face of relatively low rates of labour force participation, continuing high levels of unemployment, and the promised high rates of income replacement upon retirement. While there is considerable pride in Bismarck's model of social solidarity and insurance (Börsch-Supan 2000a), there is widespread debate about the proper response to the demographic crisis, including continuing conflict over the role and status of private pension provision. The so-called

'Reister-tax' provisions encouraging voluntary private pension and savings plans enacted in early 2001 can be identified as one step towards a 'solution' to the current and forecast retirement income problems, even if it remains unclear whether this initiative will make a substantial difference to the projected national retirement income liabilities. Similarly important, though sometime consigned to the margins of political debate over German pension 'futures', are the employer-sponsored pension institutions found in the German manufacturing industry.

Some of Germany's largest firms have provided these types of benefits for more than a century. Many of these same firms have had extensive experience with the Anglo-American funded pension schemes including DC and cash-balance systems. Whereas much of the public debate about pensions has been about protecting the status of social insurance, for Germany's largest firms there is considerable interest in the redesign of the existing supplementary pension systems including a shifting away from the *direktzusagen* (book reserve) systems that were once so important for internal investment resources. This interest has been prompted, in part, by the recent developments in global capital markets and international financial accounting rules. Here it is argued that these developments will have significant implications for the German corporate-sponsored pensions, profoundly affecting the viability of the inherited *direktzusagen* and *pensionskassen* DB systems. Whereas very little was known a decade ago about the pension liabilities of the German firms, these private pension institutions are now 'in play' as part of a more general realignment of powers between the management, labour, and shareholders.

How and why financial transparency and comparability has become so significant, and the implications of such accountability for management power and private pension systems are important topics of this chapter. To sustain our analysis requires returning to an earlier debate in the United States of America about the connection between the market value and corporate pension liabilities. While the debate was truncated by the introduction of the Financial Accounting Standards Board pension liability rule (FASB 87) and the remarkable performance of the US equity markets in the 1990s, recent trends in the US corporate pension funding and reporting are noted. In later sections of the chapter we deal with the convergence of the US, international, and European accounting standards, noting the underlying assumptions made by accounting professionals about the efficiency of the global financial markets. In detail, we consider the patterns of

German corporate pension accounting in the DAX 30 index and non-DAX 30 companies. Given that the German corporate pension systems are 'unfunded' (*direktzusagen*) or 'underfunded' (*pensions-kassen*) when compared to the Anglo-American private pension systems, the adoption of international accounting standards has revealed significant *net* pension liabilities amongst the leading German corporations.[1]

This chapter and related research sits between the disciplines of political economy and economic geography. There is a massive and growing academic literature devoted to the rival national systems of finance and corporate governance (Hopt *et al.* 1999). Similarly, there has been an explosion of work on the tensions between globalization and localization (Gertler 2001). Both sets of literature combine, in different ways, the analysis of institutions, rules and regulations with reasons for and against the convergence of the systems of corporate governance and management (see Christopherson 1993, 2002, and compare with Weiner 1999). In this chapter, it is argued that global financial integration and the international convergence of accounting rules and regulations have overtaken the inherited domestic institutions of the German employer-sponsored pensions.

PENSION LIABILITY AND CORPORATE FINANCE

Much of the literature comparing the Anglo-American and German systems of finance and corporate governance accentuate the differences, not the historical links or the overlapping, perhaps converging, institutions. Although there are good reasons to do so, while recognizing the remarkable differences of economic performance in the German and Anglo-American financial markets in the 1990s, we should not exaggerate the historical record.[2] In particular, any understanding of the current pension funding dilemmas faced by the German corporations should begin with a brief look backwards to the introduction of the US Employee Retirement Income Security Act (ERISA) of 1974 and the subsequent debate about pension liability accounting and funding. In looking at the US historical record, we can draw together informed glimpses of issues and circumstances relevant to the contemporary situation in Germany.

Prior to the passage of ERISA, the US Internal Revenue Service (IRS) was the dominant governmental institution responsible for overseeing the financial integrity of private employer-sponsored pension plans. Using powers conferred by their role in certifying the federal tax status of these plans, the IRS monitored the funding of corporate pension liabilities. While the IRS encouraged the funding of pension liabilities, according to informed observers the IRS tended to encourage funding according to minimum standards rather than the full funding of liabilities (Murray 1976: 152). Also involved in 'regulating' corporate pension plans was the Accounting Principles Board (APB), a forerunner to the Financial Accounting Standards Board (FASB).[3] This private association of accounting professionals used advisory opinions to set voluntary accounting standards, particularly in the area of reporting corporate profit and loss statements. Neither the IRS nor the APB directly regulated the corporate pension funding practices; firms had a wide discretion in setting expected interest rates, rates of return on invested assets, the timing of contributions, and the accounting of unexpected gains and losses (Weiss 1976).

The passage of the ERISA in 1974 saw the introduction of statutory provisions designed to protect workers' pension rights, and mechanisms designed to ensure that all workers were able to vest and participate in the offered pension plans. In effect, the federal government introduced concepts allied with the civil rights legislation to pension law so as to ensure an equitable and fair treatment (Sass 1997). Also, ERISA set conditions for the full funding of DB plans' expected liabilities spread over an extended period of time, while requiring an earlier recognition by plans (and hence plans) of gains or shortfalls in investment performance. In effect, the ERISA sought to redefine the financial discretion available to plan sponsors and set stricter parameters for pension funding. The move towards the full funding of liabilities in accordance with commonly accepted standards was underscored by the creation of the Pension Benefit Guaranty Corporation (PBGC). Designated as the federal agency responsible for protecting the value of accrued pension benefits, this responsibility was shared between the Department of Labor (DoL), the IRS, and the federal courts.

The available evidence at the time suggested that many pension plans were funded in a manner consistent with the ERISA standards. Even though passage of the ERISA can be traced back, in part, to widely publicized instances of corporate bankruptcy and the total loss of accrued benefits, pension plan funding was a well-established technical craft sustained by principles drawn from trust law and related common law standards of behaviour (Langbein 1997). Furthermore, the APB standards introduced in the mid-1960s, though not compulsory, seemed to have 'encouraged' some firms to report their long-term pension liability (Weiss 1976). Even so, Feldstein and Morck (1983) and their colleagues in the volume edited by Bodie and Shoven (1983) noted problems in ascertaining the true value of corporate pension liabilities. Although they argued that the market could (or should) 'see through' accounting practices and attribute market values consistent with the relative level of pension underfunding, they recognized that there were significant measurement problems and variable accounting practices. Furthermore, they were unable to distinguish a causal logic between the poor corporate financial performance and the level of pension underfunding.

In Friedman's (1983) paper, based upon the 1977 DoL data drawn from more than 7800 plans sponsored by over 1800 firms, similar problems of measurement and accounting practices were identified. Nevertheless, he found that unfunded corporate pension liabilities were a function of the level of corporate debt; the higher the corporate debt the higher the unfunded liabilities. He also found that firms with high levels of debt and firms with significant volatility in their earnings preferred predictable, low risk investment regimes. In effect, the new ERISA funding imperatives combined with the inherited pension accounting practices seemed to have encouraged firms to balance high levels of corporate risk (on one side) against low pension risk (on the other side). By contrast, firms with high rates of (predictable) earnings growth tended to be those with pension funds that pursued high risk-and-return investment strategies. In many cases, Friedman argued, firms used their available discretion in making pension contributions and the reporting of unexpected gains and losses to smooth the reported corporate earnings. Notwithstanding the legal separation between firms and their sponsored pension plans, it appeared that firms' financial strategies tended to integrate rather than divide pension liabilities from the corporate assets and liabilities.

The relative transparency of the corporate profit and loss statements and the practice of the corporate financial management in relation to pension obligations were at the heart of the FASB Statement 87 issued in late 1985. For many financial analysts, the previous APB standards confused or failed to adequately distinguish between the DB and DC plans. Further more, existing standards left too much discretion to firms, allowing the development of non-commensurate and competing reporting standards and procedures. During hearings held by the FASB on their Preliminary Views, many major industrial corporations proclaimed the virtues of discretion, arguing that disclosure of pension assets and liabilities was best achieved taking into account the particular circumstances of each firm. Moreover, the chairman of General Motors argued that the proposed current valuation of the pension assets and liabilities would be virtually impossible given the problems of fixing the values of working and sunk capital (Liebtag 1984). Financial analysts, however, were under no such illusions: the available data was not consistent enough to discriminate between corporations on the basis of their underlying pension assets and liabilities (Miller 1987).

The introduction of the FASB 87 set the parameters for the US corporate finance slowly flowing-on, as we shall see, to most other advanced industrialized economies through the national accounting boards and the International Accounting Standards Committee now Board (IASC or IASB). In brief, the objectives of the FASB 87 were as follows. (1) To provide a measure of corporations' net pension costs reflecting the nature of plans and employees' entitlements; (2) to provide a more transparent and comparable measure of pension costs; (3) to provide a means of disclosure consistent with plan sponsors' financial circumstances, and (4) to improve the reporting of the US corporate finance (paraphrasing the original FASB announcement as summarized in Ernst & Whinney 1986: 2). Basically, the FASB sought to standardize corporate pension cost reporting, ensuring that information was available in corporate earnings statements in a timely and consistent manner. While every effort was made to require the current reporting of all pension assets and liabilities, the FASB had to concede firms some discretion in the timing of reporting. Nevertheless, with the adoption of an accounting framework and standardized templates the FASB achieved its objectives.

The FASB then extended its pensions accounting standards to corporate health care benefits and related retiree benefits. Statement No. 106 was introduced in late 1992, with a limited transition period. As was the case in the FASB 87, the guiding principle behind the FASB 106 was full disclosure using consistent and comparable standards of valuation and reporting. Given that many of the firms sponsoring DB plans also provided related but largely unfunded health care benefits, it was anticipated that the FASB 106 would have significant effects on their reported profit and loss statements (Warshawsky *et al.* 1993). The available evidence at the time suggested that the market underestimated the true costs of such benefits, reflected in market prices higher than expected (Mittelstaedt and Warshawsky 1993). In subsequent sections, we look in more detail at the flow-on of these accounting standards to other jurisdictions. In doing so, our historical record closes with the announced reformation of the IASC as the IASB in May 2000, and the EC's announcement in June 2000 that it intended 'requiring all EU listed companies to prepare their consolidated accounts in accordance with... International Accounting Standards (IAS)' (p. 2).

PATTERNS OF THE US CORPORATE PENSION LIABILITIES

Through the 1990s, the FASB 87 became firmly entrenched in the US corporate financial accounting and the annual reporting of corporate earnings. Because the standards fashioned and implemented by the FASB are recognized as 'authoritative' by the US Securities and Exchange Commission (SEC), these standards must be observed by publicly-listed and traded companies registered with the SEC. As such, it has been identified as one important institution (amongst others) responsible for the shift away from the DB plans towards DC plans. Arguably, the FASB accounting standards have prompted the US corporations to separate human resource management functions from their financial functions. Not only have the costs of administering DB plans grown enormously (Mitchell 1998), the market valuation of health care and retirement benefits have effectively made such benefits a part and parcel of the valuation of traded companies and hence the market for corporate control (Siegel 1996). In effect, DC plans shift costs and financial risks to plan participants away from firms' stockholders and management.[4]

Early fears that the FASB 87 would result in corporate bankruptcies and the collapse of the PBGC proved unfounded. Notwithstanding the problems of financing corporate restructuring and the funding of defined pension benefits in the automobile and steel industries, the PBGC emerged unscathed in the early 1990s. The economic success of the first Clinton administration combined with the accelerated growth in the US equity markets from the early to late 1990s, effectively discounted the value of the inherited DB liabilities. By virtue of the extended period of transition allowed by the FASB, and a compromise on reporting year-to-year unexpected gains and losses on pension fund assets, the transition occurred in an era of economic growth. More recently, with the run-up in the Anglo-American market beginning around the 1993–4 rates of return on invested assets out-stripped the conventional expectations. By end of 1999, the annualized US equity returns were more than 12 per cent in real terms; many pension funds shifted assets towards equities and away from fixed income products (a policy they were to rue 12 months later).

We turn now to the results of a series of reports published by Bear Stearns (McConnell *et al.* 1999, 2001a, b). In their first report, the Bear Stearns accounting practice compared net pension expenditures (and income) for publicly-listed firms included in the Standard and Poor's (S&P) 500 index for two years: 1994 and 1998. As is well appreciated, the S&P 500 index is made up of the largest New York Stock Exchange (NYSE) listed firms as measured by market capitalization. Of course, including firms listed in both years and before the 'new economy' boom, bubble, and bust meant that the database looked backwards rather than forwards. As such, the index was dominated by four sectors (in order): capital goods, consumer cyclicals, consumer staples, and basic materials. Of the 500 firms, about 370 reported on DB and retiree health care expenditures and expected liabilities. The majority of firms (approximately 70 per cent) reported net pension expenditure for both years, although a minority of firms (about 12 per cent) reported shifting from a net expenditure position to a net income position (observations subsequently validated for 1999 by Towers Perrin 2000 and Watson Wyatt 2000).

Of the 350 firms included in the report, 32.6 per cent reported a decrease in their net pension contributions while another 10 per cent reported no change in their contributions. However, another 10 per cent reported a shift from the net pension expenditure to a neutral position (neither a net contribution nor a net income result). In effect a majority of the 350 S&P 500 reporting firms saw their pension contribution expenditures decrease in real terms (adjusting for wage and price inflation over the four-year period). Only 12 per cent of the firms reported a net pension expenditure increase, while a tiny fraction of the firms reported moving from a net income or neutral position to a net expenditure position. Remarkably, a significant number of firms reported a net pension income rather than a net pension expenditure as part of their consolidated corporate earnings. As noted above, about

12 per cent of the firms reported a shift from net expenditure to net income, about 6 per cent reported moving from a neutral position to net pension income, and another 5 per cent of the firms reported an increase in their net pension income. In effect, about 20 per cent of the firms added to their corporate operating income by virtue of their accounting practices.

According to McConnell *et al.* (1999: 10), the reported reduction in the net pension expenditure for many firms and the shift to a net pension income for a minority of the firms reflected, in part, change in the assumed expected return on pension fund assets. Also suggested was the possibility that some firms had benefited from the 'amortization of actual returns in excess of expected returns'. The expected return on assets was a positive function of the equity bias in the pension fund investment strategies. Because the FASB 87 requires DB plan sponsors to look forward when reporting pension assets and liabilities, there is a temptation for pension fund investment officers to follow markets upwards, thereby reducing the year-to-year financial burden on plan sponsors. In this instance, the average expected rate of return increased from 9.08 per cent in 1994 to 9.19 in 1998.[5] Even so, some 50 or more firms reported no change in the expected returns over the period 1991–8 and only a handful of the firms reported a yearly revision in their expected returns over the period 1993–8. Furthermore, there were no apparent patterns between the firms' expected return policies and the extent of under- or overfunding in relation to the expected long-term obligations.[6]

Nevertheless, there was considerable variation between S&P 500 firms' net pension cost accounting policies. For 1998, some firms held to very conservative assumptions about expected returns (e.g. Alcan Aluminium 7.20 per cent) while a few firms had very aggressive assumptions (e.g. Weyerhauser 11.50 per cent). For some firms with mature pension plans (large numbers of retirees to active participants), however, an aggressive equity strategy would be wholly inconsistent with protecting retirees' welfare and the financial integrity of the firm. Even so, McConnell *et al.* (1999) suggested that some firms seemed to manage the overall reported corporate income by varying expected returns. Because the FASB 87 requires a single net cost value firms are able to adjust, and perhaps vary according to broader corporate objectives the various components that make up the net pension cost. In effect, and notwithstanding the objectives behind the introduction of the FASB 87, firms retain considerable discretion reporting pension costs. Indeed, McConnell *et al.* (1999) suggested that in some cases the reported corporate earnings were considerably less once the 'pension income' was taken into account.

In two subsequent reports, McConnell *et al.* (2001a, b) looked again at the 'adjusted' operating income of S&P 500 firms for 2000 and beyond. They found that, notwithstanding market turmoil, more firms derived a net income from their pension plans comparing the year 1999 (109 companies) with 2000 (162 companies). Although many firms reported declining pension plan assets, the income effects of pension plans on corporate earnings was generally positive and increasing. For a select group of firms, pension income contributed to more than 10 per cent of reported income and in a few cases so significant was the income effect from sponsored pension plans that those firms would have otherwise reported a loss for the period. Looking forward, McConnell *et al.* suggested that the effects of market volatility on pension income would not necessarily result in sudden or profound shifts in the reported corporate income. They developed a model so as to assess corporate 'exposure', leading to the identification of a group of firms that may be more affected than others. But they also noted that their results were to be taken as *indicative* rather than *definitive*; there remains considerable latitude within the FASB 87 for managing reported income over time even if the pension plan assets were to fall by as much as 15–20 per cent (in contrast with other more exacting accounting standards, notably the UK FRS 17).

This finding is consistent with Lowenstein's (1996) argument that firms manage what is measured: '[i]t is inevitable, therefore, that management often will manage not for the economically better outcome but for the *measured* outcome, or they will simply manipulate the reported numbers' (Lowenstein 1996; 1355).[7] This point was underscored by McConnell *et al.* and in more recent related studies by independent analysts and consulting firms (see the report in *Pensions & Investments* 26 June 2000: 1). While it is impossible to determine the extent to which the FASB accounting measures of DB pension liabilities contributed to the growth of employer-sponsored DC plans, market analysts have become highly tuned to the potential risks associated with DB plans. There can be little doubt that increased transparency has prompted the discounting of existing and potential financial risks associated with sponsored pension plans—a pattern of behaviour increasingly apparent in the United Kingdom with the implementation of a similar accounting standard.

THE EVOLUTION OF GLOBAL ACCOUNTING STANDARDS

By this account, the FASB has become an essential cog in the web of regulatory institutions that oversee the US corporate governance and the market for corporate control. Its professional associations and independent appointment system buttress its mandate as an independent expert authority on accounting practice (not withstanding the controversy occasioned by the Enron debacle). It is a self-organizing institution that relies upon decentralized management mechanisms like self-measurement and self-reporting to sustain corporate compliance with codes of practice for the benefit of third party market agents. In this case, of course, the FASB operates in a regulatory space in part provided by the SEC. It functions in the light cast by the SEC as well as its professional membership, not just in the shadows cast by government regulation in general (compare with Power 1998: 9). In this sense, it is less an institution of trust than it is a non-profit institution with legitimate coercive powers of discipline.[8]

Arguably the FASB and its pension accounting rules should be considered a distinctive feature of the US financial markets, referencing what Hancher and Moran (1989: 290–91) would identify as *local* legal, social, and economic factors that sustain the institution. As is well appreciated, there is considerable debate about this general proposition. Some suggest that domestic elites and their interests represented and allied with nation-states are fundamental constraints on convergence. By implication, the emerging map of twenty-first century capitalism is best understood as one meditated by nation-states relying upon retained powers over property and competition, negotiated exceptions, trade-offs, and compromises, and reinforced by ambiguity over the implementation of common agreements (Crouch and Streeck 1997). Yet there are also those who emphasize the relative autonomy of large firms. The historical interests of such firms in domestic rules and regulation (concerning competition and labour-management relations) can be juxtaposed (in theory and practice) against their growing interests in access to global consumer and capital markets (see generally Mayer and Whittington 1999).

In this regard, the performance and practices of the global financial services industry are increasingly at the centre of debate over nation-state autonomy. For example, Rhodes and van Apeldoorn (1998: 423) noted that the European and global harmonization of accounting rules and regulation is an especially contested sphere of public policy. They suggested that the mutual recognition of nations' different rules and regulation would be one way forward in accommodating, on one hand, the corporate interests in a pan-European regulatory framework consistent with their increasing geographical scope of operations and, on the other hand, the traditional powers of the nation-state.[9] At the same time, the FASB, the SEC, the UK ASB, the International Organisation of Securities Commissions (IOSCO), and the IASB (amongst many other institutions) have actively pursued convergence. Identified by Braithwaite and Drahos (2000: 121) as a 'private sector business organization which is committed to a process of continuous improvement in the development of international accounting standards for financial reporting' they noted that the then IASC is '[o]f profound importance to the globalization of financial regulation'. Indeed, they argued that the IASC has sought harmonization 'to progressively higher standards'.

This reading of the IASC's goals and objectives is not entirely consistent with its evolution since being established in 1973 (see also Steinberg *et al.* 1999). Braithwaite and Drahos blur different phases of its development, ignoring the initial tentative steps towards consensus. Even so, in the last few years the FASB has found few instances where the IASC standards could be judged inferior to the US GAAP, while there are a number of instances where the IASC standards could be judged more comprehensive and inclusive than the US GAAP (Bloomer 1999). It is beyond the scope of this chapter to review the FASB evaluation of the ISAC, standard by standard. But it is worth noting that the IAS 19 (employee benefits) was revised between 1993 and 1998 in consultation with a wide variety of related organizations and individuals including the FASB and the SEC. In assessing the 'new' IAS 19 against the relevant FASB standards, Petrone (1999) suggested that there was close conformity across a wide range of issues. Where there were differences, the IAS 19 standards were judged more exacting in some cases (multi-employer plans, unanticipated extra costs, and anticipated changes in government regulations) and 'different' in other cases (especially the treatment of DC plans). One slight difference was that the IAS 19 does not require corporations to report their minimum DB liability whereas the FAS 87 does. Apart from this issue, Petrone suggested that market agents would readily understand any other differences.

For some academic analysts the IASC is an extension of the FASB being, by implication, the agent of the SEC representing the US nation-state interests in extending the geographical reach of the US capital markets.[10] According to this view, and in defence of other types of national financial systems, due respect must be accorded to 'local' interests in the design and adoption of accounting rules. While not disputing the need for nation-states to accommodate (in some fashion) to international financial standards, by this account geopolitics combined with market agents and interests 'explain' the convergence of accounting rules and standards. In this chapter, however, the SEC is not the *deus ex machina* of our argument—an all-powerful agent driving accounting professionals towards the harmonization of global accounting standards. This kind of argument ignores important differences between institutions, it ignores the independent processes of consultation and advice used by the IASC, and it ignores the competition for agenda setting amongst national and international accounting standards institutions. Furthermore, conspiracy theories skate over apparent tensions within and between national institutions and their constituent members. Witness, for instance, the political difficulties encountered by the FASB in the early to mid-1990s when it tried to introduce an accounting standard to fully account for the cost of stock-based employee compensation plans and its difficulties in dealing with 'off-balance sheet' transactions (as illustrated by the Enron scandal).

Here we consider aspects of the supply of harmonized accounting standards before focusing upon the German corporate pension liability, international accounting standards, and their implications for the provision of supplementary pensions. In the first instance, it should be recognized that the claimed conflict between international accounting standards and national financial autonomy may be less profound than sometimes implied. In McLeay *et al.*'s (2000) study of the German implementation of the Fourth European Company Law Directive (1985), they noted that the EU Directive radically challenged German accounting practices. While the Directive incorporated some aspects of the Anglo-American accounting practices related to transparency, it also retained elements of the German practice—consensus and compromise sensitive to 'local' interests were deemed as necessary steps on the path towards a common regulatory framework. More recently, however, the German federal government allowed listed companies to use the FASB or IASC standards, recognizing the interests of large German firms in gaining access to global capital markets if not the interests of many other domestic firms in lower-priced capital resources. Similarly, the SEC has allowed foreign firms to list on the US financial markets even if this has meant accepting accounting standards that are at some variance to the US GAAP.[11] In response, the UK ASB has proposed and implemented a new rule (FRS 17) on marking-to-market pension liability stronger than both the FASB 87 and IAS 19.

In the second instance, it should also be recognized that there is, more often than not, an idealized 'client' behind the SEC, FASB, ASB, IOSCO and the IASC: capital market agents whose role it is to properly price the value of traded securities. And behind these agents are the normative goals of these institutions: the enhancement of the efficiency and fairness of global financial markets (Steinberg *et al.* 1999). By this logic, the enemies of the market agents *and* market efficiency are firms *and* governments reluctant to disclose important financial information, and firms willing to manipulate the information so disclosed. But notice an implication hidden in these claims: information about corporate financial performance is a public good rather than a private matter that is the object of privileged access. Of course, information is not quite the same as reasoned knowledge; there is a vibrant market in the Anglo-American world for insight and opinion about the implications of disclosed information. But this model of markets and rules is, at base, very different from the German model of non-traded long-term banking relationships. Ideally, in the German system information is a perquisite of being an inside player. By the time such information gets to the market, insiders have surely reaped its value.

In the third instance, it should be recognized that global financial integration has had enormous implications for the autonomy of countries' accounting standards boards. There is considerable competition amongst financial markets for cross-border listings. Rapid advances in communication technologies and the development of real-time trading links have effectively opened up many remotely-located agents to London and New York. In this context, the IASC has become more important over the past five years than it may have been ten years ago as a means of avoiding any 'race to the bottom'. At the same time, pan-European alliances between financial markets to cross-list securities rely heavily upon either mutual recognition of different standards or the implementation of one standard consistent with international standards. While gross differences between whole sets of countries in relation to their legal and regulatory heritages may define the boundaries of these alliances, within these loosely related blocs of markets there are firms with global ambitions. Defection to global markets is an option even if domestic competitors may be restricted to local banking relationships because of limited resources (see Chapter 7).

GERMAN CORPORATE ACCOUNTING STANDARDS

The completion of the IASC code and its related employee benefit accounting standards has been accompanied by strong pressure from the SEC and FASB to create credible audit systems for monitoring compliance and credible sanctions for non-compliance. Partly in response, the IASC remade the Committee, introducing a Board with a membership structure and set of powers capable of implementing the new international code.[12] At the same time, a number of advanced economies moved to replace their own codes with the IASC code or, as in the German case, create an accounting board to deal with and/or implement international standards. In effect, the IASB code has become the reference point for many countries wishing to adopt accounting standards consistent with, if not exactly the same as, international standards and expectations regarding the proper regulation of global financial markets and corporate governance.

The Adoption of International Accounting Standards

German legislation allowing domiciled firms to use international accounting standards is indicative of the force behind global financial harmonization. But this legislation simply *allowed* rather than *required* the use of international accounting standards. Furthermore, as we have seen above, much of the theoretical literature on corporate disclosure and finance presumes firms are reluctant to disclose and will only report that information required by law (see Admati and Pfleiderer 1998; Fishman and Hagerty 1997). Not only are there considerable costs associated with producing this kind of information, there is also some anxiety at the corporate level about the consequences of disclosure for firms' market positions. These anxieties were put into sharp relief by the extraordinary result that accompanied Daimler-Benz's adoption of the US GAAP standards in 1993. As is well-known, and repeatedly discussed amongst market analysts, year-end earnings disclosure using these standards converted a German accounting standards' 'profit' into a US GAAP 'loss'. These kinds of 'surprises' have enormous implications for how global financial markets value individual and groups of related firms.[13]

Nevertheless, there are academic theorists who would argue against convergence in national systems of corporate governance. Invoking notions of path dependence and sunk costs consistent with economic geography, Bebchuk and Roe (1999) made the theoretical case for 'continued divergence' rather than 'convergence' in national systems of corporate governance (over 15–20 years). In doing so, they argued against simple-minded presumptions in favour of market solutions to conflicting national regulatory regimes. Even so they recognized that convergence was possible, depending upon the balance of forces between 'competitive globalization' and 'path dependence'. But they also suggested this was an empirical question, to be resolved by history not by the inexorable logic of economic theory (see also Berndt 1998a). These two authors have enviable reputations as theorists of law and economics and the institutional framework of nation-state markets. Thus, there are clearly practical and theoretical reasons to be cautious about the likelihood of German firms switching towards international accounting standards (see the related argument underpinning Rhodes and van Apeldoorn 1998; McLeay *et al.* 2000).

To summarize, four hypotheses relevant to the adoption of international accounting standards flow from the arguments and authors summarized above. (1) *Firms are unlikely to voluntarily adopt higher international standards of reporting.* Not only would transparency represent a break with past non-traded relationships and impose limits on management discretion, any 'surprises' in financial accounts may have severe economic costs for the firm and its shareholders. (2) *Given the option to adopt,* firms will tend to limit disclosure to that required by local laws rather than embracing international standards. (3) *Given an inherited capital stock and related corporate structure,* international standards of disclosure will be less relevant to the local situation than domestic standards. Alternatively, (4) *if adoption were to occur it would have less impact on corporate governance in these circumstances than in other more appropriate circumstances.* The implications of the literature are plain. German firms would not voluntarily adopt higher international standards, or would do so only in a manner that did not threaten their inherited systems of management and governance.

To assess these hypotheses, we assembled 1998 and 1999 annual reports for German publicly traded DAX 30 index (large) and non-DAX index (smaller) firms. These reports included a wide variety of corporate incomes and expenditure accounting measures, as well as statements regarding the current and adopted accounting standards.[14] It should be noted that the DAX 30 index firms included the 30 largest

German corporations, being dominated by international industrial firms like DaimlerChrysler and BASF though also including less well-known but nonetheless substantial domestic-oriented firms such as Metro AG and Henkel KGAA (see Tables 4.1 and 4.2 for 1998 data). Note that we ignored the subsequent mergers and acquisitions that have affected the structure of the DAX 30. The DAX 30 index firms dominate total market capitalization. Their share of the market far out-strips the Dow Jones index share of the total US market capitalization. At the same time, the German publicly traded firms are less significant in relation to the stock of all traded and non-traded firms compared to the US and UK markets. As for the sample of 36 smaller firms, many were very small indeed with less than DM100 million in reported assets (Table 4.3). As should be appreciated, it is much harder to collect information on these firms.

Given the expectations noted above, the patterns apparent in Table 4.1 may come as a surprise. The majority of DAX-listed firms immediately adopted the international accounting standards (IAS and/or US GAAP) when permitted to do so. Subsequently, a further 7 firms adopted international standards in 1999 and those left outside of the IAS or US GAAP regimes including Volkswagen and Siemens indic-ated that they would adopt one of these standards in the near future. By contrast, very few of the firms just outside of the DAX 30 switched to international standards. Thus, we can reject hypotheses (1) and (2) outright. But this leaves us the task of explaining the rate of adoption amongst DAX 30 as opposed to the non-DAX 30 firms.

Explaining Patterns of Adoption

Adoption is rarely studied in the Anglo-American literature because of the mandatory nature of accounting standards.[15] Explanations of adoption that would invoke firm size, industry affiliation, and export orientation are not convincing. Each sector like automobiles, chemi-cals, and engineering has exceptions making comparisons between industrials and retail commercial sectors (for example) less than compelling. Thus, we leave aside the option of an econometric mod-elling strategy and concentrate on the four propositions that explain early adoption *within* the DAX 30 environment.

Being included in the DAX 30 signifies a distinctive status with respect to competition between international financial markets, therein

Table 4.1. The DAX 30 Index firms' reported market capitalization (DM bn), accounting standards, and industrial sectors, 1998

Company	Market capitalization	Accounting standard	Industrial sector
Adidas-Solomon	4.399	IAS	Household and textiles
Allianz	83.148	IAS	Insurance
BASF	20.523	US GAAP	Chemicals
Bayer	27.388	IAS	Chemicals
Bayerische Hypo Vereinsbank	25.979	IAS	Banks
BMW	12.702	German	Automobiles
Commerzbank	13.771	IAS	Banks
DaimlerChrysler*	87.652	US GAAP	Automobiles
Degussa Huels	7.682	German	Chemicals
Deutsche Bank	28.142	IAS	Banks
Deutsche Lufthansa	7.498	IAS	Transport
Deutsche Telekom*	87.250	US GAAP	Telecommunications
Dresdner Bank	18.891	IAS	Banks
Fresenius Medical Care*	—	US GAAP	Health Care
Henkel KGAA	4.677	IAS	Personal & household
Karstadt Quelle	—	German	Retail
Linde	4.446	German	Engineering and machinery
Man	2.718	German	Engineering and machinery
Mannesmann*	42.883	US GAAP	Telecommunication
Metro	21.842	German	General retailers
Munchener Re	18.502	German	Insurance
Preussag	6.485	German	Engineering and machinery
RWE	23.461	German	Diversified industrials
SAP*	17.258	US GAAP	Software and computer
Schering	7.504	German	Pharmaceuticals
Siemens	37.287	German	Electronics and electrical
Thyssen Krupp	5.714	German US GAAP	Engineering and machinery
Veba*	26.749	US GAAP	Diversified industrials
Viag	13.600	IAS	Diversified industrials
Volkswagen	22.894	German	Automobiles

*Company listed on the New York Stock Exchange.

Table 4.2. The DAX 30 Index firms' pension liabilities (Euro ml), 1998

Short code	Company	Pension liabilities	Short code	Company	Pension liabilities
AD	Adidas-Solomon	N/A	KQ	Karstadt Quelle	N/A
AL	Allianz	3 387	LN	Linde	624
BF	BASF	4 062	MA	Man	1 648
BY	Bayer	4 717	MN	Mannesmann	2 305
BH	Bayerische Hypo Vereinsbank	1 828	ME	Metro	800
BM	BMW	1 394	MR	Munchener Re	163
CO	Commerzbank	1 269	PR	Preussag	2 824
DC	DaimlerChrysler	16 618	RW	RWE	11 030
DH	Degussa Huels	686	SP	SAP	22
DB	Deutsche Bank	3 855	SC	Schering	1 134
LU	Deutsche Lufthansa	2 760	SI	Siemens	10 124
DT	Deutsche Telekom	3 130	TK	Thyssen Krupp	N/A
DR	Dresdner Bank	1 846	VB	Veba	4 845
FM	Fresenius Medical Care	51	VG	Viag	2 891
HE	Henkel KGAA	1 773	VW	Volkswagen	7 955

Source: Annual Reports (*Financial Times* 1999).

requiring reporting systems consistent with the standards of those markets. This argument has two parts. Firstly, we should recognize that the demand for country-specific index-based passive equity investment products grew dramatically over the 1990s. The realization that the costs of active investment, more often than not, outweigh the returns from stock selection in the soaring markets of the late 1990s prompted investment strategies that discounted firm-specific information in favour of indicative bundles of stocks. Secondly, the interest of European markets in being competitive with the burgeoning Wall Street and London markets prompted those European markets to actively encourage index listed firms to adopt accounting standards that would facilitate the trading of assets between markets. Adding to this pressure, of course, was the introduction of the Euro in January 1999 and the prospect of European sector-wide market indices. Continental policy makers sought to increase the European share of cross-border financial flows—being within the DAX 30 was to be a willing (or not so willing) partner in this competitive strategy amongst financial centres. For firms

Table 4.3. Smaller German Dax-listed companies' pension assets and liabilities (DM ml), and accounting standards, 1998

Company	Pension assets	Pension liabilities	Accounting standards
Barmag	577.1	65.3	German
Brau und Brunen[1]	1 546.4	429.9	German
Buderus	2 205.8	480.1	German
Cewe Color Holding[1]	363.9	7.6	German
Deutsche Beteilungs[1]	472.9	12.2	IAS
Deutsche Pfandbrief- und Hypothekenbank	236 038.2	146.7	German
Dr Scheller Cosmetics[1]	51.8	6.9	German
Durr	1 084.3	26.9	German
Elexis[1]	358.5	81.1	German/FAS
FAG Kugelfischer	3 623.7	875.2	German
Fielman	613.1	0.57	German
Gerresheimer	1 583.0	376.1	German
Gesco[1]	105.1	0.52	German
Gold Zack	162.9	7.0	German
Graphitwerk Kropfmuhl[1]	98.5	8.5	German
Hanover Re	22 212.0	52.1	[German]
Heidelberg[2]	7 676.8	834.7	IAS
Herlitz[1]	1 925.8	47.3	German
Integrata Training	20.7	0.38	German
IWKA AG	1 906.8	187.6	German
Jenoptik AG[1]	2 122.3	132.4	German
Metallgesellschaft	6 925.8	1 047.0	German
MWB[1,3]	23.7	1.0	German
Net.Ipo[1]	—	—	[German]
R. Stahl[1]	142.7	16.1	German
Sauer Inc[1]	—	—	[German]
Schleicher	48.1	1.4	German
Schwarz Pharma	1 291.9	40.6	German
Sudzucker	7 112.3	585.7	German
TFG Venture Capital[1]	47.2	—	[German]
Uzin[1]	89.3	0.5	German
VEH Valora	5.8	—	[German]
WCM	2 217.7	17.0	German
Wedeco[1]	29.6	—	IAS
Wesumat Holding[1]	132.3	0.38	[German]
Wunsche[1]	631.8	4.5	[German]

[1]Listed on Deutsche Börse.
[2]Converted from Euros at DM-fixed rate €1 = DM 1.95583.
[3]Annual, not consolidated balance sheet data.

included in the DAX 30 index, disclosure according to internationally recognized accounting standards is a necessity if the Frankfurt Börse is to realize its global ambitions.

For German firms with global ambitions, conventional sources of finance are expensive relative to global finance markets. The simplest and most obvious reason for early adoption identified by industry insiders has to do with the sheer size and significance of the global (UK and US) equity markets compared to the Frankfurt and continental European markets. Whereas the first proposition implies that DAX 30 index firms were hostages to the ambitions of the Frankfurt Börse, these same firms have sought cheaper pools of finance to expand in eastern Europe and North America. Just as German banking relationships have not been as competitive as global markets for new finance, the Frankfurt market has neither the depth of resources nor the experience for level of valuing corporate global investments and competitive strategies. In this context, disclosure is a vital informational signal in any move to attract the interest of Wall Street ratings firms and the expertise of Anglo-American investment institutions. At the same time, expanding commercial relationships and market alliances between the related German and Anglo-American firms have required open disclosure of interests and market value—common standards of disclosure have become an essential ingredient in establishing the 'terms of trade' between firms coming from very different cultural and industrial traditions. Notice, however, that only 5 of the DAX 30 index firms are listed on the NYSE.[16] The adoption of international accounting standards may be a way of avoiding this prospect.

For German firms with significant Anglo-American holdings, their managerial experience with international accounting standards has developed their capacity to adjust and adapt to the putative new regulatory regime. A significant portion of the DAX 30 index firms have US and UK holdings, allowing for learning between jurisdictions within the firm while reinforcing the need to rationalize accounting standards between units. For example, Allianz, BASF, Bayer, and DaimlerChrysler all have US units with local employees and sponsored pension plans. They use systems of accounting and financial reporting that meet the US standards. This is especially apparent in areas like pension accounting where BASF and Bayer, for example, manage both the DB and DC plans in ways consistent with the US federal ERISA regulations and the US GAAP (see Chapter 5). The fact that many of these types of companies switch managers internally between jurisdictions encourages overlapping knowledge, and in some cases convergence upon common internal standards. Of course, overlapping jurisdictions within firms does not always translate into convergence on one managerial system. An added incentive for the adoption of common international accounting frameworks has been the need to centralize investment decision-making, drawing assets and liabilities oftentimes together across the firm in ways that allow these firms to make new investments to match or dominate their Anglo-American competitors.

Diversification of shareholding has become a desirable goal for managers and their traditional investors. By convention, the German firms are described in terms of their overlapping shareholdings, managing investor relationships on the inside rather than the outside (the market). For some firms, this remains the dominant logic underpinning corporate strategy and management (witness BMW). But in other firms shareholding, if not control, is far more diverse (e.g. Mannesmann-Vodafone, DaimlerChrysler, and Deutsche Bank). Diversification of shareholding is increasingly a desirable option, especially as continental capital and consumer markets become more competitive. On the management side of the equation, diversification of ownership has two advantages. One is greater discretion, recognizing the limits on innovation posed by the close and overlapping interests of their traditional shareholders. Another advantage of diversification of shareholding is the opportunities for managers to tap expertise outside of their home jurisdictions. For traditional shareholders, over-invested in selected numbers of German firms, diversification allows the dilution of interest and the spread of financial assets into new areas of the German and European economies. In this respect, then, a precondition for diversification of shareholding is greater transparency, consistency, and comparability. Therefore, the FASB and IAS standards offer neutral reference points for new shareholders suspicious of the privileged position of traditional shareholders.

On balance, and with respect to those firms included in the DAX 30 index, the forces of competitive globalization seemed to outweigh path dependence (compare Bebchuk and Roe 1999). Slowly emerging is a form of German corporate capitalism perhaps more consistent with that described by Berle and Means (1933) for the United States of America than that associated with the traditional German industry organization (Berndt 1998b). Thus, even hypothesis 3 should be rejected, at least for those large German firms included in the DAX 30 index.

THE GERMAN CORPORATE PENSION LIABILITIES

This, then, brings us to the 1998 pattern of *net* corporate pension liabilities reported in Table 4.2 and represented in Figure 4.1. Before considering these data, we should acknowledge three important caveats about the reported data. First, few annual reports made mention of the various mechanisms for funding German supplementary pensions. Included here are data for at least the *direktzusagen* and *pensionskassen* pension systems, the two most important private retirement income systems. While this is consistent with the IAS 19 and the FASB 87, some analysts would dispute the assumption that *direktzusagen* systems are properly treated as 'unfunded'. Notice as well, the data includes corporations' pension liabilities summed together from all countries in which it operates even if these liabilities reflect different regulatory regimes. Second, we should also recognize that the age of employees, the expected working lives and wages of employees, and the tenure structure of the firm are important variables determining DB plan liabilities. Third, by definition, pension 'liabilities' match pension 'assets' in DC plans; while we know that most if not all the DAX 30 firms have DB plans, some may have unreported DC plans.

Two points stand out from Table 4.2. First, there was considerable diversity amongst firms with regard to their total net pension liability. DaimlerChrysler stood out as the 'leading' firm with reported liabilities of over 16 billion Euro, compared to the utility RWE (11 billion Euro) and Siemens (10 billion Euro) the diversified manufacturing and engineering company. At the other end of the spectrum, BMW reported (using German accounting standards) liabilities of just 1.3 billion Euro. Many of the DAX 30 firms reported significant liabilities in the billions of Euro. A second trend or pattern was that manufacturing firms *tended* to have higher liabilities than service firms or banking firms. The significance of these data can be overplayed. But it is important to acknowledge that the total volume of net pension liabilities is important to financial analysts valuing German firms against their Anglo-American competitors. Given the incentives in the Anglo-American world to fully fund DB expected liabilities, Anglo-American firms that might be thought direct competitors have little or no net pension liabilities. Furthermore, as we saw in previous sections of this chapter, there are a significant number of Anglo-American firms that have managed their discount rates in favour of corporate earnings.

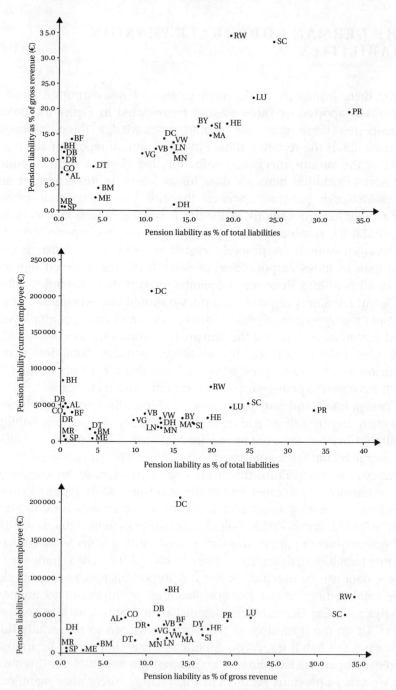

Fig. 4.1. Pension liability (1998) for the German DAX 30 firms.

To better appreciate the underlying patterns of pension liability, we set total net pension liability against three variables: total reported employment, total reported liabilities, and total reported gross revenue. This is rarely done, if ever, for Anglo-American firms (for a good reason, see above). In the German case, however, clear patterns emerged from this analysis. Most obvious, from Figure 4.1 was the significant correlation (0.75) between company pension liability as a per cent of gross revenue against pension liability as a per cent of total liabilities. Also significant but less strong was the correlation between pension liability per employee set against gross revenue (0.56). Initially, there was no significant correlation between pension liabilities per employee and total liabilities. But excluding DaimlerChrysler (DC) from the second and third tests of correlation, the underlying correlations were stronger and more significant (0.57) and (0.59) respectively. Finally, there were distinct patterns by industry, with significant clusters according to banking and insurance compared to heavy industrials. Note that the low pension liability per employee almost always meant low pension liability against gross revenue. But there are interesting patterns: compare Deutsche Bank (DB) with Mannesmann (MN).

Clearly pension policy, and pension liability management varies a great deal within the DAX 30 index firms (but seems fairly stable from one year to the next; comparing 1998 with 1999 data). To make more sense of these patterns requires a greater knowledge of the circumstances of individual firms. In general, we have shown that the DAX 30 index firms are closely connected with the evolving international accounting standards regime. We have also shown that reported pension liabilities amongst these firms are very significant. And for those firms not reporting liabilities, the inherited German accounting standards regime is not a refuge from global finance. Whether adoption of these standards will affect corporate governance (hypothesis 4), however remains unclear.

MANAGEMENT DISCRETION AND RETIREMENT PLANS

There are a variety of implications to be drawn from this discussion for German corporate structure (in general) and the future of German corporate-sponsored supplementary pensions (in particular). To assess hypothesis 4, let us begin by making three entirely obvious comments about the goals behind international accounting standards. One goal has been to displace the interests of insiders for the interests of outsiders. This means displacing those with special access to price-sensitive information in favour of market agents and shareholders without privileged channels of access (Clark and Wójcik 2002). Another goal has been to regulate managers, not just by imposing rules and regulations on their behaviour but also by imposing rules and regulations on the disclosure of information about the performance of their firms. Yet another goal has been to improve the economic efficiency of resource allocation between firms and between sectors. According to the FASB and the IASC, access to capital is a better economic process if it is a disembodied process of market supply and demand. For German firms traditionally biased in favour of insiders, reliant upon overlapping and reinforcing supervisory boards, and the beneficiaries of non-traded preferential financial terms and conditions, harmonization to the IASC rules presages a very different world of markets and competition for financial resources.

The introduction of international accounting standards will alter managers' discretion, will change their available options, and will impose constraints on the use of inherited modes of financial decision-making. This will not, however, mean the end of managers' discretion. Evidence, noted above, about earnings management within the existing US GAAP regime is evidence enough about the remaining scope for action (and subversion). Moreover, the new regime of market inter-mediation may actually strengthen the German corporate management in relation to claims for special status made by other stakeholders. We suggest here that the introduction of the IASB accounting standards may actually drive a wedge between the interests of corporate management, the interests of their supervisory boards, and the process of (labour-management) co-determination. To illustrate, consider the implications of these observations for German employer-sponsored supplementary pensions given the under-funding of *direktzusagen* and *pensionskassen* pension systems.

By default, the IAS 19 and its variants blur historical distinctions between the various ways German firms finance retirement income. Recall that the *direktzusagen* pension system is a means of recycling employer pension contributions as self-managed investment funds. Assuming success, corporate long-term retirement obligations are to be paid out of the resulting proceeds of long-term growth (measured by revenue flow and higher labour productivity). Many theorists of comparative corporate governance believe that the *direktzusagen* system underwrote post-1945 German economic growth. Furthermore, the existence of these systems of internal finance are often invoked to account for the distinctive capital-rich profiles of German industrial firms compared to their Anglo-American competitors (Hopt *et al.* 1999). However, international accounting standards are neither required to be sensitive to the national economic significance of this institution, nor are they necessarily sensitive to the implied social contract between successive generations of company workers. Annual net pension cost, the IASB prospective corporate balance sheet entry, stands instead of the various social mechanisms of funding long-term corporate pension liability.

International standards may rewrite long-term pension liabilities, not counted against current income in German accounting practices, as short-term liabilities. Thus the underfunding of long-term pension obligations, characteristic of *direktzusagen* systems and common to corporate *pensionskassen* funds, will be charged against the current value of the firm. Given the extent of net pension liabilities in many leading German industrial firms, it is possible that these liabilities could translate into lower corporate quoted market prices relative to similar Anglo-American firms operating from the IASC and the FASB compliant jurisdictions. Even if firms were to remain loyal to German accounting standards, market agents are likely to draw implications about their underlying pension liabilities using the information available on German firms that report according to international standards. A low relative market price accompanied by modern capital assets and advantageous market positions are, as well, opportunities for rival firms to mount hostile takeover offers. In effect, the German corporate supplementary pensions may be implicated in the pan-European market for corporate control. This would replay the recent history of the US employer-sponsored pensions, including the interaction between the pension liabilities and corporate restructuring.

Importantly, the discounting of corporate value may also be accompanied by the introduction of external benchmarks for judging investment returns. In the absence of deep German and European equity markets, for many years the benchmark for internal investment was long-term government bonds. Also, given the quantitative regulation of asset allocations in favour of bonds and against equities, long-term bonds were the favoured investment class for *pensionskassen* funds. But as the integration of European financial markets has accelerated over the past five years, bond rates have converged and yields have declined. In the context of the development of pan-European sector-based equity portfolios by institutional investors, it is increasingly difficult to justify a benchmark rate of return set to bond rates. Even so, the adoption of equity related benchmarks would be quite problematic. There are few obvious ways of increasing the internal rate of return (and reducing the opportunity cost of capital) without tackling the organization of the firm (or other firms, the possible targets of hostile take-overs). Just beyond the horizon lurk global financial institutions with interests in the corporate restructuring of German and European industry.

Thus, the disclosure of under-funded pension liabilities is a threat to, and an opportunity to remake, managers' discretion in relation to historical privileges. Not surprisingly, there has been a significant shift over the past ten years amongst the large German firms away from *direktzusagen* systems. Another response has been to slowly increase the funding of *pensionskassen* obligations thereby reducing the overall reported corporate pension liability. These trends imply, of course, significant short-term financial costs for corporate stakeholders in the form of lower profits, rates of return, and lower real wages. And there are conflicting interests embedded in German firms that make this strategy more problematic than often supposed. Whereas corporate managers have a short-term interest in sheltering from the emerging European market for corporate control, not all stakeholders may accept the nature of reorganization, and boards of supervisors may be compelled to defend their historic claims for preferential status. Similarly, the threat to co-determination posed by Anglo-American investment practices amplifies political debate about the funding of German PAYG social insurance as workers and beneficiaries are charged with the costs of full funding.

The prospects for extensive voluntary savings schemes and employer-sponsored supplementary pension plans may be entwined within domestic political negotiations. But I have also suggested here that these arrangements and institutions are also now part of the global financial system either directly or indirectly. As such, the imperatives of capital markets embedded in international accounting standards pose significant challenges to the accepted practices and relationships. The current and long-term funding of the German corporate pension liabilities may require rewriting internal corporate relationships in favour of corporate managers and external shareholders. These are the issues addressed in Chapter 5.

CONCLUSIONS

In this chapter, we have traced the evolution of the US corporate accounting practices from the APB Opinions through to the current SEC and FASB co-sponsored regime of Generally Accepted Accounting Principles (GAAP). The focus of argument and discussion was the treatment of pension liabilities, and inevitably those liabilities associated with DB or final salary pension schemes. Drawing upon debate around the time the FASB 87 and 106 were introduced, we demonstrated that issues raised then (over twenty years ago) are highly relevant to the German scene. In fact, recent evidence drawn from the German corporate annual reports suggests that many of the largest DAX 30 index firms have rapidly embraced these standards, notwithstanding the apparent implications for pension funding from such adoption. As the FASB, the IASB, and the ASB have converged upon a harmonized set of accounting standards that promote transparency, consistency, and comparability, financial and corporate governance systems outside of these standards have had to adapt to, if not always adopt, these standards.

In doing so, we assessed the evolution of core systems of financial accounting in the Anglo-American world against changes at the margins of the German financial and corporate practice. Our argument took the historical evolution of the US accounting standards over a period of about 40 years and set the results of that history against German institutions in the context of EU integration over the past five years or so. There are clearly significant conceptual and empirical dangers inherent in such a strategy. Whereas history was assumed to slowly unfold in one context (the United States of America), we have argued that history is currently under threat in another context (Germany). In one, path dependence is the motive force of history, in the other lock-in is almost immediately resolved by the forces of global finance and economic logic. This may well be the case, empirically speaking. Remarkably, the largest German firms have proved far more responsive than theory would suggest. But it does not do justice to the coherence and persistence of German institutions and traditions; we also need to look more closely at the ways in which such threats are accommodated within these institutions rather than accepting the proclaimed 'end of history'. This is the subject of Chapter 5. It looks at the ways in which nation-specific social expectations and co-determination interact with the German corporate investment practice.

Still, notwithstanding reasonable doubts about the force of this argument, it should be noted that the process of harmonization to international accounting standards is quite unlike many other multi-lateral negotiations over trade etc. Whereas we have come to expect that nation-states are the active agents behind such negotiations, balancing internal social and economic interests against the interests of global trading partners, in corporate finance independent accounting professionals have become the negotiators and standard setters. As recent debate about the restructuring of the IASB has shown, the idea that accounting professionals ought to 'represent' or in some way 'balance' their underlying 'national interests' with the professional harmonization of global accounting standards has been soundly rejected. The IASB has eschewed 'representative nationalism' in favour of the interests of their idealized clients in global capital markets. This has been a difficult lesson for the regulatory institutions of large countries. On the other hand, for many smaller advanced economies, it is an ideal readily accepted and incorporated into national regulations.

Whatever the interests of nation-states, the international accounting profession has moved far faster and far more comprehensively than many believed possible. They have done so in the context of the interests of private market agents, thereby sustaining the globalization of markets for financial services. In these ways, the market valuation of corporate earnings against accepted international accounting standards has become the *raison d'être* of private rating agencies, investment firms, and mutual funds companies. Indeed, the FASB, the IOSCO, and the IASB and their related partners have made possible the growth of a global market for corporate control as opposed to the long-term non-traded relationships that dominate the German economy. This rule-based system of valuation has become a key element facilitating globalization, and a key element driving the externalization of corporate information to remotely located electronically linked buyers and sellers of corporate securities. If incomplete in terms of its coverage of the advanced industrialized world, each new initiative aimed at harmonization according to international standards brings global capital market integration closer to national systems of corporate governance once assumed fundamentally different and impervious to change. As powerful economic nations like Germany come to terms with global finance, the pressure on other European nations to reassess the relevance of their own institutions can only be thought to increase.

NOTES

1. To characterize corporate *direktzusagen* pensions as 'unfunded' runs the risk of mis-representing the distinctive financial structure of such systems. When firms set aside each payroll period an amount equal to the present value of earned pension benefits, they are required to utilize a mandated interest (discount) rate. Such systems may be thought, by some, to be fully funded not unfunded even if 'all pension assets are invested in a single security: the debt of the sponsoring firm' (Pesando 2000: 352). Pension benefits are also protected by a mandatory insurance scheme, analogous to solvency insurance. However, for financial agents the intermingling of corporate and pension financial assets and liabilities is very problematic. See the IASC (2000: 634) where mention is made of the necessity of providing accounting reports that show 'the net assets available for benefits' (IAS 26, Accounting and Reporting by Retirement Benefit Plans).

2. See Allen and Gale (1994) where they begin by identifying Germany at 'one extreme' and the United States of America at 'the other extreme'. In their view, the German financial institutions and instruments are controlled by dominant banks in contrast with the US model where markets play crucial roles in the allocation of financial assets. La Porta *et al.* (1998) develop a comprehensive cross-national data base for the comparison of countries' legal systems, their financial structures, and the robustness of financial markets. Again, the German model is explicitly identified as a system different from the Anglo-American model (amongst others). Here, though, doubts are raised about the effects of such differences on nations' relative economic performance. See also Carlin and Mayer (1999) who dispute the generality of any connection between the financial structure and economic performance. Berndt (1998a, b) also assesses the robustness of the German model, weaving together sectoral and firm-based studies with geographical differentiation. He is less sanguine about the persistence of the German model in the context of globalization.

3. With the Enron scandal, there is now a great deal of interest in the FASB. The American Institute of Certified Public Accountants established the Financial Accounting Standards Board in 1973. It is an autonomous professional body, with a large membership drawn from a wide variety of sectors and industries. As part of its mandate, it sets so-called 'generally accepted accounting principles' (GAAP) for its members. These principles incorporate many of the original APB opinions but has evolved a research and development function in keeping with the demand for accounting standards perceived by its leadership and membership. Details on its role and status can be found at www.rutgers.edu/accounting/raw/fasb/facts/fasfact1.html

4. See also Ford (1994) on the financial and human consequences of the introduction of the FASB 106 for the provision of retiree health care benefits. By her account, and the experience of industrial unions, the transition to reporting the full costs of such liabilities resulted in the termination of many retiree health care plans.

5. This was a modest increase in the average expected return (10 basis points). The minimum reported expected return increased one hundred basis points (from 5.00 to 6.00 per cent), and the standard deviation increased from 0.89 to 0.93 not withstanding a decline in the maximum reported expected rate of return from 13.00 to 11.50 per cent. Note that less than 50 per cent of S&P 500 firms reported their expected rate of return for 1994 and 1998, indicating in a crude way the shift towards DC plans amongst the largest US firms.

6. Furthermore, there were few, if any, apparent trends by industry. For example in capital goods and basic materials, most firms were clustered around the 5–10 per cent mark (pension expenditures as a percentage of reported operating income), with a

decreased pension contribution in 1998 compared to 1994. Indeed, given the close clustered patterns of firm 'locations' with respect to pension expenditures as a proportion of operating income in the S&P sectors (except technology and health care stocks), the particular circumstances of individual firms seemed more important than the sector.

7. See also the comments of Arthur Levitt (June 29, 1999) the previous Chairman of the Securities Exchange Commission (SEC) at an Audit Committee Symposium decrying the common practice, it seems, of 'earnings management—the practice of using accounting tricks to mask true operating performance'. www.sec.gov/news/speeches/spch289.htm

8. It should be noted, however, that the enthusiasm of the US accounting profession and the SEC for the FASB rules disclosing the market value of assets and liabilities does not always translate into ready acceptance by other finance professionals. Writing much before the Enron scandal, Kaen (1995: 7) raised doubts about the value and meaning of the common US accounting rules that emphasize earnings per share. He argued that this measure is at once arbitrary in relation to the real interest of investors in cash flow, and often too short-run in orientation. Relevant for this chapter, he also noted the important problems of interpretation that arise when attempting to compare different jurisdictions' measures of earnings per share (comparing the Swedish and US standards).

9. There is considerable doubt about the long-term viability of such a EU regulatory strategy. In a study comparing the US and EU business law more than a decade ago, Conard (1991) suggested that a model of EU regulation based upon 'federal' minimum standards and nation-state discretion could easily degenerate into interjurisdictional rivalry. He wondered how it would be possible to stop some jurisdictions adopting so-called 'lax' standards within the 'federal' umbrella, thereby initiating a 'race of laxity' amongst the EU nation-states. More recently, Swaine (2000) has noted that member states lack a firmly entrenched constitutional principle of subsidiarity that could protect them from liability when discriminating between private actors like corporations on the basis of their national origin.

10. Arthur Levitt, the previous Chairman of the SEC, referred to the relationship between the FASB and the SEC as a 'partnership with the private sector [providing] a way to build input into the standard-setting process from all stakeholders, including preparers, auditors and users, as well as regulators'. See his September 29, 1997, speech at www.sec.gov/news/speeches/spch176.txt

11. See the arguments by Cohen (1994) and Novak (1998) about the consequences of global financial market integration for the status of the US securities markets in international finance and the need for the SEC to relax its stance regarding the primacy of the FASB and the US GAAP. Note the related comments of Arthur Levitt accepting the need to respond to globalization and the effects of new communications technologies, notwithstanding the imperatives of sustaining the virtues of full disclosure and market transparency for market efficiency, fairness, and economic stability (October 18, 1999). www.sec.gov/news/speeches/spch304.htm

12. For a general introduction to the SEC position on the IASC proposals see the comments of the SEC Commissioner Hunt (February 17, 2000) at www.iasc.org.uk/news/cen8_159.htm See also the news releases of the SEC at www.sec.gov/news/intlacct.htm (including a fact sheet, Levitt's remarks, and a detailed assessment—Concept release 34-42430). Details on the IASC strategy are to be found at www.iasc.org.uk/news/cen8_058.htm (including the discussion paper, its appendices, and summary). Doubts about its prospects as a robust international system of governance can be found in Licht (1997), being a critical analysis of the value of international securities regulation using the game theory.

13. Arthur Levitt used this example to argue the case for high quality international accounting standards characterized by 'transparency, consistency, and comparability'. www.sec.gov/news/speeches/spch304.htm Transparency refers to the mode of reporting, declaring the available information on corporate earnings, assets, and liabilities in a manner that allows market agents to economize on information collection. Consistency refers to the nature of period-to-period reporting, allowing market agents to develop coherent accounts of the market value and circumstances of firms under scrutiny. Comparability takes transparency and consistency one step further, relying upon common accounting standards implemented in accepted ways that facilitate comparison between firms over time. In effect, comparability allows market agents to scrutinize corporate reports for 'value' across time and space.

14. In the few instances where accounting standards were not reported, we labelled these companies as German rather than international. In essence, it was assumed that non-reporting standards meant 'German' by virtue of customary practice and the need to disclose any *change* in reporting standards.

15. One of the few studies related to the introduction of the FASB 87 concluded that just one variable could explain 'early adoption': increased reported earnings. Neither size, nor debt, nor industry affiliation was found significant. In this respect, Langer and Lev (1993) concluded that this was evidence of 'earnings management' denying even the importance of administrative costs and resistance to compliance.

16. As of March 2000, these firms were DaimlerChrysler, Deutsche Telekom, Fresenius Medical, SAP and Veda. No DAX-listed firms are listed on the NASDAQ, although there are six very small German firms so included. Of course, this does not preclude the possibility of further listings; BASF announced that it would seek a listing in June 2000.

Stakeholders, Shareholders, and German Co-determination

There is widespread debate in the academic, media, and policy communities about the continuity of diverse national systems of accumulation versus convergence to a dominant model. Whole schools of thought are arrayed like jousting armies across the economic and political landscape. Concepts like path dependence and sunk costs underpin claims on behalf of continuity, while capital mobility and financial arbitrage provide the intellectual weapons for those that foresee convergence. Like Berndt (2001), however, we have doubts about the coherence of national models theoretically and empirically, just as we contend that large firms have considerable room to manoeuvre in the global economy as opposed to the small- and medium-sized firms with limited geographical scope and competence (compare Guerrieri 1999 with Kluth and Andersen 1999). In this chapter, we are concerned with the reconfiguration of German corporate decision-making focusing upon employer-sponsored pensions (*betriebliche Altersversorgung*), their management and their investment protocols given the Anglo-American practice and international accounting standards (subjects of the previous chapter).

We aim to show that the German model is under attack from within; there are important incentives driving managers away from inherited commitments and relationships, while the Anglo-American management practices are being copied and adopted by virtue of the cross-jurisdictional character of large German firms. This is not an entirely new argument, witness the research by Gertler (2001) and others in economic geography on the nature of technological exchange within German firms and between national systems of regulation. We also suggest, however, that the process of convergence is conditioned by the changing interests and loyalties of managers in relation to workers and shareholders and the introduction of new German private pension institutions that may 'map on' to the Anglo-American institutions and practices in ways not previously anticipated. Our emphasis on corporate pension policy reflects the importance of this issue for the financial integrity of large German firms, and the putative importance of private pensions relative to the underfunded national social insurance system. As we have shown previously, the adoption by the DAX 30 firms of international management practices and accounting standards may have far-reaching implications for the provision of German supplementary pensions.

The analysis begins with a brief review of the various modes of German corporate retirement income provision. This takes us from summary data regarding coverage rates through to the role and status of 'unfunded' *direktzusagen* (book reserve) and 'underfunded' *pensionskassen* (mutual insurance) pension systems in the context of German labour-management relations and co-determination.[1] Little of this material will be new to experts in the field. But it is important to set out the nature of inherited institutions and practices, recognizing that analysis in the latter sections of the chapter takes aim at these remnants of past struggles over the balance of power within and between firms. Not only do these institutions and practices reflect the foundations of post-war power sharing and economic growth, they are often legitimized by the reference to idealized conceptions of German society. In our analysis of corporate decision-making we introduce economic imperatives and management interests that challenge continuity with the past. Globalization and the promise of bonuses and stock options geared to the market value of the firm are 'threats' to the past, while inherited institutions and practices are 'constraints' on collective decision-making.

Sustaining the chapter is a set of linked arguments that cumulate to an overarching position on the disputed tension between globalization and localization. In doing so, we argue that the German employer-sponsored supplementary pensions are more important than often acknowledged; coverage rates are comparable with the Anglo-American world and promised benefits may become a significant component of retirement income. Furthermore, we suggest that many large German firms have extensive experience with the Anglo-American pension benefit systems, providing valuable insights into the advanced management of assets and liabilities not readily available to their workers or most other German firms. Interviews with corporate management suggest that the German co-managed pension institutions tend towards consensus given workers' risk aversion. This regime is under threat from German managers concerned to enhance their wealth rather than their long-term share of corporate income. Continuity with the past is vulnerable to defection and the interests of market agents operating in global financial markets.

SOCIAL INSURANCE AND SUPPLEMENTARY PENSIONS

The looming crisis of continental European social security systems is widely debated in academic and policy circles. In Germany, notwith-standing the adverse demographic and fiscal trends, policy initiatives have stalled, stumbled, and restarted—caught between a commitment to comprehensive but largely unfunded social insurance and a reluct-ance to introduce the tax incentives that would promote private pension provision. At one level, the issues are entirely political and deeply embedded in domestic social affairs having to do with the role of social insurance as a force for social cohesion. At another level, however, these issues have enormous importance for the future of the German industry in the global economy. Any effective tax initiative for encouraging the private provision of pensions must deal with the cost to capital, recognizing the existing very high social (benefit) costs of labour relative to international competitors.[2] Resolution of these economic and political tensions has been identified by the financial community as an important test of German political capacity in the light of globalization (Deutsche Bank 1999: 27–30).

For many social commentators, the German retirement income system is believed to have a number of virtues. Being comprehensive in coverage with benefits proportional to workers' income, the social insurance system provides a level of retirement income that is equit-able within and between successive generations. Also, the system provides related disability, early retirement, surviving spouse and family benefits. By comparison, many would argue that the employer-sponsored supplementary pensions are irrelevant. Some suggest that the new policy aimed at encouraging supplementary pensions will not, and could not, make a significant difference to the financing of social insurance. Older workers, the generation who dominate the expected long-term PAYG financial burden, would not be able to accumulate sufficient assets to retire with incomes equal to the promised benefits of the PAYG system. And younger workers, who might benefit from the enhancement of supplementary private pensions, may have to pay twice: for the retirement costs of their parents and for contributions to their own retirement accounts. In any event, or so the argument goes, coverage rates are low, benefits are limited, funding is inadequate, and expected benefits risky.

Social Market and Private Pensions

The priority attributed to social insurance is an indication of the significance of the social market: the interrelated institutions of collective welfare, finance, and governance that together, according to many commentators, differentiates Germany from the Anglo-American world (O'Sullivan 2000). See also Hutton (1995: 20) where he compares various countries arguing that 'the behaviour of the economy can only be understood in terms of the whole of each country's social and political system and where it stands in the global order'.[3] All this is well appreciated in the academic literature, being the staple diet of comparative corporate governance and regulation based on the idea that nation-states are persistently different by virtue of their internal organization (history and geography) (see Hopt *et al.* 1999). Less appreciated is the extent to which the social market is under threat from 'insiders' *and* the changing global environment. An exclusive focus upon social insurance would seriously underestimate the changing status of employer-sponsored supplementary pensions as a putative solution to the crisis of social insurance (Sinn 1999).

For analysts familiar with the German economic and social policy, the social market is a comprehensive system of interdependent and reciprocal systems of governance. Each system of governance, like the social insurance system, relates in a concomitant manner to the other parts of the whole system. In combination, these sub-systems of governance add up to a *comprehensive and coherent* web of self-sustaining institutions and practices. This structure-oriented view of German society is more than just an empirical observation; it can be found as a theoretical argument in its most developed form in Luhmann's (1995) treatise on social systems. By his account, social systems are sets of self-referential systems of governance that together constitute the whole while regulating relationships between the constitutive elements. If social systems are properly thought to be the products of agency (action) and contingency (events), in the German case the social system is knitted together by reciprocal relationships and collective delibera-tion. So, for instance, the role and status of collective bargaining is at once determined by an ideal conception of the proper relationship between management and labour *in* society and the need for dispute resolution relevant to the immediate circumstances of industries and firms.[4]

Echoing this logic, Reynaud (2000: 4) suggests that commitment to German social insurance reflects the 'network of various contacts and multiple forms of cooperation between the social partners and the government'. Cooperation on this issue is believed to sustain coop-eration at other points in the system of mutually reinforcing economic, social, and political systems. Reynaud goes further, and beyond Luhmann's theoretical enterprise, to suggest that social insurance has a distinctive status in German society. Any forced change in its status, bowing to global market imperatives and the interests of private agents, would be detrimental to the integrity of related systems of industrial and social governance. In this model, private pensions are deemed to be *outside* the parameters of the social market. This is despite the fact that 45 per cent of the workforce are covered by supplementary schemes even if coverage is biased towards public employees and employees of large manufacturing firms located in western Germany (Deutsche Bundesbank 2001: 50).

Data on German supplementary pensions are variable in quality and difficult to obtain (Queisser 1996). The available evidence suggests that these types of pensions are more important than often believed. About 32 per cent of firms offer supplementary pension benefits; most often relying upon DB or final salary schemes managed in a variety of ways (see below). Significantly, 87 per cent of firms with more than 5000 employees offer such benefits in their compensation packages. In manufacturing, coverage rates are higher, involving 68 per cent of all enterprises and 64 per cent of all employees (Koenig and van der Lende 1999: 5).[5] Large corporations have had supplementary pension systems for many years, in some cases being established in the late nineteenth century. In terms of value, some German corporate plans contribute a significant share of retirement income. Of the nine firms identified in Table 5.1, all firms sponsor plans that contribute 20 per cent or more to the final retirement income. In most cases, firms bear the burden of

Table 5.1. The German employer-sponsored occupational pension schemes' contribution rates as a percentage assuming 35 years of service, 1996

Firm	Employer contributions	Employee contributions	Total (%)
BASF	24	4	28
Bayer	25	3	28
Bosch	26	—	26
Daimler Benz	30	—	30
Degussa	25	3	28
Henkel	33	—	33
Hoechst	27	4	31
Merck	35	—	35
Siemens	27	—	27

Note: Assuming a defined benefit pension without regard to the particular institution managing the pension plan assets and liabilities.

contributions. Where they do not, employees' share of contributions is quite small. For the employees of large firms, private pension provision will be of greater importance if proposals to cap the value of social insurance benefits effectively shift the burden of income replacement to private institutions and individuals.

Social Systems and the Environment

Implied by the structure-oriented argument is a certain relationship between the social systems and their environments. For Luhmann, social systems are organically related to their environments. Although conceived as a passive 'correlate' of the social system, the environment is nevertheless a constitutive element of the social system by virtue of its relative complexity. Accordingly, social systems are *made* coherent by what is deliberately excluded from these systems recognizing that coherence requires the exclusion of anything that would directly challenge the integrity of the whole. Hence, that which is deliberately excluded is left unincorporated and 'located' in the surrounding environment. In this respect, Luhmann, like many other commentators on the German scene, has suggested that social systems are conceived, in part, in opposition to the apparent disorder and disharmony of the market economy. Various implications follow from this logic. Most importantly there is an implied hierarchical ordering of institutions and their systems, distinguishing between those that are endogenous (for instance, social insurance) and exogenous (for instance, private pensions). Employer-sponsored private pension arrangements may coexist with social insurance; coherence is a logical ordering of significance as much as it is a process of lexical exclusion.

Even so there is a paradox in theory and, as we shall see, in practice. Notwithstanding the claimed irrelevance of private pensions such arrangements are inevitably governed by existing overlapping and interrelated social systems even if these systems have as their goal the mediation of endogenously defined social relationships. This is most apparent when considering the governance of employer-sponsored private pension institutions like *pensionskassen*. Even though these institutions are deemed irrelevant to the core institutions of social insurance, employment law and the collective bargaining system overlap with and dominate *pensionskassen*. This point is also made by Weiss (1995). Therein he sketches the basic principles underlying the federal German law, noting the relationship between labour law (based upon private contract law) and labour-management relations (based upon collective rights). He suggests, in fact, that these two aspects of law are 'closely interrelated', just as social security law is 'closely interrelated' with labour law even if each system is 'strictly separated' (Weiss 1995: 24–5). More specifically, social security law is a branch of public not private law.

As each social system selects from and responds against its environment, it evolves over time in ways that forge a distinctive relationship to the environment. By this logic, we can go one step further in the argument noted above: as social insurance has evolved in relation to concomitant systems of social organization, private pensions have remained peripheral to the German retirement income provision. The implication is plain. The likely effect of new tax incentives designed to promote private pension provision could be muted because of the continued significance of otherwise dominant interrelated social systems. This is another version of path dependence and institutional persistence, so important in economic geography and comparative corporate governance. Still, we should not exaggerate the significance of path dependence. Although social systems tend to exclude incompatible institutions, or relegate them to the margins of existing institutions, this is not an absolute process. Rival modes of social organization can lie dormant or function within the shadows of existing systems of governance. Likewise, the process of selection within and without social systems is surely a contested political process. Social agents may call upon excluded or marginal modes of social organization as weapons in attempts to redefine their relationships to social systems.

For Luhmann (1995: 433), evolution is a process of selection and adaptation in relation to changing circumstances. Systems immediately affected pass on their response to change to other interrelated systems, being a cumulative process of incremental accommodation even if the end result may be less predictable than the immediate effects of changing circumstances. If this appears to be a rather benign process, it is because it presumes the continued integrity of the whole. But there are reasons to suppose that the recent changes in the environment of German social systems are neither incremental nor benign in effect. Three points can be made summarizing the basis of this claim.

First, the environment in which the German social systems and social agents operate has begun to change scale, a process described by Swyngedouw (2000) as 'rescaling of the economy'. While the nation-state remains important for most firms and the social partners, the international economic environment has become more important than ever introducing new imperatives and circumstances not previously encountered or incorporated into the post-war German social structure. At the same time as economic upscaling has come to be important, downscaling in terms of the effective unit of response (from nation to region, from industry to firm, and from social partners to management) to these imperatives has also become important. Collective institutions, the bedrock of German co-determination, may be 'at risk' in this new order.

Second, both the large German firms' management and nation-state elites have an interest in responding to these imperatives. The former are engaged in competition for a global position, while the latter have claimed the opportunity to provide economic and political leadership in Europe and beyond. Both have an interest in creating national champions, competitive in the global economy. Whereas Luhmann and others suppose that social systems evolve by balancing interests and by reflexive responses to changes in interrelated systems, these types of responses may be too slow relative to the speed of globalization or too cumbersome in the light of changed priorities. In play is the historical pattern of interrelated social systems in the light of claims about what is now relevant for the global rather than the national environment.

Third, whereas institutions and practices like employer-sponsored pensions were once considered peripheral to core social systems and were relegated to a marginal status, as globalization accelerates these institutions may be especially important even if their integrity is threatened by the imperatives driving global finance. In effect, and notwithstanding the particular formation of German financial institutions with German social systems, the Anglo-American financial practices now threaten to undermine both the German banking practices and the coherence of inherited relationships between the systems of finance, labour, and retirement income provision.

GLOBAL FINANCE AND GLOBAL LEARNING

Many DAX 30 listed firms operate throughout continental Europe, the UK, and North America. Of course, the geographical scope and intensity of external operations varies between firms and industries. By virtue of their merger with Chrysler, Daimler Benz is now deeply immersed in the North American auto market compared, for example, with BMW notwithstanding their own US operations. There is, for many of these firms, a tension between the management of their German operations and their international operations. Simply, the issue is the extent to which management practices within the firm and different jurisdictions ought to be resolved in favour of a common company-wide practice. For the most part, this issue has been resolved in favour of local practice because management has been required to respect local customs and regulations pertaining to employment and labour relations practices. So, for instance, Gertler (2001) has shown that the application of common production technologies within German manufacturing firms across the world has almost always led to local solutions rather than the application of company-wide standards; the *local* environment is an important mediating variable.

For German firms, of course, there is a further complication. Not only are many aspects of management practice caught up within the fabric of interrelated systems of economic and social regulation, these systems are defined, in the first instance, by reference to the German environment rather than other countries' environments or the global environment at large. In fact, many would contend that other countries' environments are not simply at a distance from the German environment but are irrelevant to the German social systems. This is surely the argument deployed by those concerned to protect the integrity of the German social market. There are significant barriers to the use of experience in Germany from outside Germany.[6] Even so, for German firms operating in the Anglo-American world the 1990s brought home important lessons regarding the management of employer-sponsored pensions. These lessons were drawn from their own experience, the experience of other German firms, and the experience of their competitors.

In Table 5.2, summary data are presented on the numbers and types of pension and retirement income benefit plans operated by leading German firms in the United States of America during 1997 and 1999. This data was accessed through corporate reports to the US Department of Labor (DoL) concerning the funding and investment status of those plans (Form 5500). Notice these plans were almost always fully funded as required by statute, the US GAAP and the Financial Accounting Standards Board (FASB) (Chapter 4). Here, we make three broad-ranging observations. First, many of the large German firms operating in the United States of America have had extensive experience in the full range of pension and retirement benefits including the DB plans, 401(K) DC plans, profit sharing, savings and flexible benefit plans. Second, many German manufacturing firms provide pension benefit plans in union and non-union environments, thereby having to manage trustee boards with and without employee representatives. Third, even firms with relatively small US operations have had considerable experience with the financial services industry that underpins the US private pension and retirement benefit system.

Of course, some German firms may have had less direct experience with these types of benefit systems than implied by Table 5.2. Mergers and acquisitions between the German and US firms have not always led to mutual understanding. But consider, in brief, the (1997) experience of Bayer (Table 5.3). One of their plans (003) was a DB plan funded by employer contributions on behalf of 336 active workers and about 118 retirees represented by the United Paperworkers Union. During the year, the net rate of return on a base asset market value of $6 million was approximately 31 per cent. Another plan, a 401(K) plan (019) with more than 18 thousand active participants and about 12 thousand retirees was funded by employer contributions ($35 million). Over the year, the net return on an asset base of about $1.6 billion was approximately 19 per cent. Embedded in this brief comparison is an important story about the equity boom of the 1990s, and the benefits reaped by

Table 5.2. The US pension and related income plan experience of German Dax-listed corporations excluding death, disability, health, and dental care plans, 1997–1999

Firm	No. of plans	DB	Defined contribution				Union	Acquired firms
			401(K)	Profit	Savings	Flexible		
Adidas	4		√	√	√			√
Allianz	2		√					
BASF	5	√	√		√		u	√
Bayer	14	√	√	√	√	√	u	√
Bayerische Hypo-und-Vereinsbank	1		√	√	√			
BMW	25		√	√	√	√	u	
Commerzbank	7	√	√		√	√		
Daimler	1		√					
Daimler/Chrysler	10	√	√		√		u	√
Degussa	3	√	√		√	√		
Deutsche Bank	3	√	√	√	√	√		
Deutsche Telecom	2	√	√				u	
Dresdner Bank	6	√	√	√	√	√		√
Fresenius	1			√				
Henkel Corp	17	√	√	√	√	√	u	√
Linde Ent.	9		√	√		√		√
Lufthansa	5	√	√				u	
Mannesmann	10	√	√		√	√	u	√
Preussag	2		√	√		√		
RWE	1	√						
Schering Corp	5	√	√	√	√	√		√
Siemens	46	√	√	√	√	√	u	√
Thyssen	14	√	√	√	√	√	u	√
Krupp	2	√	√	√	√	√		√
Volkswagen	11	√	√	√	√	√		√

Source: freeERISA.com. For definitions of these various different types of pension and retirement income plans see the web site www.freeERISA.com/info/glossary.asp. Notice there are many different versions of defined contributions plans. For example, flexible benefit plans sometimes called cafeteria plans rely upon an IRS tax provision, and may or may not supplement other benefits. A savings plan is a type that defined contribution plans in which participants may make discretionary contributions either matched or partially matched by their employers. Normally such contributions are made after tax rather than before tax (the preferred basis of pension fund contributions).

Table **5.3.** Summary of the Bayer Corp. employer-sponsored US pension plans, 1997

Plan no.	Plan type	Participants			Year-end ($ml)		Year-end investment return (%)	Net ($ml) income	PBGC covered
		Vested	Non-vested	Retirees[1]	Assets	Expenses			
003[2]	DB	216	120	118	7.27	0.23	31.4	1.39	✓
006[2]	DB	Fewer than 100 participants			0.97	0.014	15.3	0.22	✓
009[2]	DB	Fewer than 100 participants			1.13	0.006	19.3	0.26	✓
010[2]	DB	231	176	102	13.67	0.241	16.3	2.15	✓
015	DB	121	7	60	2.39	0.039	51.8	0.48	✓
019	401(k)	14 541	4 175	12 696	1946	44.37	19.1	286.51	✓
021	401(k)	588	66	242	73.29	2.15	18.0	17.79	✓
023	N/A								
025	401(k)	384	55	6	7.77	0.411	N/A	3.05	✓

[1] Including separated employees with deferred entitlements.
[2] Union identified as representing covered workers.

Source: freeERISA.com.

plan sponsors. Also embedded in this comparison is a complicated story about who bears the risks of pension liability, the shift towards employee contributions and DC plans, and the quite different benefit systems of union and non-union employees. We do not wish to belabour these points made so often elsewhere. Our point is the recognition of a common experience amongst large German firms in the United States of America.

Returning to Chapter 4, we noted that McConnell *et al.* (1999) have shown that the (1998) reported expected rate of return on pension assets for US S&P 500 companies was 9.19 per cent up from 9.08 per cent in 1994. They have also shown that a significant number of these firms reported expected rates of return between 9.5 and 10.5 per cent. By comparison, our research based upon the annual reports for the DAX 30 German firms for the same year indicated that the reported expected rate of return on pension assets were in the range of 5.5–9.7 per cent, with most around the 7.0 per cent mark. Unfortunately, this data was sparse and of limited quality. More detailed are the data on the reported discount rate, ranging between 5.5–6.5 per cent. In effect, the German firms expected consistently much lower rates of return on their unfunded or under-funded German plans compared to the actual and expected rates of return on their funded US plans. Now, of course, the German situation is quite different than the US situation. For instance, in Germany there have been significant quantitative limits on asset allocations by asset classes, biased in favour of bonds against equities (national and international). This has been the subject of considerable debate in Germany and the EC (Chapter 2).

Most important has been the realization amongst German firms that their Anglo-American rivals have utilized much more aggressive investment strategies. Many US firms have managed the investment of their DB pension fund assets so as to decrease their pension fund contributions and, in some cases, contribute to their net reported corporate income. This point has been elaborated by Bear Stearns (McConnell *et al.* 2001a, b), and has been subsequently validated by industry analysts (see Towers Perrin 2000; Watson Wyatt 2000) and interviews with the UK and US firms.[7] This kind of investment strategy can be characterized as a maximization strategy, using the most advanced financial methods to drive rates of return in a manner consistent with corporate financial objectives. It stands in contrast to the objective function commonly attributed to the US pension fund management; optimizing the value of current assets against expected liabilities (Logue and Rader 1997). Not surprisingly, the German firms operating in the United States of America have developed similar investment strategies. And given the free flow of information within the global investment management community, the management of large German firms in their 'home' jurisdictions have become very much aware of these developments.

MANAGEMENT MOTIVES AND THE SOCIAL MARKET

As noted above, over the 1990s large German firms accumulated the Anglo-American experience and/or knowledge at odds with German customs and conventions. Information was acquired either directly through overseas affiliates or through the analysis of the actions and behaviour of competitors. If none of these channels worked, actuarial and investment consultants were more than willing to fill in the gaps. We have intimated, however, that notwithstanding the acquisition of this information, domestic pension management and investment practices remain firmly entrenched in the reciprocal web of the social market. Such is, or was, the power of the institutions and regulations underpinning the German model. Yet this logic ignores or leaves un-explained the introduction of new kinds of corporate pension institutions as well as the adoption of international accounting standards relevant to the reporting of corporate pension liabilities.

It is suggested in this section that the management of large German firms have learnt another important lesson from the Anglo-American world, a lesson that has profound implications for the coherence of the social market and the management of employer-sponsored pension plans. During the 1990s the German corporate management, unlike many of their Anglo-American colleagues, were excluded from the benefits associated with the run-up in global equity markets.[8] Compensation remained tied to corporate income, discounting the importance of corporate national and global market value. Whereas significant numbers of senior and middle managers in the large US firms became wealthy by virtue of their bonuses and stock options, the German managers were locked into compensation agreements balancing their interests in income growth with those of workers and shareholders. If, in the early 1990s, bonuses and stock options appeared less significant compared to conventional forms of remuneration, by the end of the decade a significant segment of the US managers had shifted their aspirations from income growth to wealth creation through company stock market value.[9]

Clearly, these kinds of compensation plans were very important in the telecommunications, media and technology (TMT) sectors concentrated in Silicon Valley (California) and Rt 128/495 Boston (Massachusetts). While now associated with the TMT boom, bubble and bust, bonuses and stock options remain very important for the large US corporations. Twenty years ago, this form of compensation was introduced to align the interests of senior corporate officers with their principal shareholders. But broad-based employee bonus and stock option plans are now essential elements of compensation in most S&P 500 corporations (Laing and Sharpe 1999). In theory, the alignment of interests between senior officers and shareholders is believed to be a better mechanism for driving the growth of corporate market value than conventional compensation packages. Moreover, it is widely believed that bonuses and stock options encourage risk taking among senior management otherwise cautious about the consequences of corporate restructuring for their own careers and income. In effect, bonuses and stock options are designed to redefine the natural partners in any corporate enterprise—from management *and* labour to management *and* shareholders. Even if corporate management may not have an interest in the welfare of stockholders, they are assumed to have a strong interest in the 'cash-out' value of their claim on the value of the firm.

A variety of reasons can be invoked to explain the diffusion of this compensation device down through the corporate hierarchy. Through the 1990s, it became apparent that if corporate management were to remake the US corporations through mergers and acquisitions they would have to buy the loyalty of their immediate functionaries. For a variety of reasons, and the reasons are many and complex, as dividend yields declined in importance relative to stock market capital appreciation it became vital for managers to 'manage' corporate market value through quarterly reported income flows than traditional profit and loss accounts. Furthermore, it is apparent that the cost accounting of stock options was less than ideal. The FASB was not able to introduce reporting rules entirely consistent with the interests of financial markets in properly pricing the true cost of such options. The debate over initial proposals spilled over into Congress, and through a coalition of the 'new technology' and 'old economy' firms a compromise agreement was forced through on reporting the current value of stock options.[10] Consequently, bonuses and stock options may be thought to be a *partially* accounted transfer of wealth to participating employees as it is a benefit to shareholders concerned with the future market value of traded firms (Aggarwal and Samwick 1999).

For German firms, operating in the United States of America and/or global markets with Anglo-American competitors, bonuses and stock options have been identified as essential for overcoming the inertia of the social market. Such compensation strategies are believed to enhance the power of corporate bureaucrats by shifting their reference standards. As in the Anglo-American world, these devices are thought to reward risk-taking notwithstanding the widespread social apprehension about the possible costs of risk-taking. But, of course, encouraging risk-taking via bonuses and stock options is only plausible if there is a market for German corporate control. And a market for corporate control is only possible if institutional investors are confident in the value of their investments relative to the traditional claims for privilege made by internal stakeholders (management, labour, and banks). Inevitably, the development of a vibrant German market for corporate control has required the adoption of reporting systems recognized by international investors (hence the importance of the US GAAP and International Accounting Standards). Furthermore, the prospects for a market for corporate control have been encouraged by legislation enabling current domestic investors to reduce their cross-holdings without incurring significant tax penalties. Even bankruptcy law has been reformed in the interests of encouraging corporate restructuring, deliberately implementing (in 1999) a model based upon the US Chapter 11 code (Kamlah 1996).

It can be argued that the large German firms (their management and principal shareholders) and the federal government have put in place institutions and policies consistent with the imperatives of global finance. In part, these reforms may enable corporate managers to take advantage of an emerging national and European market for corporate control (recognizing the highly differentiated and slow nature of this political and economic process; see Wójcik 2001a, b). They have done so in order to remake the distribution of power within large firms, and to enhance managers' shares of market-defined corporate value. As a result of greater financial transparency and accountability, inherited systems of employer-sponsored pensions and retirement income are now part of the process in managing corporate market value. Whereas these institutions may have been thought to properly belong in the sphere of co-determination and the social market, the embedded commitments are being revalued in terms of global finance. Inevitably, the costs of funding existing pension liabilities will have to be accounted for and shared between various stakeholders: by the workers (in the form of lower relative wages), the shareholders (in the form of lower dividends), and perhaps the management (in the form of lower shared income).

In this respect, a number of the largest German firms (including DaimlerChrysler and Siemens) have restructured their pension systems into the so-called contractual trust arrangements (CTAs). These special purpose institutions are separate legal entities, isolating pension assets (but not liabilities) from the immediate financial commitments of the sponsoring firms. Having segregated the pension assets from the corporate assets, and being managed by a nominated trustee or board of trustees, the CTAs are deemed to operate outside of the immediate corporate context and the norms and conventions of the social market (Koenig and Mahnert 2001). Quite deliberately, these institutional innovations are designed to satisfy the international accounting standards. By doing so, these institutions are required to operate beyond the immediate influence of the traditional practice of using pension assets as inexpensive sources of internal capital investment. These institutions are believed to be a means of introducing advanced financial instruments away from the scrutiny of German insurance regulators. In these ways, the German corporations have sought to match and mimic the UK and US employer-sponsored pension funds in the hope of repeating their remarkable growth in assets over the 1990s (thereby discounting massive inherited corporate pension liabilities). The passage of the much debated, revised, and delayed pension reforms will also provide these institutions with a preferred tax status.

THE GERMAN CORPORATE STRUCTURE AND GOVERNANCE

To comprehend the significance of global finance and learning for the social market, requires a series of analytical moves designed to elucidate the structure and logic of decision-making. In this section, we set out an idealized model of German corporate structure relevant to the inherited systems of decision-making. In the subsequent section, we return to global finance and learning in order to show the interaction between spatial rescaling and corporate pension management and investment decision-making. In order to develop this argument, however, we need to link basic assumptions about the nature of German institutions with changing circumstances. It should be apparent that we do not accept the assumption made in much of the social science literature that social agents are so profoundly rational that the existence of rational expectations obviates the need for an analysis of institutional processes. On the other hand, we would also assert that decision-making is an ordered process affected by context and events.

Behavioural Assumptions

For many theorists, it is enough to assume that people are naturally utility maximizers. By this one assumption the complex matters of context, deliberation, and planning are resolved at a stroke of the pen (Gigerenzer and Todd 1999). It does not matter how and where people assess their options and it does not matter what their plans are in relation to their options. What matters is the application of the golden rule to different circumstances. If some people were to deviate from the best path of action, it is assumed that the market imperatives provide sufficient discipline to limit systematic departures from this logic. Those who systematically depart from the best practice could not and would not survive (economically speaking). Amendments can be made to this logic that recognize the world as we know it even if nothing really changes in the underlying theoretical edifice. For example, it could be noted that people rarely have sufficient information to act in an entirely error-free manner, and it could be noted that there are limits to the value of processing information.

This characterization is, admittedly, crude. It focuses upon conventional theorizing at the expense of attempts to remake economic decision-making with a psychological core (Camerer and Weber 1992). Even so, a binary distinction is made in much of the literature between rational (good) behaviour and non-rational or irrational (bad) behaviour. For those with a clear, uncluttered conception of rationality the concept is thought to refer to action that has an unequivocal connection between the means and the ends. By definition, to be rational means choosing the best means to achieve the most desired end. On the face of it, the value of this kind of proposition may be judged empirically: we could set a test of the veracity of the proposition. But this is less important than the fact that binary models of rationality are presumed to be universal in their application; it should not matter if the economic agents are American, British, or German—the logic applies or should apply if the institutions are sufficiently benign (as they should be).

In this chapter we take four steps away from this conventional logic. In terms relevant to the German context we assume the following conditions.

(1) Desired goals often depend upon the context in which actions are contemplated;

(2) available means to ends are, more often than not, also affected by the context, and;

(3) there may be good reasons for acting consistently within a given context just as there may be reasons for defecting from the norms that define that context. Of course, we also assume

(4) that context is not a prison (profoundly limiting the scope of action and knowledge). Agents may use geography purposively and strategically.

Economic Agents as Stakeholders

Much of economic theory is focused upon economic agents with thin social roles. That is, economic agents are individuals with utility functions that happen to occupy certain positions and spaces in institutions and society. So, for example, individuals may be workers, or managers, creditors or shareholders each with their own goals and objectives. It is also tempting to suppose that each *type* of economic agent has a set of common goals and objectives being, in effect, more similar within the type than between types once we suppress the details of individual interests. While we can begin with individuals in their own right, the next move would be to show how and why they may be summed together under distinct headings (like worker etc.). Of course, the process of summing-up to a 'representative' agent involves arguments about the nature and scope of cooperation and collective action, topics that dominate the literature on bargaining and negotiation.

We also use the analytical device of the representative agent: introducing workers, managers, and shareholders. And we could also introduce a related agent called the banker to help the analysis along. But we do so recognizing that these categories have a particular

German significance, the product of deliberate attempts to regulate firms' labour-management relations. To explain, recall that the standard theoretical move is to sum up individuals into categories and attribute to that category actions and interests that represent their type of person. In our case, however, we should recognize that a worker is a person with social roles nested in a hierarchy of interrelated social institutions. Each worker (for example) is an employee of a firm, and is represented by his/her union on the firm's Works Council. Each worker is a member of a union, itself affiliated with its parent industry union and the national union organization, and; each firm and its local union are represented on the regional industry council where much of the bargaining over wages and benefits takes place. From the firm through to industry associations, workers and managers sit side-by-side in elected or nominated roles as representatives of their respective constituencies.

Joint representation is a common feature of German industrial life though often dependent upon the firm size, its industry affiliation, and co-determination status. Joint representation does not necessarily translate into common interests or ready agreement over corporate strategy. Nevertheless, we do assume that managers and workers share one basic goal: an overriding interest in the anticipated growth in the real value of their lifetime earnings. This may be portrayed as a zero-sum game, where the workers' share of corporate income is equal to 1-managers' share. More likely, however, the workers and managers collude to minimize the shareholders' share of income (dividends). Our opinion on this matter is developed in more detail below. We should also note, of course, that the expected growth of lifetime earnings is the product of at least the following: continuity of employment, growth in corporate market share, and higher rates of productivity. Sustaining these conditions requires the cooperation of workers and managers. But this does not mean that workers and managers need agree on the strategies for attaining these conditions.

Corporate Governance and Control

We must also consider the relationship between the shareholders and managers, the classic principal–agent problem that figures so importantly in the Anglo-American literature. We assume, as most theorists of the modern corporation assume, that managers have considerable

discretion—the power to initiate corporate strategy including investment in plant and equipment subject to periodic review by the
shareholders. In the Anglo-American world, corporate management
has considerable room to manoeuvre because of the dispersed nature
of share ownership. Not only is it difficult to monitor manager actions,
imposing discipline is quite problematic. While it can be contended
that the Anglo-American managers are vulnerable to their firm's
share price volatility, few managers are ever actually held accountable
except in the most extreme circumstances (Bliss and Flannery 2000).
Amongst the large German firms, of course, share ownership is often
quite concentrated and dominated by firms and financial institutions
that hold each other's stock. This has been widely documented, and
is an aspect of German corporate structure that draws the bulk of
commentary from inside and outside of Germany (Edwards and
Mayer 1998).

Considerable academic attention has focused upon the supervisory
boards of large German firms, where the representatives of institutional
cross-holdings are located. However, the firms' management boards
are often closer to corporate decision-making, the control of resources,
and the distribution of income between various internal stakeholders.
In fact, in many cases there is a presumption in favour of the management board as the operating core of firms. By contrast, the supervisory boards should be thought (for the moment, at least) of as
institutions of appointment and review rather than of policy initiation.
Just as management boards tend to represent internal stakeholders
so too do the management boards of corporate-sponsored and
jointly-managed *pensionskassen*. The structure of governance of these
institutions is much like the Dutch industry pension funds and many
continental corporate pension funds (Chapter 6). The boards of
management overlap with each other relying upon agreement at one
site (the firm's management board) to manage pension benefits at
other sites (including the corporate pension fund board of management). By contrast, the *direktzusagen* pension arrangements are firmly
ensconced within corporate treasuries that are closely controlled by
the management.

It is widely believed that insider knowledge is a by-product of
shareholder dominance, and that it provides participating institutions
an advantage over market agents located in the global financial markets. We do not dispute this argument directly. But we do want to
suggest that dominance without an exit option is less valuable than
assumed. For a number of our industry respondents, the cross-holdings

of stocks between related firms and institutions actually limits the power of supervisory boards. There is a strong albeit implicit culture of mutual respect but mutual disengagement with respect to each other's interests. As a consequence, and notwithstanding the potential power of such boards, supervisory boards are often of secondary functional importance to management boards. Even setting shareholder dividends is highly constrained (see Andre 1998; Roe 1998a). Here our assumption is that large firms' management boards, being the representatives of the interests of internal stakeholders, tend to dominate their supervisory boards, the representatives of external shareholders. Management power is firmly entrenched and is rarely directly challenged by the supervisory boards.

MODELS OF INVESTMENT MANAGEMENT

Relying upon the basic principles underpinning the German model sketched above (along the lines suggested by Streeck 1997 amongst others), the issue here is whether the CTA-like private pension institutions may be consistent with the social market. To do so, we compare and contrast the current German corporate pension institutions and practices with the CTA institutions. Necessarily, our discussion is brief and argumentative being based upon three idealized models of management.

Model A: Consensus Seeking (Satisfying)

In the basic model of the German firm, assumptions were made about the behaviour, motivation, and relationships between management and labour, and management and shareholders. Let us assume a world so described. We assume that management and labour are joined together in systems of governance, and have as their common goals the maintenance of their expected long-run income. We also assume, like many other writers on the German model, that any costs of collaboration are borne by the shareholders in the form of lower dividends. Of course, there are probably two types of shareholders. One type may have preferential status (being an internal principal) while the other type has less status (being denied the benefits of internal knowledge).

Consequently, the costs of such an income distribution policy may weigh more heavily on one type (the latter) than the other (the former).

To understand the implications of this logic, consider investment management in relation to *pensionskassen* assets and liabilities. In Model A, the investment management process is characterized as one of consensus seeking (satisfying) rather than optimizing or maximizing. Why? For a variety of reasons. It should be readily appreciated that the co-determination process dominates the management board appointment process, the decision-making process, and the allocation of risk and uncertainty between those represented on the board of management. Representation on such boards is more often than not a function of institutional career than it is a function of expertise and/or knowledge. Being concerned to maintain expected long-term income, management and labour representatives are highly risk adverse in circumstances where their decisions may affect the constituents' share of current and expected corporate income. In particular, worker representatives are assumed very resistant to any changes in their members' contributions (if any) to occupational pensions. In these circumstances, it is widely believed that consensus seeking results in decisions that complement board members' relationships in related organizations (the firm, the union, the region, the industry, etc).

In effect, the board members are focused upon a negative (minimizing risk) rather than a positive goal. Having protected against any downside risk, the various interests and relationships present on the *pensionskassen* drive decision-making recognizing that the costs of poor decisions are more likely than not to be borne by shareholders. There are significant moral hazard problems in such systems of decision-making, being even more significant in multi-employer industry *pensionskassen*. March (1994) suggested that in these types of circumstances there are many possible outcomes because there are so many different interests competing for attention. Consensus seeking results in satisfying; it is a means of balancing the heterogeneous interests and relationships.

Model B: Optimizing (Within Constraints)

Notice that consensus-seeking is, in effect, the default model of decision-making. All we need assume are competing interests organized by virtue of the background pattern of relationships. There are no doubt German firms and industries so easily characterized (Gorton and Schmid 2000). In many respects, these are expensive institutions in terms of the costs of decision-making, often poorly managed and poorly focused upon the management of pension assets and liabilities. Whereas some would argue that consensus seeking results in common commitment, there does not seem to be any clear reason why this should necessarily be the case. Here, however, we wish to emphasize that optimizing (within constraints) is a likely model of decision-making because government regulations concerning private insurance arrangements, loom large in management practice. In fact, it is probably easier to understand decision-making in large German firms and their pension institutions as a problem of decision-making by rules, rather than imagining that decision-making is as unstructured as implied by the satisfying model.

As *pensionskassen* are governed and monitored by the insurance regulator, these institutions operate within well-defined boundaries. Not only are there regulations concerning liabilities, for many years limits have been imposed on the allocation of assets to traded equities, government bonds, and the like. These quantitative limits on asset allocation effectively narrowed the scope of investment strategy.[11] Also, given the importance of actuarial expertise in the decision-making process, professional standards are deemed by many to be as important as official regulations. In this context, pension board members can be thought to act so as to optimize a complex objective function made up of separate goals and objectives related to matching year-to-year assets and liabilities. By contrast, unfunded *direktzusagen* plans are not so burdened by regulations nor are they so exposed to the close scrutiny of external professionals. Indeed, there appear to be few limits on the allocation of *direktzusagen* assets. Rather, there is considerable discretion available to firms' treasurers in driving the rate of return on self-invested assets. Of course, for the global finance industry the problem is that most firms' *direktzusagen* pension assets are co-mingled with corporate assets.

Interestingly, most writers on the theory of decision-making distinguish only between consensus-seeking and maximizing behaviour. If optimization is addressed it is seen as a mode of maximizing behaviour. In the German case at least, optimization is a mode of decision-making that fits between these two options; it is a form of decision-making that is based upon the observance of external rules and articulated limits. Can management boards maximize within constraints? Would they want to do so given the immediate set of relationships that overlap with and affect board decision-making? It is difficult to answer these two questions in any conclusive manner. Answers to these questions depend upon the circumstances of individual firms and industries. For some firms that have cultivated close relationships with their workers and union representatives, maximizing within constraints may be possible. In play may be the joint commitment of management and workers to the financial integrity of the firm rather than their fealty to the so-called external relationships.

In this situation, it is important to have advice and experience from outside the immediate environment. Hence, the experience of German firms in the Anglo-American world returns as important reference points in setting guidelines for decision-making. Likewise, the advice of investment consultants separate from the close-knit community of German banking and actuarial consultants may help establish new options and possible relationships.

Model C: Maximizing (as if the Firm is a Global Corporation)

For many German firms, caught within the web of regulations and professional practice, optimizing (within constraints) best describes the leading edge of German investment management. By contrast, the maximizing model assumes an unfettered decision-making process, and presumes the existence of a clear, unambiguous objective: the highest rate of return on invested assets. Here, the reference point is the Anglo-American practice, recognizing that over the past decade this model has provided the UK and US plan sponsors many benefits including contribution holidays, supplements to corporate income, and (presumably) dampened market price volatility. Even so, we should not exaggerate the scope of such a model; there remain important constraints in any such management regime. The relative maturity of the DB plans can have significant consequences for the allocation of assets between asset classes. Likewise, government regulations relating to minimum funding requirements can affect investment decision-making. Nevertheless, over the 1990s it is apparent that those Anglo-American firms that based their investment regime on Model C benefited enormously from the explosive growth of the global equity markets.

It is arguable that even if *pensionskassen* plans have been restricted to optimizing or consensus-seeking, *direktzusagen* plans have had the opportunity to match and mimic the Anglo-American maximization strategies. Yet it appears that this option has been rarely taken. Until recently, it would seem that the *direktzusagen* assets have been deployed to promote the growth of the firm in ways consistent with the long-term income objectives (growth and stability) of managers and workers. Also, it seems that fixed capital (new plant, technology, and infrastructure) has been the ultimate destination for *direktzusagen* assets. Advanced financial products found in global capital markets have not been favoured investments. Only recently, many German firms have come to realize that higher rates of return may be found outside the firm and outside of Germany, or in human capital as opposed to physical capital stock; senior corporate managers have come to appreciate the value of alternative options. Indeed, it could be observed that as corporate management have shifted their focus towards the market value of the firm rather than the flow of income, the *direktzusagen* assets have become more valuable just at a time when the global financial markets are increasingly aware of the unfunded nature of *direktzusagen* obligations.

Faced with the heterogeneous interests represented on *pensions-kassen* boards, it would seem that *direktzusagen* plans have greater potential value than *pensionskassen* plans *if* funding could be resolved in accordance with the expectations of the global financial markets. In effect, this would mean segregating *direktzusagen* assets and liabilities from corporate assets and liabilities to become an identifiable internal investment organization. As some larger German firms have established CTAs, they have done so in order to protect the financial interests of managers and shareholders. Inevitably, to join together these interests with those of the workers into dedicated investment institutions involves considerable political tact; implicitly, workers' representatives are required to support the interests of the firm as it reaches out to the global economy. A subtle shift in loyalty is required, moving from the system of collective bargaining and industrial co-determination and the related systems of social insurance and welfare, to the core objectives of the firm (its managers and shareholders). One possible reward for such a shift in loyalty are enhanced pension and retirement benefits.

This strategy may redefine the constituency of workers' representatives. At the same time, as the EC moves towards an accounting standards regime modelled on international accounting standards, and as it moves towards European capital market integration by dismantling country-specific quantitative limits on assets classes and cross-border investments, the conditions for a maximization model are being put in place. Indeed, notwithstanding the debate over various EC proposals to implement a common set of prudential standards and investment guidelines (as developed in De Ryck 1999), it is apparent that Model C has strong advocates amongst the larger German firms. The introduction of the Euro has made these types of pan-European regulations more important than ever before. If the market value of the firm is to be the most important management target, Model C is a necessary institutional reform: the market value of the firm can only be maximized if the value of the pension assets in relation to liabilities is also maximized. In these ways, the 'up-scaling' of the German economic environment has begun to undercut the common interests of large German firms' management *and* workers in domestic industrial relations systems.

CONCLUSIONS

In this chapter, we have focused upon the imperatives driving changes in the German corporate pension management policies. This is an important issue in its own right, and an opportunity to contribute to the debate about continuity and convergence. It is widely assumed that the nation-state institutions and traditions tend to persist in the face of competing institutions located in other jurisdictions. This is not necessarily an absolute argument; some analysts would suggest that any tendency of persistence must be balanced against the forces of competition (see, e.g., Bebchuk and Roe 1999). Lock-in does not, and cannot, persist forever. Nevertheless, it is difficult to account for instances of German institutional change when so much of the literature and national political debate are set against the imperatives driving globalization. Given the current paralysis in German public policy concerning the underfunding of social insurance liabilities it may seem surprising that, in the corporate arena at least, there have been such changes in the management power and practice.

Our account of German corporate pension policy has focused upon the motives of corporate management in relation to workers and shareholders. We noted in Chapter 4 the competitive advantages of access to global financial markets. In this chapter, we considered the significance of management interests in remuneration policies that are increasingly focused upon the market value of the firm. It was suggested that large German firms operating in the Anglo-American world during the 1990s learnt a great deal about advanced financial management; specifically, they learnt the value of maximization strategies (for their own wealth). In order to make this point, three competing models of corporate and pension investment management practices were identified: maximization, optimization, and consensus-seeking. For German corporate management, knowledgeable about the costs and benefits of competing investment management practices, one lesson of the 1990s was that the consensus model is a most expensive option whether pension liabilities are funded, unfunded, or underfunded. In an integrated global financial market with common accounting rules, the implications of pension liabilities for corporate market value are all too clear.

To sustain the argument, I emphasized management motives. In particular, it was argued that the historical agreement between management and labour to share corporate revenue within and without the firm is slowly breaking down. Corporate management has less of an interest in sharing the current and expected income with labour than it has in generating their own wealth in the form of bonuses and stock options linked to the market value of the firm as determined in global financial markets. This is a very different model of corporate governance than that which dominated, and still dominates in many sectors and small and medium firms, the German political economy for more than fifty years (Pistor 1999).

We must be careful, however, not to exaggerate the argument. Bonuses and stock options are not the most important issues in German corporate governance. There remain important political barriers to the full implementation of such systems of executive compensation even with the recent introduction of a tax regime designed to promote private employer-sponsored pensions and the break-down of cross-holding of shares. In any event, any widespread introduction of bonuses and stock options would presuppose political agreement on many issues still outstanding in the public arena. On the other hand, it seems that the prospect of some form of executive compensation based on the market value of the firm now drives the management of large German firms. Inevitably, in this context, pension liabilities have become an important part of the management corporate strategy. Given the experience in the Anglo-American world, the funding and management of inherited pension obligations is an essential ingredient in any plans aimed at maximizing the market value of the firm.

There maybe, of course, other motives important in understanding the recent corporate pension initiatives. We have only touched the surface of a complex issue. Witness the recent studies on hostile take-overs in Germany (Jenkinson and Ljungqvist 1999) and the industrial and regional dissembling of the German model (Berndt 1998a). Even so, we have argued that the adoption of international accounting standards given significant corporate pension liabilities can be traced back to a basic issue deeply embedded in the German political economy: the changing relationship between the management, workers, and share-holders. We have suggested that this relationship is being rewritten within large firms, even if debate over the proper form of this rela-tionship has been stymied in the public arena. It is as if the German national interests in global economic champions has necessitated their leaving the complex array of interrelated national social systems (the social market) for the global market place. If large German firms are to be allowed to float free of the core systems underpinning German social structure, mimicking and matching their Anglo-American com-petitors, what is the long-term future of the social market? As they move into the world of financial accountability and transparency, the funding and management of inherited pension liabilities loom large as issues likely to distinguish the German firms from the Anglo-American firms.

NOTES

1. These two types of employer-sponsored pension institutions are emphasized because they are the most important private pension institutions, measured by accumulated assets and enrolled employees. In combination, they account for about 70 per cent of all pension assets (around DM 430 billion of a total DM 530 billion in 1998). Furthermore, these two types are most relevant to large firms as opposed to small firms. For further commentary on the other two types of pension institutions, their assets, coverage rates, and investment regimes see Koenig and van der Lende (1999) and Deutsche Bundesbank (2001).
2. Industry and academic commentaries have also focused upon the economic costs of social insurance for industrial competitiveness and the long-term unsustainable financial burdens of the current PAYG system. Some analysts have suggested the radical reform of social insurance, including the introduction of notional accounts, partial funding, and capped benefits (Börsch-Supan 2000a, b). There are also those that advocate the promotion of tax-preferred employer-sponsored occupational pensions, matching and mimicking the claimed desirable attributes of the Anglo-American DC pension plans (Deutsche Bank 1996).
3. Even so, in his recent book Hutton (2002) contends that Britain's 'natural' partners in the global economy are European rather than North American. In the main, his analysis of the performance and structural attributes of western European countries is far more optimistic than mine: whereas I suggest in earlier chapters of this book that the new economy has made a significant and long-term difference to Anglo-American real rates of economic growth, Hutton thinks that in the end the social contract underpinning western Europe will deliver sustained higher rates of economic growth

with social justice. No doubt turmoil in global stock markets provides evidence for his optimism.

4. This point is made by numerous authors. See, for example, Wolfgang Streeck (1997: 37) where he suggests that firms 'are social institutions, not just networks of private contracts or the property of the shareholders. Their internal order is a matter of public interest and are subject to extensive social regulation, by law and industrial agreement. Also, the managers of large German firms face capital and labour markets that are highly organized, enabling both capital and labour to participate directly in the everyday operation of the firm and requiring decisions to be continuously negotiated'.

5. The idea that such coverage rates are too low or too narrowly focused on particular segments of the German industry is surely a reflection of the more general claim on behalf of the comprehensive nature of social insurance. These coverage rates are not so unusual or limited if compared to the Anglo-American world. See Clark (2000) on the UK and US coverage rates, noting the bias towards large firms, unionized industry, and manufacturing.

6. In this vein, Reynaud (2000: 8) suggested that the value of international comparisons was 'not to import ready-made solutions from abroad to solve problems faced at (the) domestic level'. Going further, he said 'national pension systems are the product of the societies concerned and inevitably reflect the series of specific characteristics, especially concerning the relationship between the state and society, political traditions, industrial relations, structure of the economy, and perceptions of justice and equality'.

7. See also a report by the industry analysts Towers Perrin (2000). They show that in 1999 the reported earnings of 25 of the 30 firms included in the Dow Jones Industrial Index were positively affected by pension income (including reductions in pension contributions) derived from DB programmes. Also, reported pension liabilities were smaller because these same firms were able to increase their discount rates (used to determine the present value of obligations). The 1999 effect of the DB pension plans was stronger than even the 1998 effect on net corporate income.

8. German firms most affected by this issue have been those that have acquired or have established Anglo-American firms staffed by UK or US nationals. The problem for such firms has been to attract and retain the best staff where their compensation packages have been deemed 'uncompetitive' by virtue of their fealty to the ideals of the social market. Where German firms have introduced bonuses and stock-options for the UK or US nationals but have restricted access to such compensation to their German staff, the internal tensions occasioned by such inequities have made management across systems of corporate governance and financial markets more difficult than hitherto recognized in the literature.

9. It should be noted, however, that although managerial stock ownership has increased in recent years, it remains true that many other forms of executive compensation are used to regulate the principal–agent relationship. See the study by Holderness et al. (1999) on the trends in the managerial ownership of US corporations since the Great Depression of the twentieth-century.

10. For details of the FASB standard accounting for stock based compensation see their October 1995 (154-C) Statement of Financial Accounting Standards No. 123. The Board recommends rather than requires that firms report stock based employee compensation using a fair value method. The FASB also goes into some detail about the controversy surrounding their proposal and the compromise forced upon it by Congress. It remains a highly contentious issue, witness the controversy surrounding a very similar proposal by the UK Accounting Standards Board (July 2000).

11. Details on the nature and implications of these regulations for German investment policy are to be found in Heubeck and Baum (1998). Their article was also devoted to (then) recent proposals for a new 'concept for occupational pension financing', much like the CTAs, combining aspects of the Anglo-American world (including the UK and the US) with solvency protection and independence from plan sponsors.

6

Dutch Fund Governance and Financial Services

While it is commonplace to refer to the pending fiscal crisis attending the ageing of European countries' populations, it would be misleading to suppose that all continental European countries will be similarly affected. There are significant differences between countries in their reliance upon social security retirement income, just as there have been many country-specific initiatives designed to anticipate and ameliorate the possible effects of the 'demographic bomb'. The Netherlands, for example, would seem to be more like continental Europe with respect to the importance attributed to the institutions of social security than the Anglo-American economies. However, over the past decade or so the Dutch government has sought to shift an increasing proportion of individuals' projected retirement income costs to employer-sponsored funded pension plans. The Dutch retirement income system is a 'mixed' system of pension institutions with a volume of pension fund assets more akin to the Anglo-American world than continental Europe: the OECD (1999c: 13) estimated that the Dutch accumulated pension fund assets were 93 per cent of the GDP compared to the UK and US pension fund assets of, respectively, 77.5 and 64.4 per cent.

The Dutch retirement income system is perceived by policy makers to have a number of advantages over the Anglo-American model. It has been suggested by German commentators that the Dutch system preserves the elements of co-determination and collective bargaining so essential to post-war European political stability, while providing scope for financial growth and innovation so important in the Anglo-American securities' markets. Notwithstanding its modest economic size compared to France and Germany, the Dutch economy has been closely connected with the global economy for many years. As such it is widely perceived to have a (European) corporate governance structure and (an Anglo-American) financial system that usefully combines social solidarity with robust international competitiveness (Chirinko *et al.* 1999). If the Anglo-American pension system would be difficult for European countries to emulate, the Dutch system may be an effective compromise providing a beneficial mixture of pension institutions.[1] The chapter begins with a brief account of the relationship between the Dutch social security and pillar II pensions and moves on to the structure and governance of sector-wide pension plans.

Basically, three points are made in this chapter. First, the principles of Dutch social solidarity have been the basis of a two-tiered national pension system that has extensive coverage of eligible workers and equitable consequences in relation to the long-term distribution of retirement income. The European Court of Justice (1999) opinion in the *Maatschappij Drijvende Bokken* can be read as a defence of the integrity of such national solutions to the 'demographic bomb'.[2] This point is made through an analysis of the logic underpinning the court decision, set in the context of the structure and organization of sector-wide pension funds and their 'captive' financial service firms.[3] Second, the governance of sector pension funds combined with their intimate connection with collective bargaining raises important issues of selection bias and moral hazard. While many sector funds may be efficiently managed, the lack of an effective means of disciplining the entrenched board members and their managers may have discouraged a competitive cost-efficient market for financial services. Third, we dispute the idea that national pension systems and financial markets are properly or naturally off limits to geographical scope. Even so, we do not doubt the importance of sustaining progressive models of retirement income given the claims made by those who would discount national goals in favour of a standardized Anglo-American pension model.

It seems inevitable that Dutch citizens will rely more and more upon supplementary pensions for their retirement income. This also means that they will be more and more exposed to the global market for financial services and all that implies in terms of the governance of risk and return. Not only are the institutions of the Dutch economy and society increasingly sensitive to the imperatives of market competition, these same institutions are also implicated in the rapidly evolving

European financial services industry. Can co-determination survive in these circumstances? What are the roles and responsibilities of jointly-trusteed institutions as they come into the market for financial services? Recent initiatives by the Dutch government designed to make pension funds' performance accountable to the market for financial services carry with them a 'map' of the financial services industry that is pan-European and global in scope. Closely-held institutions, close personal and social relationships embedded in history and geography may be at odds with the imperatives of European integration and globalization. By this logic, the Dutch 'miracle' may be slowly restructured from the top-down according to the imperatives of market competition.

SOCIAL SECURITY AND SUPPLEMENTARY PENSIONS

The literature on comparative social welfare and public policy tends to associate the Netherlands with the institutions of Scandinavian social democracy. For example, in Esping-Andersen's (1990) three-way classification of welfare state regimes the Netherlands was grouped with countries like Denmark and Sweden. His quantitative scoring and qualitative assessment of welfare programmes and policy principles resulted in a three-by-three classification of advanced industrialized states, distinguishing three clusters of states according to three measures of strength (strong, medium, and low) (see Esping-Andersen 1990: table 3.3, 74). In Esping-Andersen's analysis the Netherlands was strongly associated with the 'socialist' regime in contrast to Austria and Germany (in the conservative cluster) and Australia, Switzerland, and the United States of America (in the liberal cluster). For the most part, the clusters were well-defined and exclusive. The only anomaly appeared to be the United Kingdom, scoring low on conservatism, medium on liberal-democratic, and medium on socialism.

Reinforcing this image Ploug and Kvist (1996: 84) suggested that the Dutch have 'one of the most comprehensive pension schemes in Europe'. Relying upon another comparative classification of pensions systems (Salminen 1993), they also associated the Netherlands with Sweden under the schematic model of 'citizenship'. In both cases, the old age public pension systems were designed for universal coverage and the entitlement to a retirement income according to citizenship (or legal residence) and prior earnings. A worker's *Algemeine Onderdoms-wet* (AOW) entitlement is based, in part, on compulsory contributions in relation to a minimum benefit biased upwards in favour of low-wage workers and against high-wage workers. In combination with private pension entitlements, the allowed maximum retirement income benefit is 70 per cent of the final wage. In this sense, the goal of social security is equitable income replacement not just 'welfare'. It was designed to be a form of redistribution applied to the entire population rather than a programme of basic income benefits (compare with the United Kingdom; see Budd and Campbell 1998).

Much more can be written about the subsidiary benefits and effects associated with the Dutch state and European welfare states. For instance, the Dutch social security system and in particular disability and unemployment benefits appear to encourage early retirement when compared to the Anglo-American countries like Canada and the United Kingdom (see Gruber and Wise 1999: table 1, 29). Here, however, we should recognize another important aspect of the Dutch retirement income policy: the extensive coverage of Dutch workers by employer-sponsored private pension plans. Indeed just as Ploug and Kvist (1996) observed that the European social security systems are, in general, in retreat in terms of benefit levels and coverage rates, Blomsma and Jansweijer (1997) noted that the Dutch private pension system is increasingly important as a supplement to the AOW benefits. Not only do private pensions often contain significant early-retirement options, as a matter of public policy supplementary pensions have been required to take up an increasing share of workers' retirement incomes. In effect, the state has sought to shift a portion of promised retirement income to the private sector thereby discounting its looming social security obligations.

Though not mandatory, the most recent data suggest that nearly 90 per cent of Dutch workers were covered by supplementary employer-sponsored pension schemes (Prins 1999). These schemes can be divided into four types; see the 1997 data published by the Dutch insurance and pension funds regulator (Verzekeringskamer 1999): the privatized public sector pension fund Algemeen Burgerlijk Pensioenfonds (ABP); nearly 850 corporate pension plans; about 82 sector (multi-employer) pension plans; and 11 professional association pension funds. There were also about another 40 000 insured pension schemes used by small enterprises. Much of the subsequent discussion is focused around the sector pension funds, in part because of their share of the total Dutch pension fund assets (approx. 66 per cent) and their share of covered workers (3.850 of 5 million total covered workers). Note that the privatized public sector plan remains the largest Dutch plan with about 900 000 participants and assets reputably worth nearly NLG300 billion (1999). While there are a handful of large sector plans accounting for the majority of all sector plan participants, most of the 82 sector plans are small in terms of participants and assets. Indeed, based on the available data (1994) 55 plans had fewer than 10 000 participants (Table 6.1).

Plan size is an important issue in pension fund management (Clark 2000). As we shall see in subsequent sections of this chapter, plan size also figures prominently in pension fund governance. In many respects, economies of scale determine the costs of service provision inside and outside of pension funds. Furthermore, the US evidence shows that the larger the fund or cooperating funds the more sophisticated are financial control systems, member services, and investment management products and services (Greenwich Associates 1999). Just as many sector funds have relatively few members, given the year-to-year full funding of expected liabilities the size of managed assets is also often small by international standards. In Table 6.2 we report the distribution of corporate and sector-wide pension funds by asset size (NLG 1998). This data was provided by the association of sector funds Vereniging van Bedrijfspensioensfondsen (VB) for their 50 participating funds and for the 56 participating funds in the corporate funds association. More than half of the sector funds had assets valued at less than NLG1 billion (about Euro 455 million) while about a third of corporate funds were so valued. A significant proportion of corporate funds were valued at

Table 6.1. The size distribution of Dutch sector plans, including the total number of participants by size class (000s), 1994

Size (000s)	Number in class	Total number of participants	Per cent share of all sectors' participants
< 1.0	12	6 769	0.2
1.0–4.9	27	69 693	2.2
5.0–9.9	16	118 761	3.7
10–49	12	215 141	6.7
50–99	3	223 438	8.0
100–499	8	1 013 817	33.0
> 500	2	1 465 918	46.0
Total	80	3 113 537	100.0

Source: Vereniging van Bedrijfspensioenfondesen, Rijswijk, the Netherlands.

Table 6.2. The size distribution of Dutch corporate
and sector pension funds by value of assets (DLG ml,
1998) and numbers in class, 1998

Value of assets	Corporate pension funds	Sector pension funds
< 100	2	2
100–499	11	17
500–999	6	10
1 000–4 999	21	12
5 000–9 999	10	5
10 000–19 000	—	2
20 000–49 000	5	1
50 000–99 999	—	1
> 100 000	1	—
Total	56	50

Source: Vereniging van Bedrijfspensioenfondesen, Rijswijk, the
Netherlands.

between NLG1 and NLG5 billion in size, and another twenty per cent
were even larger. Note that the ABP was included on the corporate side
of the ledger in Table 6.2. The largest Dutch sector funds are in the
metals industries, manufacturing, and banking and financial services.
The largest corporate pension plans include firms with a global reach
like Royal Dutch Shell, KLM, and Philips.

The Dutch pension funds are fully-funded DB plans. There are
exceptions especially the ABP which, prior to privatization in 1996, was
significantly under-funded. Unlike the Anglo-American world, Dutch
pension funds are directly monitored year-to-year by the insurance
regulator. As is customary in DB plans, the benefits are determined by
the age, years of service, and final salary. These plans provide a variety
of benefits including disability, death, and surviving spouse benefits.
While many sector funds cap benefit levels, in effect applying a policy
of redistribution based upon sector-wide salary levels, corporate pension funds tend not to cap benefits to the same extent. The value of
offered benefits varies between plans, depending upon the corporate
and sector wage levels. Similarly, there are significant variations in
the employer and employee contribution rates, more often than not
depending upon the relevant collective bargaining agreements. Furthermore, the government provides tax relief on pension contributions
and investment returns, taxing pension benefits as income during
retirement.

The Netherlands is a small country of less than 16 million people and a workforce of about 7.5 million (see Chapter 1, Table 1.1). And yet, in terms of total pension fund assets, by European standards it is one of the largest economies. By virtue of funding regulations, the insurance regulator Verzekeringskamer (1999) estimated total pension fund assets to be worth about NLG700 billion of which NLG480 billion were managed by sector funds and NLG210 billion by corporate pension plans. In terms of asset allocation, however, there were some significant differences between the sector and corporate plans, and between the Dutch and UK plans. While both types of plans tend to split assets equally between stocks and bonds, on an average the corporate plans have had about 10 per cent more assets allocated to these two categories (approx. 35 per cent). Both types of funds have had significant real estate and mortgage holdings as well as private placements. In should be recalled that the UK funds tend to split their assets between stocks (on an average about 80 per cent), bonds (13 per cent), real estate (2 per cent), and cash (5 per cent). Davis (1995) and Davis and Steil (2001) provide greater information and a comparative international analysis of these patterns.

THE INSTITUTIONAL STRUCTURE OF SOCIAL SOLIDARITY

Like the UK and Germany, there have been Dutch employer-sponsored pension plans since the middle years of the nineteenth century. But unlike Germany, the Dutch pension plans have developed and grown significantly in relation to social security (compare with Börsch-Supan 2000a). Therefore, it is tempting to suppose that the Dutch plans are, in fact, just like the Anglo-American pension plans. We might imagine that any apparent differences are a product of continental European history and geography, being slowly erased by time as recent trends in the Anglo-American world come to dominate policy and practice. So, for example, we might anticipate a slow but inevitable transition from the DB to the DC plans, especially in the corporate sector, and greater interest amongst plan participants in individual savings plans, and the international diversification of market-traded securities. There can be little doubt that the Dutch pension industry is far more knowledgeable about the Anglo-American developments and expertise than many of their German colleagues.

Despite the obvious similarities, Dutch pension institutions can be described in very different terms from those that would describe the Anglo-American industry. With specific reference to sector pension funds, the Dutch government and defendants in the *Maatschappij Drijvende Bokken BV* characterized supplementary pensions using the concept of social solidarity. While perhaps an elusive concept for an Anglo-American audience, it could be thought to combine the principles of equality and fraternity with mutual protection and insurance (see Chapter 3 on France). Equality can be thought to refer to the value of benefits due to plan participants and their equitable treatment with respect to other plan participants. Fraternity can be thought to refer to the governance of pension funds, linking collective interests with collective decision-making and accountability. Mutual protection and insurance can be thought to refer to risk sharing and risk pooling, preferring the mutual indemnity of risk to the individual purchase of risk-adjusted insurance policies. Using this notion, the Dutch government and defendants sought to distance the Dutch sector pension funds from market principles, and the application of European competition policy.

This definition of social solidarity, relying as it does on secondary concepts related to the history of social democracy, mirrors government policy and is sustained by deep connections to the roots of contemporary Dutch politics (see Goodin *et al.* 1999 on the political foundations of the Dutch social democracy). It also resonates with German notions of the 'social market' and can be linked to the French concept of the social contract. More generally, it also has parallels with the mandate of the DG Employment of the European Commission in that it refers to the relationship between 'social partners' (unions and employer organizations) in markets and society. This last connection will be developed in more detail below, noting the importance of related clauses to be found in the Treaty of Rome. In suggesting these connections, we do not mean to defend an argument in favour of a pan-European social philosophy. But there is a considerable difference between the Dutch social solidarity and Anglo-American social theory. For instance, Coleman's (1990) treatise on social theory is practically silent about social solidarity, assuming individual interests are the primary building blocks behind collective action and institutional organization.[4]

To illustrate, consider the four building blocks of social solidarity relevant to Dutch pensions policy. A remarkable aspect of the Dutch system is the near-universal coverage rates *within* sectors offering supplementary pension benefits. Not only are employees required to participate in employer-sponsored pension plans, employers are required to participate in multi-employer sector plans unless they offer their own plans paying benefits at least equal to, and preferably superior to, the relevant sector plan. In *Maatschappij Drijvende Bokken BV* a firm objected to being required to participate in the sector-wide pension plan. Like a number of other companies in other sectors, it argued that it had a right to make alternative arrangements (in this instance, with an insurance company). When challenged, the sector plan was able to invoke a government mandate to sustain its claim for compulsory membership, drawing upon a state-protected agreement made by employer and employee sector representatives in the early 1950s. Furthermore, the sector plan's decision was deemed final and binding. There were no immediate avenues for an independent review of the sector plan's decision on this matter.

Even so, and not withstanding the judicial argument, we should not over-emphasize the market–nonmarket contrast implied herein. The Dutch government has sought to increase the market accountability of the sector-wide pension funds. Through legislation adopted in late 1997, the government introduced the prospect of a common standard for measuring pension fund investment performance. In essence, after a prolonged implementation stage (through to the end of 2001), the performance of individual pension funds are to be assessed against the industry average and deviations measured according to standardized Z-scores. Systematic deviations (presumably on the down side) over time may be then used by participating employers to petition for permission to leave the consortium. While clearly a significant step towards market competition, Z-scores need not concern most funds. One obvious response is to converge on common standards of investment and administration. An individual fund may take into account other funds' actions and strategies. At the same time, these competitive pressures may encourage shared administrative and management services, internalizing rather than externalizing competitive pressures. See below for more details.

If compulsory membership is one building block of social solidarity, the second is the equal representation of employers and employees on the boards of Dutch sector and corporate pension plans. These boards and their constituent members act on behalf of plan participants and beneficiaries, being legally responsible for their decisions regarding the administration and management of the plan and the prudent investment of pension plan assets. For readers familiar with the powers of

Anglo-American pension plan trustees, this arrangement is consistent with the evolution of the Anglo-American trust law and statute (Langbein 1997). Though not as common in the Anglo-American world, in the United States of America there are many small- and medium-sized jointly-trusteed multi-employer pension plans in industrial crafts such as plumbing, electrical work, and the construction trades. Dutch pension boards have wide powers consistent with their responsibility for the integrity of sector plans. Furthermore, the board membership is often congruent with the board membership of 'captive' financial services organizations, and may also overlap with the membership of the boards responsible for sector-based collective bargaining. The institutions and practices of collective bargaining permeate the structure and management of Dutch sector and corporate pension funds.

A third element underpinning social solidarity has to do with the determination of benefit levels. As noted above, sector plan benefits are set in accordance with sectoral compensation standards; there are significant differences between sector plans in terms of the value of their benefits, reflecting the relative place of sectors in the national, EU, and global economies. Sectors dominated by industries characterized by high value-added per unit produced have higher benefit levels and a wider range of benefits than those industries operating at the low-wage margins of the global economy. Within sectors, however, the benefit levels are standardized between firms and between workers. Firms within the sector indemnify each other with respect to the risk of default on their pension obligations, just as individual participants indemnify each other with respect to the risks of death and disability (for instance). Neither the firms nor individuals pay risk-adjusted premiums. Pension benefits are, in effect, averaged across age groups and across firms for the benefit of all even if, in some situations, specific firms and workers may have a claim for special treatment.

With respect to the offered pension and insurance benefits, there is little scope for competition between firms within sectors. Furthermore, in accordance with the year-to-year and long-term financial integrity of their plans, pension boards set standard contribution rates. But notice that the determination of wage and pension benefits are the responsibility of the sector-wide collective bargaining processes. Likewise, allocation of the relative shares of pension plan contribution rates between the employers and employees is also left to collective bargaining. Three factors impinge upon the determination of benefit levels and the allocation of contribution burdens. As noted above, compensation is closely related to the value of output which, in turn, is related to labour productivity and the accumulated capital stock. In many industries there are incentives to set benefits and allocate contribution rates in ways that would sustain long-term competitiveness. Second, in industries dominated by a few large firms and linked networks of smaller firms, economic interests may be thought more homogeneous than sectors not so organized. Third, by implication, there are mechanisms that protect participating firms and workers from exploitation by those that dominate the collective bargaining process.

To summarize, firms and individuals face significant barriers to defection. Joint representation in the collective bargaining process and on sector-wide pension boards is thought to dampen interfirm rivalry, and may sustain the long-term value of pension and insurance benefits. Mutual indemnification of risk encourages collective responsibility and solidarity, limiting the possibility of exploitative standard setting by those who control the institutions of social solidarity. Ideally, the legal independence of pension boards insures the financial integrity of sector pension funds while their close relationship to the collective bargaining process ensures benefit standards and contribution rates consistent with economic circumstances. In these ways, the advocates of the Dutch model argue that the national institutions of social solidarity properly regulate the risks of selection bias and moral hazard.

PENSION FUND GOVERNANCE AND PERFORMANCE

Dutch pension plan participants and beneficiaries are the 'principals' of their plans. Their agents are board members who are appointed by their employee representatives (unions) and plan sponsor employers. In turn, board members monitor and control the managers of plans. As board members, they have a legal duty to ensure that all current and expected obligations are met in full. Notwithstanding this principle, the board members also represent the considerable economic interests of unions and plan sponsors in the costs and performance of their pension funds. Nominally, Dutch pension plans are non-profit mutual insurance institutions. Any accumulated net returns over and above the current and expected liabilities are identified as a 'surplus' rather than a 'profit', the distinction being driven by deeply held beliefs in the difference between firms based upon private property rights and collective associations based upon mutual agreement. Nonetheless, there is considerable debate in the Netherlands and elsewhere over the proper disbursement of surplus returns. While plan sponsors and current employees have an unmistakable interest in using any surplus to reduce contribution rates, retiree groups have a vocal interest in added benefits and the prompt adjustment of benefits to increases in real wages.

In theory, it can be argued that the (non-profit) sector pension plans are more cost-efficient than competing (for profit) insurance companies. Because of the compulsory nature of firm and worker participation in sector plans, there is little need for advertising and marketing. Plan participants are enrolled at the participating firm, obviating the need for a large sales force or telemarketing site. The costs of administering deductions are not trivial. But in the first instance these costs are borne by the firms rather than sector funds. Since it is very unusual for a firm and its workers to leave a sector plan, there are practically no switching costs on either side (plan sponsor or sector plan). Perhaps as important, the use of standardized as opposed to individualized risk-adjusted benefit and premium schedules imply a low average per-unit processing cost. At the same time, this may also mean limited services for participants and little in the way of a service culture in the plan. Finally, the over-arching non-profit mandate may mean lower compensation rates for the board members compared to their colleagues in insurance companies as well as compressed internal salary structures referencing sector salary norms rather than the salaries accorded similar functions in the financial services industry.[5]

While the reality of these cost advantages has been disputed by the insurance industry, it appears that confidential government inquiries confirmed their existence. For the Dutch government, concerned to shift the burden of retirement financing to pension plans in a socially equitable manner, the preferential status of sector plans has the twin virtues of cost efficiency and social inclusion.[6] Even so, there remain two substantial objections to the putative monopoly status of these institutions. The first has to do with the robustness of the claimed distinction between collective associations and firms. Does the non-profit mandate make such a difference that competition issues can be put aside in favour of social solidarity? The second issue bears upon the economic performance of sector plans. If their costs per unit are less than competing insurance companies, it does not follow that their investment performance is similarly superior. In fact, the net performance of a sector fund could be less than a competing insurance company. If so then the monopoly status of sector funds would amount to a subsidy to those participating firms and their workers who would otherwise pay higher premiums for coverage from the insurance industry. These two issues can be combined into a common question: how significant is pension fund governance with respect to their functional performance?

It is difficult to answer this question with precision. Though many funds use cost and performance benchmarks for internal management purposes, the costs of Dutch funds with respect to each other and with respect to the insurance industry are difficult to obtain. As for invest-ment performance, the introduction of legislation requiring the pub-lication of the so-called Z-scores has introduced the possibility of switching between funds. Even so, Z-scores have drawbacks. As is well-known, a major component of investment performance is the initial allocation of assets between asset classes. Over the 1990s, investment strategies driven by equities would have *ceteris paribus* delivered higher returns than strategies driven by bonds. Asset allocation, however, is determined by a variety of factors including the underlying profile of expected liabilities. Therefore, we must be cautious in drawing con-clusions from the available data.[7] In Figure 6.1 we report Dutch pension fund investment performance by type (corporate and sector) for 1998 (provided by VB). On an average, sector plans outperformed corporate plans (13.3 against 12.8 per cent). But the difference was slight given the higher dispersion of returns amongst corporate funds. It was difficult to draw distinctions in terms of the distribution of returns according to the fund type, fund size, or the pattern of asset allocation—a conclu-sion repeated for the following year (to the end of 1999).

Ownership and Governance

As is well appreciated, the Anglo-American corporation is characterized by the 'separation of ownership and managerial control' (Viscusi *et al.* 1995: 456). Ownership is diffuse with many shareholders holding 'a small or negligible percentage of shares'. Managers control the firm, relying upon implied and delegated powers over a wide number of topics (Roe 1994). Discipline is based upon the market for corporate control. Boards of management can be deposed, managers penalized by the sale of the firm, and bankruptcy declared by disenchanted creditors. Theoretically, the overarching behavioural imperative is profit maximization and, in turn, shareholder value. Of course, there is

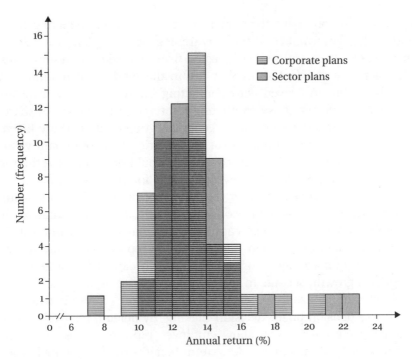

Fig. 6.1. Distribution of investment returns for selected Dutch pension funds (1998).

considerable debate over the efficiency of market discipline, and the degree to which profit maximization as opposed to managers' vested interests rule decision-making (Jensen 1993). By convention, the continental systems of corporate governance are deemed 'different': shareholder control is believed more direct, being in the hands of interlocking networks of large investors not the market for corporate control (see Hopt *et al.* 1999 for an exhaustive cross-country survey). Even so, problems of ownership and control loom large albeit less understood (Jenkinson and Ljungqvist 1999).

This account of the Anglo-American corporation suggests commonalities with the Dutch sector pension plans. More often than not both are characterized by diffuse ownership. In sector plans, it could be reasonably argued that the 'owners' (participants and beneficiaries) voice in the management of the plan is muted by poor coordination amongst the large numbers of individual 'shareholders'. The affiliation of workers through their sponsoring firms implies competing interfirm cost profiles, adding to the problem of coherence. A common labour union is one means of routinely coordinating the interests of 'owners'.

Even then unions have their own interests in the participating firms and in the performance of the overarching pension plan (see below). In practice, there are no disinterested firm or worker representatives. Managers are confronted, as they are in the modern corporation, by boards of directors riven with conflicting interests, yet, nevertheless required to manage those conflicting interests on the behalf of share-holders (see Eggertson 1990 for a general argument along these lines).

It might be protested that as social solidarity is the dominant value, problems of coordination and coherence would be less severe than in the modern corporation. However, social solidarity may not be so vir-tuous or so laudable. Consider the following possibilities. In a sector characterized by long-term economic decline, the representatives of older workers may, in effect, capture policy making. Their interests in early retirement and a high rate of income replacement may not be consistent with younger workers' interests in capital investment and long-term growth. Second, in sectors characterized by large numbers of relatively unorganized smaller employers, workers' representatives may dominate pension board decision-making. By default, relatively unco-ordinated employers may allow employee representatives to protect workers' current income and long-term benefits by shifting the burden of contribution rates to employers. The temptation exists to spread the benefits of pension income while concentrating their costs. Third, none of the institutions of social solidarity may have the capacity to affect, or a compelling interest in monitoring, the costs of pension and insurance benefits. The legal independence of pension board members may be so pronounced that they are able to shift the added costs of institutional inefficiency to the collective bargaining process. Given the power of pension boards over the firms in sector plans, the costs of board decision-making are inevitably transferred to individual firms and their workers. Whether performance Z-scores will make a substantial dif-ference to these 'tendencies' remains an open question.

Sector Funds as Financial Conglomerates

There is another, related issue of pension fund governance. So far, we have been silent about the sector funds' purchase of financial services. This is not the occasion to go into detail about the nature and scope of the pension funds financial service needs. In Clark (2000: ch. 4), there is an extensive treatment of this issue based upon the Anglo-American industry, entirely relevant to the Dutch pension fund system. It is sufficient to observe that pension funds normally consume a wide variety of financial services, ranging from actuarial services, custodial management and banking services, to advanced investment management services (developed in more detail in Chapter 7). Over the past ten years, it has become apparent in the Anglo-American pension world that there are considerable scale economies in the provision of many types of financial services (Berger *et al.* 1999). Witness the use of companies such as the State Street of Boston as the custodial managers of the flow of funds between various internal and external service providers. Many of the largest Anglo-American funds combine internal service provision with external sub-contracting, utilizing consultants to act as gate keepers between the boards of pension funds and the financial services industry. Not surprisingly, the issues of trust and comparative cost are important in the assessment of competing service providers (Clark 2001).

In the Anglo-American pension world, the governance of these fund-to-market relationships is a vital component of the pension fund performance (Ambachtsheer and Ezra 1998). However, in the Dutch model many sector funds have become financial conglomerates in their own right or the shareholders with other pension funds in mutually-owned financial firms. Many of the largest funds operate financial firms from their administrative offices, using boards of directors drawn from the fund's own board of directors. In effect, the fund directors are the representatives of (first) plan participants, (second) plan sponsors or unions, and (third) the funds in wholly-owned financial subsidiaries. It is also not unusual for the managers of sector funds to act as the managers of services provided by these 'firms'. Furthermore, a significant number of smaller sector funds are the exclusive shareholders in larger financial conglomerates, offering the whole range of complimentary financial services (from custodial services to insurance and investment management). Boards of management are drawn from the participating funds. These captive firms then sell to the constituent funds the services required for the management of the funds, based upon purchasing policies or protocols set by the funds' board of directors and implemented by the funds' managers.

Compared to the Anglo-American pension funds, these are unusual ownership patterns and relationships. In defence of these arrangements, sector fund representatives have argued that vertical integration is more cost effective than the purchase of separate financial services from market vendors. As noted above, the internalization of service functions allows fund managers to strip out vendor marketing costs, the switching costs of moving mandates between vendors, and the transaction costs associated with contracts and their enforcement. Because of non-profit mutual ownership, profit is less important than meeting the costs of service provision (including the costs of depreciation and capital replacement). Similarly, because salary costs are managed with respect to sectors' standards and norms rather than the global market for financial services, salaries tend to be compressed. At the same time, because funds' managers have multiple overlapping responsibilities, salaries can be set higher than would otherwise be justified by reference to his or her sector fund functions.

These ownership relationships between funds and their firms combined with incentives to minimize changes to contribution rates also encourages sector funds and their plan sponsors to standardize internal reporting functions: accounting systems, custodial systems, and investment products and management regimes. There are significant savings to be had from standardization; increasing returns to scale at lower per unit cost thresholds. Standardization also locks-in commitment to commonly designed and governed systems of financial services. If performance Z-scores were to prompt defection from sector-wide plans, plan sponsors could face significant switching costs given the evolution of these complex functional and information systems. Notice, however, that standardization has its limits. Requirements that plans actuarially match assets with liabilities means that board members and their financial service firms must ensure that, for example, investment regimes are tailored to the particular liability profiles of participating plans. Each participating plan within these financial institutions requires an investment strategy. Even so, the largest pension institutions have developed sets of investment products allowing for the pooling of assets between plans, while maintaining common reporting systems capable of discriminating between the assets of constituent plan sponsors.

In fact, the largest Dutch pension institutions have come to replicate many of the reporting systems of competing global investment management firms (Chapter 7). For instance, the format used by firms like Deutsche Bank, Fidelity, and Merrill Lynch, to report on the context, goals, portfolio structure, and performance of their various investment products is very familiar to the Dutch sector funds. Reporting on the volume of equity investment products' assets, their largest holdings, and the benchmarks used to assess comparative performance are features that are in common with the Anglo-American market for investment management. With the introduction of performance Z-scores, there is clearly a temptation amongst the largest sector funds-firms to mimic the procedures of their market rivals. In this sense, the Dutch sector funds are increasingly exposed to the global market for financial services. Indeed, as these funds match and mimic the services and reporting systems of the global investment groups, there is a temptation for these funds-firms to seek more members, to market their services beyond the statutory borders of the sector. Thus, some funds-firms have sought to acquire related financial products, health insurance products, and even banking services with existing or potential retail bases in the Benelux countries. At the margin, the Dutch funds-firms are rivals in the European financial services industry.

Sector funds as financial institutions increasingly need external specialized expertise. The design of financial systems is increasingly sophisticated, being driven by consultants with close relationships with advanced software companies. Also, all pension funds require actuarial services recognized and respected by Dutch insurance regulators. For the Dutch funds-firms it is neither cost effective nor is it legally possible in many cases for these institutions to hire and retain such specialized expertise. Thus, many sector funds have come to rely upon selected external service providers, often developing long-term relationships with those firms able to appreciate the complex governance and ownership patterns associated with these institutions. Inevitably, trust relationships are the dominant rationale behind sector funds' purchase of market-based financial services. Alternatively, as the imperatives of performance Z-scores have become clear, inherited trust relationships have been increasingly threatened by market relationships.

FINANCIAL STRUCTURE AND EUROPEAN COMPETITION

In the *Maatschappij Drijvende Bokken BV* the ECJ was petitioned by the Dutch high court to rule on the legality of sector funds' exclusive domain. Specifically, Article 85 (competition in the common market), Article 86 (abuse of dominant market position), and Article 90 (states' grants of exclusive rights) were identified by the plaintiffs as grounds for objecting to the monopoly status of Dutch sector pension funds.[8] This case was one of a group of three related cases, brought by firms deemed to be within the domain of existing sector funds but seeking to make alternative arrangements for the provision of pensions and insurance with external insurance companies. In *Albany*, the textile sector fund (with about 6000 participants) had required the firm to become a member of the fund, denying the right of the firm to provide equivalent or superior benefits. In the headline case *Maatschappij*, the firm had been incorporated into the dock workers sector fund (about 14 000 participants) in the early 1991 by virtue of a government decree covering all similar firms. And in *Brentjens*, the building materials sector fund (about 200 000 participants) had incorporated the firm within its domain, denying the validity of existing arrangements with an insurance group.

In all three cases, the insurance industry was excluded from the provision of pension and insurance benefits to individual firms. Prior to initiating court proceedings, two of the three firms affected had appealed to their sector funds for exemption, and had then appealed to the Dutch Insurance Board to overturn the sector funds' negative decisions. Although the Insurance Board had recommended in the *Albany* case that the fund reconsider their decision, the fund refused. The ECJ was asked to rule on the legality of these arrangements, putting in play the status of national social solidarity in relation to the EU competition policy—the status of national solutions to the demographic bomb given the overarching interest of all EU governments in an integrated market for financial services.

Against hopes and expectations in the Anglo-American financial world, the ECJ ruled that the Dutch system was legitimate invoking Article 3(1)(g) and (j) of the Treaty of Rome and Article 1 of the Agreement on Social Policy (OJ 1992 C 191).[9] Basically, the ECJ ruled that the objectives of EU competition policy had to be balanced against the objectives of economic and social cohesion (Article 3(1)(j)) and dialogue between the social partners (labour and management) (Article 1, Agreement on Social Policy). The advantages of sector-wide social solidarity in matters pertaining to pensions and insurance were explicitly linked to the EU treaty and its objectives of sustaining the collective bargaining process. The court noted the importance of risk sharing and mutuality in setting standard pension benefits within sectors and across participants, distinguishing their decision in this set of cases from previous decisions that had favoured the claims of the insurance industry.[10] At the same time, the court held that the Dutch government regulations allowing sector funds with the agreement of the relevant social partners to petition for compulsory affiliation did not contravene the EU competition policy. Even though sector funds were properly regarded as economic undertakings, the social objectives of these institutions were such that issues like competition and the abuse of dominant position could be set aside (for the moment).

The narrowest version of competition policy suggests that its only proper objective is economic efficiency (hence maximum consumer welfare) (Hay 1993: 2). From this proposition, arguments can be made regarding various kinds of market behaviour, including individual (predatory) and collective (collusive) pricing practices with respect to the apparent patterns of resource allocation (Rees 1993). Inevitably, this proposition relies upon the analysis of market structure, including the actions of existing market participants in relation to actual or potential new market entrants. In general, there is a presumption against any actions that result in or sustain market dominance; in turn, there is a presumption in favour of competition and the rights of competitors to enter markets (see Faull and Nikpay 1999: ch. 1). Article 85 prohibits any 'agreements', 'decisions', and 'concerted practices' amongst economic undertakings that would adversely affect competition in the European common market. It specifically prohibits price fixing, and other trading agreements that would exclude or harm competition. Article 86 prohibits undertakings from using their market position to place existing or potential competitors at a disadvantage, thereby affecting the welfare of consumers. Article 90 prohibits member states from granting exclusive rights of market access to selected undertakings, thereby limiting competition indirectly or directly.

While the Dutch insurance industry had reasonable grounds to claim against the monopoly status of sector pension funds, the EU competition policy is not an end in and of itself. According to Schaub (1998) of the DG Competition, the EC competition policy is best understood as a means to an end. That is, the achievement of objectives enshrined in the Treaty of Rome including the creation of a single market, convergence between member states in economic performance, and the promotion of social cohesion and mutual respect amongst the social partners. Thus, the EU competition policy is inevitably caught up in the whole fabric of policy making, and the balancing of contending political objectives. This does not mean that the competition directorate is ultimately responsible for balancing or adjudicating claims from outside their statutory mandate. As acknowledged by competition policy makers, given the anti-competitive actions of many market agents and many governments, their role is to advocate solutions that have as their objective greater EU market efficiency.[11] The role of the ECJ adjudication is to balance the programmatic objectives against the legitimate claims of other overarching objectives contained in the Treaty of Rome and its progeny.

In the foregoing discussion, we have posed an argument to the effect that European competition policy should not be thought to inevitably 'trump' national social objectives. More will be made of this point below. Before doing so, however, it is important to acknowledge that within the EU competition policy 'community' there are two related arguments that the geographical scope of the market for financial services is, in any event, smaller (national and local) than the market for manufactured goods (European and global). On one side there is a positive argument, suggesting that this is in fact empirically true. On the other side there is a normative argument that the market for financial services should be treated as if it is geographically smaller than Europe given local preferences, competence, and the flow of information. In effect, it might be suggested that European competition issues with respect to national systems of financial services have less significance than otherwise assumed. Therefore the Dutch supplementary pensions model warranted protection from the ECJ by virtue of the assumed geographical scope of European competition within the financial services industry.

Sapir *et al.* (1993) advanced the empirical argument, suggesting that imperfect competition dominates the European market for financial services. They began by arguing that capital investment per unit produced is lower in services than in manufacturing and that the switching of costs between alternative uses of capital are also lower in services than in manufacturing. More specifically they suggested that the market for financial services does not meet the standard tests of contestability. Because of the distinctiveness of local needs there are few potential entrants; because reputation is an essential ingredient in assessing the value of potential competitors, established relationships dominate local markets; and because locating and servicing customers is such a labour-intensive activity, few potential competitors are capable of raiding established markets. Sapir *et al.* (1993) also argued that dispersed cross-border transactions from remote sites of production are very difficult because of the nature of financial products: they are information intensive and characterized by informational asymmetries favouring selling agents over potential customers. Market access relies upon established relationships to overcome the distrust of potential clients. Therefore, local reputation is a significant barrier to (pan-European) entry.

These empirical claims about the geography of the financial industry can be disputed. For instance, the economies of scale apparent in processing financial products and services are such that producers must recurrently invest in information technology of all kinds to remain competitive. Indeed, in the United Systems of America it seems that mergers and acquisitions in the financial services industry have been driven by the need to spread the increasing costs of electronic information-processing investment (DeYoung and Hunter 2001). Furthermore, it seems very unlikely that these types of investments can be switched between alternative uses, given their rapid obsolescence and disposal as junk. In this context, information technology is better treated as a sunk cost than as a fixed cost (Clark 2000). This point is set forth in the previous section of the chapter, suggesting that the Dutch funds-firms have evolved as multi-functional financial conglomerates in part because of the economies of scale to be had in standardizing benefit, accounting, and reporting systems between complementary functions and between plan sponsors within sectors. While there may be few competing financial service firms willing or able to match the configuration of those internal sector-wide systems, over the long term it seems unlikely that continued geographical concentration and vertical integration will be consistent with increasing economies of scale.[12]

On the issue of information asymmetry, Sapir *et al.* (1993) can be brought together with those who argue the normative case. For instance, Rees and Kessner (1999) amongst others would argue that given the sophistication and complexity of many retirement benefit systems, the potential for exploiting customers' ignorance is so significant that overall consumer welfare is best protected by limiting the potential of 'hit-and-run' competition. No doubt some firms would find value in opting out of sector-wide plans, principally because they are either not yet incorporated into sector-wide systems or are subject to competitive pressures that require benefit discounting. The so-called UK pensions 'mis-selling' scandal is evidence for the real costs to individuals and society involved in promoting opting out of systems of social solidarity. There remain, however, industry observers who dispute the significance of information asymmetries. Furthermore, the rapid development of the cross-border sales of financial products utilizing internet technology and voice-based remote calling centres suggests that many consumers are willing to take the risk of information asymmetry if the product is significantly cheaper than the conventional local relationship-based modes of transacting.

But notice neither the empirical nor the normative counter-arguments need undercut the status of Dutch sector-wide pension plans. The goals of comprehensive coverage and equitable retirement income are probably best achieved by compulsory affiliation. But sector plans are vulnerable to claims that the funds-firms' vertical integration of financial transactions into captive financial firms go well-beyond achieving the substantive goals of the pension system. In this system of funds and firms the consumers of financial products are not individual beneficiaries but skilled financial professionals, the agents and representatives of plan beneficiaries. Given their experience in global and European financial markets it is difficult to sustain any argument that these 'consumers' of pension fund financial services need protection from the European financial services industry by granting a monopoly over the provision of those services. This does not necessarily mean that the global and European financial services industries would deliver cost-effective products consistent with the sector plans' benefits of common systems of management and reporting. Our argument is that, without effective fund governance transparency and accountability, the only plausible test of the cost efficiency of funds-firms is direct competition.

CONCLUSIONS

The Dutch model of retirement income has been promoted as an important option for the future of European pensions. It provides for equitable income redistribution, comprehensive coverage, and funded supplementary pensions. And it provides for a partnership between the state and the market in determining retirees' total retirement income. Not withstanding the slow discounting of the Dutch state's share of total retirement income, many commentators argue that the Dutch model has been a significant success in accommodating various social and economic interests in the context of outstanding economic growth (see Goodin et al. 1999; OECD 1998b). Not only have supplementary pension coverage rates remained high over the past twenty years, the Dutch model has avoided some of the most pernicious aspects of insurance systems including selection bias. Indeed, it is arguable that the often-times compulsory nature of sector-wide pension benefits provides for the long-term welfare of many employees at average rates of compensation above that which could be offered by systems of insurance. In this respect, the economic virtues of social solidarity are significant and deeply implicated with national politics.

For continental Europe, long accustomed to modes of collective decision-making involving various stakeholders, the Dutch model also provides an important model for the roles of social partners in the organization and management of pension fund institutions. As in a number of continental European states, the explicit link between the institutions of collective bargaining or co-determination and the institutions of retirement benefits provides employee representatives a significant role in managing workers' current and future incomes. Moreover, the sector-wide system of benefit levels and their negotiation is deliberately designed to remove interfirm rivalry from long-term compensation; the system was conceived to achieve a variety of social objectives including the equitable standardization of intra-sector retirement income. In this respect, retirement income is an integral element of the social market much admired by some UK commentators; see Hutton (1995). In their *Maatschappij Drijvende Bokken BV* opinion, the ECJ distinguished insurance systems from systems of social solidarity in relation to these objectives of social policy.

Therefore there are legitimate reasons to celebrate the distinctiveness of the Dutch system, rather than presume that its design and organization as a set of financial institutions is necessarily antagonist to the EU competition policy.[13] On the other hand, we have also argued that the ECJ decision mistook form for substance. The court recognized the virtues of social solidarity in determining Dutch pension coverage rates and benefit levels, an important conclusion given the possible disadvantages of pension systems offered by potential competitors from the insurance industry. While doing so, the court also properly recognized that sector pension funds are functionally economic undertakings. But notice our argument has been that the court failed to take its functional logic far enough. The court seems to have assumed that pension funds are simply the representatives of beneficiaries' interests, ignoring the important financial institutions owned and operated by those funds. Most importantly, the court failed to appreciate the hidden costs of sector fund economic organizations—that is, the potential costs associated with the vertical integration of funds' financial services borne by pension fund beneficiaries, plan sponsors, and/or participating employees. There is a real risk of moral hazard; that is, the costs and risks of organization transferred to those without an adequate voice in its operation.

It is not clear that insulation from market competition afforded Dutch sector funds by virtue of the ideal of social solidarity, should extend to protecting pension funds' captive financial institutions. In theory, sector-wide pension funds could maintain their interests in social solidarity while decentralizing to the market the purchase of financial services. Of course, a counter-argument would be that the internalization of transactions combined with lower overhead costs of this particular form of organization would effectively exclude competition from the market. However, embedded in this argument are a variety of other possibilities. One is that the internalization of transactions mask cross-subsidies between financial service functions, sheltering some functions more efficiently provided by the market while draining the surplus of other functions that could add value to plan sponsors and participants. Another possibility is that these funds-firms are actually the creatures of their administrators and managers, providing opportunities for patronage and extra income (rent). This type of arrangement may be a vital ingredient in lowering the overall costs of production—there may be mutually-realized benefits not available to plan agents from the market. It is also entirely possible that funds-firms are actually more expensive than the market for financial services.

The problematic issues here are twofold: agency and transparency. It is difficult for firms and their employee participants to judge fund-firm performance. The introduction of Z-scores is one step towards greater transparency. But more information may be needed to allow a competitive market to flourish. It is rare for funds-firms to produce costs of servicing data separate from the bundle or integrated web of internal transactions. There is also a danger that individual plan sponsors and their participants become the captive 'owners' of funds-firms. This is especially a risk for smaller firms, in sectors dominated by dispersed 'ownership' and concentrated union representation. The ECJ failed to consider the importance of a legitimate appeal process underpinning compulsory affiliation. The apparent equation made between co-determination and pension fund governance confuses one set of interests (stakeholder representation) with different interests (efficient fund-firm governance). This may not have been so important in years gone by; limited international competition in many sectors of the Dutch economy may have effectively sheltered these arrangements from close scrutiny. But with the increasing interpenetration of the global, EU, and national competitive pressures, many plan sponsors and their participants have an interest in the cost efficiency of pension fund governance.[14]

NOTES

1. See Goodin *et al.* (1999) on the virtues of the Dutch social democratic welfare model and see the October 2001 statement issued by Fondazione Rodolfo Debenedetti (Milan) on behalf of leading European academics arguing in favour of a 'portfolio' of pension institutions (and retirement income commitments) (at www.frdb.org). Over-reliance upon one pillar (social security) is widely perceived by many expert commentators to be very troubling given all the pressures on nation-state finances now and in the future (see the related volume edited by Boeri *et al.* 2001a and the assessment by Feldstein and Leibman 2002).

2. Cited as case C-219/97 Maatschappij Drijvende Bokken BV v. Stichting Pensioenfonds voor de Vervoer-en Havenbedrijven and incorporating Albany International BV v. Stichting Bedrijfspensioenfonds Textielindustrie and Brentjens' Handelsonderneming BV v. Stichting Pensioenfonds voor de Handel in Bouwmaterialen (decision rendered 21 September, 1999). The Advocate General Francis Jacobs' opinion, which focused upon Albany (C-67/96), was delivered on 28 January, 1999.

3. In this chapter, we emphasize the EU regulation rather than the national regulation of the financial services industry. We note, however, that there may be significant national jurisdictional issues involved in the crossover of funds-firms between different kinds of financial products and markets. Whereas the Dutch insurance regulator may be rightly concerned with the financial integrity of funds (assets to liabilities), there may be significant 'gaps' in the regulatory regime with respect to the funds' other financial products. This is an important issue throughout Europe, the United Kingdom and in the United States of America. See, for instance, the May 5th, 1999, testimony of Arthur Levitt, the SEC Chairman before the US Congress House Committee on Commerce regarding the Financial Services Act of 1999 (and repeal of the Glass-Steagall Act) [www.sec.gov/news/testimony/tsty/o99.htm].

4. It is worth noting, however, that the concept of social solidarity is currently in vogue in Anglo-American management consulting. For example, Goffee and Jones (1998: 28) develop their well-known Harvard Business Review paper on corporate culture, arguing in favour of '[s]olidaritic relationships [that] are based on common tasks, mutual interests, and clearly understood shared goals that benefit all parties. Labor unions are an archetypal example of high-solidarity communities'. By their assessment, the coherence of shared goals drives the organization even if the external environment is hostile and economically unforgiving. Closely related, of course, are notions of stakeholder society and the like (see Hutton 1995, for a UK take on the same issue).

5. I have resisted the temptation to explicitly link these cost advantages to the theory of market competition. More detail on the types of costs referred to in our argument can be found in Vickers (1997) and Viscusi *et al.* (1995: chs. 6 and 11). See especially their discussion of switching costs. These points are taken up in more detail in the following chapter on the production of financial products and London's place in the global economy.

6. Private insurance companies would inevitably select amongst eligible plan participants reducing the costs for some (firms and younger workers with clear health records) but increasing the costs for others (firms and older workers with health complications) to the point where coverage rates must decline. There is a risk that the insurance industry would not offer coverage to those types of workers most in need of coverage (selection bias) thereby thwarting the goals of government policy. Mandatory coverage would then become the only alternative (witness the Australian and Swiss examples; see Edey and Simon 1998).

7. It must be emphasized that drawing precise implications from pension funds' investment performance is very difficult. In Clark (2000: chs. 4 and 5), there is a detailed treatment of this issue, noting the significance of unaccounted (random) year-to-year volatility of performance against accepted bench marks. In many respects, trends over longer time frames (up to 5 years) are more acceptable empirical measures of performance.

8. Throughout the chapter, Articles 85, 86, and 90 are referred to in accordance with the Treaty of Rome and the deliberations of the ECJ. Of course, this numbering system has changed in accordance with the Treaty of Amsterdam (now Articles 81, 82, and 86). Evans (1998) provides a useful historical commentary on the various treaties, and the consequences of the Treaty of Amsterdam for the system of numeration.

9. Notice in the AG Jacobs opinion, that doubts were raised about the status of collective bargaining agreements in relation to the EU competition policy. The AG provided an extensive analysis of the facts of the case, and the issues raised in the EU law. He also reviewed the current exemptions and modes of treating collective bargaining in the western world, arguing that the legal status of the various international social charters on workers' rights to organization were problematic, to say the least. Nevertheless, he managed to find reasons to conclude that the Dutch sector plans were outside of the scope of Article 85 and that the sector funds were, in fact, properly treated as economic undertakings. He suggested that if the ECJ were to allow the sector funds privileges, it would be an exceptional decision in the light of previous related decisions.

10. The court referred to a set of cases involving countries' social security schemes, including Hofner and Elser [1991] ECR-I-1979, Poucet and Pistre [1993] ECR U-637 and Federation Francaise des Societes d'Assurance and Others v. Ministere de l'Agriculture et de la Peche [1995] ECR I-4013. The court noted re Hofner its functional definition of undertakings, the distinction to be drawn between social security systems based upon contributions as opposed to social solidarity (Poucet and Pistre), and the irrelevance of an organization's profit-making status for determining whether such an organization was 'carrying on an economic activity' (p.12) (referring to the Federation decision).

11. A recent evaluation of the ECJ decision-making and the regulatory actions of the DG Competition questions the coherence and significance of the EU competition policy (see Neven *et al.* 1998). Here, I am more sympathetic to the need for a balance approached to the EU policy making, in general, than Neven *et al.* and I find merit in the ECJ decision excluding Dutch sector pensions from the scope of Article 85. Social policy has, and deserves, its own arena even if this affects economic integration.

12. Faull and Nikpay (1999: ch. 9) provide an authoritative review of the EC's treatment of the geographical dimensions of financial markets. In the main, they stand by the conventional national definitions of such markets, referring to issues such as the scope of existing distribution channels (see 9.139–9.141). But they also acknowledge that some kinds of financial institutions and some kinds of financial firms may need to spread risks across larger geographical units, like Europe. To economic geographers, the commission's assumed geography of European financial markets appears hard to justify.

13. The issue of national spheres of influence and responsibility with respect to the EU mandates and decision-making is far more complicated than this brief commentary allows. See de Burca (1999) on the principle of subsidiarity, arguing that it is a guide for institutions' powers rather than a judicial right conferring powers or limiting powers within a multi-tier system of governance. Shaw (2000) is similarly instructive on the contested issue of national powers, noting the evolution of the pan-European legal norms and customs regarding the separation of powers between tiers of government.

14. In this respect, De Ryck's (1999) report on European pensions was arguing for reforming pension fund boards endorsed by the DG Internal Market. Drawing upon recent developments in the US mutual fund industry (Brennan *et al.* 1999) and related concerns raised in the United Kingdom in the wake of the Maxwell scandal, De Ryck suggested that boards be properly composed of a significant majority of independent trustees or members.

London's Place in the World of Finance

More than 130 years ago, Bagehot (1873: 330) lauded the vitality of the city of London. Referencing Paris, he predicted that London would maintain its 'natural pre-eminence' as the 'clearing house' of the world. For Bagehot, London's growth could be traced to the Reform Act of 1844, which effectively created a market for credit. More recently, Smith and Walter (1997: 302) suggested that the (current) pre-eminence of London in Europe can be traced to the UK Financial Securities Act of 1986, which effectively liberalized the market for private securities' transactions. Even if Wall Street is much larger in terms of domestic traded volume, listed securities, and total assets, London dominates cross-border transactions and is the favoured international location of many global banks and market intermediaries. London and New York represent in space the dominant global financial system of the late twentieth and twenty-first centuries.[1] Their relationship is at once competitive and reciprocal, being joined together by a common legal and economic heritage (compared to continental Europe; see La Porta *et al.* 1998).

The continued success of London is a matter of enormous importance for the UK economy (GDP, trade, employment, and income) (IFSL 2001). Nonetheless, the dominance of London (and the south-east in general) has prompted recurrent geographical and sectoral tensions; the growth of regional income and employment inequalities over the past twenty years or so has been linked to the concentrated economic and political power of the city financial institutions (Martin and Minns 1995). Likewise, the role of London in the emerging European single market for financial services has prompted considerable debate in

Europe. Ironically, the Franco-German alliance that has driven monetary union and the Euro has been mediated and priced in the London and New York markets (Szasz 1999). Political claims for respect for nation-state financial systems have been directly challenged by the economic opinions and power of these markets. Whereas some suppose that the competition between European financial systems is unresolved, it is arguable that London has reaffirmed its dominance over Frankfurt and Paris over the past ten years (compare Story and Walter 1997).

More specifically, research on continental European social security systems suggests that Anglo-American financial markets will play increasingly important roles in the investment of retirement income assets. This much is apparent from the structure and performance of the Dutch and Swiss pension systems. But it is also apparent in France and Germany. The introduction in both countries of state-codified private retirement savings instruments, implies the discounting of the long-term value of state-sponsored social security benefits; private arrangements will be required to make-up the difference. While these institutions may not be like the Anglo-American funded pension plans, the long-term retirement income of many European citizens will depend upon the cost efficiency and investment performance of these private savings institutions. In this regard, London casts a large shadow across Europe: as the dominant European centre of financial expertise and as the most obvious market through which to mobilize pension and savings assets for global investment. Recent moves by the EU to develop a single market regulatory framework for pension and retirement income products suggests that London will continue to grow in significance relative to Frankfurt and Paris.

My goal is to explain how and why London occupies such a vital role in the European and global financial services industries. In doing so, I focus upon the production of financial products relevant to the retirement incomes of European citizens. Notice that I draw a distinction in principle if not entirely in fact between the geography of financial production and the geography of financial trading. It seems likely that financial trading will be increasingly concentrated in fewer markets as electronic communication and trading systems replace dispersed trading floors and market places (Laulajainen 2001). Consolidation in European financial markets is one expression of the increasing significance of such technologies, just as the EMU and the introduction of the Euro have provided strong imperatives for integration. Pan-European and even trans-Atlantic trading platforms may become a reality in the next five to ten years. This does not mean that financial products will also be produced in virtual space, nor does it mean that virtual markets will necessarily overcome existing and deeply-entrenched differences between jurisdictions in their regulatory cultures, instruments, and standards of accountability.[2]

To sustain my argument, I emphasize the competitive dynamics of the financial services industry, the nature of financial products, and the distinctive place of London in the 24-hour global financial trading and transaction systems. Having developed an analytical perspective on these issues, I focus upon the long-term spatial configuration of the European single market for financial services. It should be acknowledged that this issue is the subject of considerable academic and policy debate. I do not intend to cover all the relevant literature, nor do I intend to engage or in any sense qualify the extensive and detailed historical treatments of the topic.[3] Rather, my perspective is analytical and informed by recent developments in economic geography. Invoked are economic concepts like product range and threshold just as I consider the importance of agglomeration economies, increasing returns, and path dependence allied with economic geography. To do otherwise would be to impose space and time on agents rather than seeing both adapted and produced through the actions of agents.

CATEGORIES AND CONCEPTS

There are a variety of ways of approaching the topic.[4] In geography, attention has been paid to differences in the local informal customs and norms regulating market transactions (and hence sustaining spatial differentiation). Consequently, there are studies that assess the distinctive cultural milieu and transactional relationships that characterize the city of London (see for example Amin and Thrift 1992). Appreciation of the cultural rudiments of industry organization is one expression of a consistent interest in the changing nature of firm and industry organization as they affect the geographical configuration of production (in general) and the tensions between localization and globalization (in particular). In fact, economic geographers have paid far closer attention to the internal organization of firms and industries than economists similarly interested in the economic geography of contemporary economies. At the limit, there are interesting overlaps between the disciplines of economic geography and finance. Witness the work of geographers on the management of modern corporations (O'Neill 2001; and Schoenberger 2001).

By contrast, economists interested in economic geography have sought to develop and explicate the spatial implications of golden rules. Krugman's (1991) argument about the significance of increasing returns for the localization of agglomeration economies has provided a macro-economic logic for understanding the differentiation of the economic landscape. Assuming an initial (arbitrary) assignment of economic activity, increasing returns allows for the cumulative development of places along distinctive paths of accumulation that tend to persist notwithstanding the arbitrage mechanisms of an equilibrating spatial economic system. In terms of industry organization, one implication from this kind of analytical perspective is the evolution of specialized industry-regions, industrial districts, and the like. Put slightly differ-ently 'there is a priori a great deal of flexibility in the choice of locations but a strong rigidity of spatial structures once the process of agglom-eration has started' (Ottaviano and Thisse 2001: 177). In this sense, London can be seen as an instance wherein an initial advantage has become a dominant process. History matters even if there is unease about the predictive force of the new economic geography.

In this chapter, I focus upon the micro-economic imperatives driving firm location decision-making in the context of an inherited European and global landscape. This allows us some flexibility with respect to the behavioural logic that we might attribute to corporate decision-makers. One disadvantage of the golden-rule approach of Krugman and others is the necessity of assuming a rational signal-response mode of decision-making (as shown in Arthur (1992) and elsewhere). At the same time, I am not convinced that the inherited landscape is as compelling as assumed by those that believe in path dependence. Firms assess and reassess time after time the costs and benefits of particular locations. This is especially true of the Anglo-American 'bulge-bracket' financial houses that maintain and manage their global operations on a daily basis, through advanced information and com-munication technologies. Basically, the analytical approach I use is focused upon the production of financial products (or services) draw-ing upon the previous arguments provided, in part, in Clark (2000) and Clark and O'Connor (1997).

Firms and Industry Competition

Let us begin with the objective function of financial service firms. It is assumed that these firms maximize reported income, being sensitive to the link between reported income and the quoted stock market prices of their parent institutions. It is also assumed that corporate managers tend to protect against 'negative surprises' in reported income, managing expectations about the flow of reported income quarter-to-quarter and year-to-year. At the senior level, it is further assumed that corporate executives' compensation packages are tied (in part) to changes in the stock market prices. But it is assumed that lower down in the corporate hierarchy the cost of employment packages is a significant factor in managing reported income. While we assume that these firms manage reported income, we should also assume that there are strong incentives to minimize the costs of production (one important component being labour costs). Finally, it should be apparent that there are significant agency issues both between the senior managers and stockholders, and between senior managers and employees. Executing corporate strategy requires a level of active management that can be very hard to sustain down the corporate hierarchy.

It is also assumed that acknowledged expertise and demonstrated track records of success are at a premium in the industry. The combination of reputation and consistency of outcomes drives the prices that firms can charge for their financial services. However, it should be acknowledged that the outcomes of investment management (for example) are only revealed at the end of regular periods of time. In many cases, the value of any financial product is predicted against an accepted benchmark rather than guaranteed (Shleifer 1985). Consequently, while firms may accumulate clients and mandates for the provision of financial services on the basis of their past performance, the competitiveness of financial firms is very sensitive to their relative performance. Consistently poor relative performance can prompt sudden and sustained client defection, the loss of mandates, and the discounting of hard-earned reputations. Not only is reputation a vital means of attracting talented employees and clients, it drives the accumulation of financial assets so important for reaping firm-specific economies of scale (Clark 2000: ch. 4).

For a variety of reasons, the industry is dominated by a relatively small number of very large multi-jurisdictional and multi-functional firms. At the same time, there are a myriad of small, highly specialized firms providing distinctive and particular sets of skills and services to large firms and to the market in general. Competition is rife in the industry. The potential entry and exit of rival firms combined with the predatory employment and price practices of the larger firms drives corporate strategy. Witness, for example, the flow of mergers and acquisitions over the past 10 years, the spin out firms created by those leaving larger firms, and the impact of technology on the costs and quality of service provision. In part, scale economies are important because they allow firms to spread the cost of product innovation, recurrent investment in information technology (year-to-year), and the costs of managing reputation in the global marketplace. However, the economies of scale are not so important that they can insulate dominant firms from poor relative performance. In fact, the growth of US firms in London through the acquisition of UK firms is an indication of the costs of complacency and inertia.

In sum, the financial services industry is characterized by oligopolistic behaviour and competition. Following Waterson (1984: 17), 'the quintessential feature of an oligopoly is interdependence: the actions of all the individual firms in an industry are affected by the actions of the other firms'. Equally important, of course, is product differentiation (see Viscusi *et al.* 1995). This is a vital component of most firms' competitive policy, being driven by interfirm rivalry as well as by those who demand increasingly specialized and tailored financial products.

London and Industry Organization

London's financial industry is much more than the city of London. It has spilled out towards the west-end of London and in recent years it has been joined by massive developments at Canary Wharf (to the east). It is now a set of related nodes spread across London, and a set of isolated locational choices connected to systems of national and international communication and transportation rather than immediate market relationships. Whereas much of the economic geography literature on industrial districts assumes an intimate connection between the citizenship of firms and their location, London is an 'industrial district' that has attracted and retained firms whose home location could place them elsewhere in the world (in the United States of America and Europe). For many such firms, locating and developing a significant presence in London has been a conscious locational choice made both in relation to competitors and related firms, and in relation to the preferences and needs of customers.

London relies upon four rather different but overlapping markets. The domestic UK market is significant. The volume of institutional and pension fund assets is very important, being ranked third in the world after the United States of America and Japan (in that order) (Davis and Steil 2001). When compared to continental Europe, this element is sufficient to distinguish the UK economy and London (its financial hub) as a profoundly different type of financial system (Davis 1995). A second, most important, market is the interchange between the United States of America and Europe, facilitating and mediating a wide range of transactions flowing from Europe to the United States of America and from the United States of America to Europe. This is a traditional function provided by the city of London; it represents a market that is global in scope, joining London with Asia, Asia with Europe, and the Americas. A third important market is to be found *in* continental Europe. London provides financial products and services not found in continental markets, or financial services provided in London by institutions with acknowledged superior reputations and costs and prices. A fourth important market is the rest of the world; private and sovereign institutions whose ties to London stretch back to the Empire and beyond.

The largest bulge-bracket financial service companies, bring together all four markets (and related markets), locating in London to service their diverse client base. Notice, these institutions tend to be organized according to asset categories or classes and related products rather than geographic markets. For example, foreign exchange functions encompass the entire globe on a 24-hour basis rather than being segmented and managed by local offices in countries and regions. Similarly bond trading, equities trading, and private placements of all kinds tend to be functionally centralized according to expertise rather than dispersed according to the specific needs of geographic markets. In part, this kind of functional and product specialization reflects the evolving market for expertise and talent and the increasing flow of assets into London and the global markets. Of course, this organizational logic must be sensitive to the tastes and preferences of markets. Function and product teams often combine research with marketing, trading, and execution with local regulatory requirements, and product design with client needs. Ideally, combining markets according to product groups enables firms to reap economies of scale on the processing, reporting, and execution side of the firm.[5]

Of course, as noted above, the industry is actually comprised of a handful of self-enclosed bulge-bracket firms and a myriad of small highly specialized firms. Whereas the former aim to reap the apparent economies of scale, the latter aim to reap the benefits of agglomeration.[6] For smaller firms, close proximity enables specialization, relying upon interfirm networks rather than the collection under one roof of all necessary and related functions. The combination and growth of markets, the co-location of rival bulge-bracket firms, and the growth of related small firms have brought together to one place a remarkably diverse labour market and an enormous range of financial services. Inevitably, there is a neat symbiotic relationship between the pool of talent and the provision of financial services. For all financial firms, large and small, London is an invaluable resource as it is a location at the junction of diverse local and global markets.[7]

PRODUCT DIFFERENTIATION AND QUALITY

We suggested above that product differentiation is a common competitive strategy in oligopolistic industries such as financial services. It was also suggested that financial products and services have a variety of elements or components including, for example, (1) an asset designation, (2) a market designation, (3) a measure of relative performance, (4) a recognized accounts system, (5) a price, and (6) reputation.[8] So, to illustrate, a Swiss pension fund might come to London to purchase investment and management expertise for an emerging-markets equity product, comparing competing firms' relative prices, performance, and reputations against accepted benchmarks. Price is partly dependent upon the volume of managed assets, there being discounts for larger tranches of assets. However, price is also a function of perceived product and vendor quality. And quality is a combination of all six attributes or components of the product. Not surprisingly, firms compete with one another on the basis of perceived product quality, while seeking to differentiate their products from others' rival products.

Why come to London to purchase an emerging-markets equities product?[9] There are at least three plausible answers. In the first instance, London has been the dominant European centre providing such products reflecting a historical legacy as much as current competence. In this respect, a firm's reputation may depend upon the reputation of its financial centre as much as its own competence. In the second instance, there is a choice of potential vendors in the London market, whereas in the local (Zurich) market there may be only one or two vendors. Therefore, it may pay the producers of such products to co-locate with other producers of similar financial products and services recognizing that the purchasers of such products directly compare and evaluate potential vendors. This is a version of Hotelling's (1929) theory of locational choice. In this case, the formality of investment decision-making on the demand side of the equation may require a similar level of formality on the production side of the equation. In the third instance, London may be better able to provide related financial services including third-party advice about the respective virtues of competing vendors. Inevitably, just as firms have strong incentives to differentiate themselves they also have strong incentives to co-locate with one another.

We must be careful, however, not to suggest or imply that there is only one global location from which to supply financial products and services to each and every market. In fact, there are many financial centres around the world providing a variety of similar and some times dissimilar products to their local markets. At this point in the argument, I must explain how and why financial centres coexist with one another, and why there is a hierarchy of centres differentiated according to the nature of offered financial products and services. In doing so, we need history and geography (in the first instance), and a typology of financial products distinguished according to the nature and sophistication (and therefore quality) of the product (in the second instance; see also Clark and O'Connor 1997).

History and geography provide a simple but compelling story. Countries of the world can be sifted and sorted into a set of financial systems characterized by very different legal and regulatory regimes (see especially La Porta *et al.* 1998). These systems carry with them markedly different historical legacies, reflecting the accumulated effects of economic and political forces at work in these countries over the past 200–300 years (Roe 1994). This topic is, of course, the subject of detailed and extensive historical study. In terms of the contemporary political economy, the role and status of these different systems is expressed through debate about the proper regulation of corporate governance, the role of financial markets, and the inherited responsibilities of institutions such as banks. See, for example, the compendium edited by Hopt *et al.* (1999), the recent analysis of the German and US systems of corporate governance by O'Sullivan (2000), and the assessment by Ronald Dore (2000) of the conflict between rival systems and the possible costs of resolution of conflict through the increasing dominance of the Anglo-American system of corporate governance. Whereas London collects in one place a variety of markets, it also collects together expertise relevant to very different regulatory requirements.

Three implications immediately follow from this point. First, some regulatory regimes internalize and isolate to privileged financial institutions the production and consumption of financial products and services. By contrast, some regulatory regimes encourage (and sometimes require) the provision of financial products and services through third-party agents located in financial markets. Second, some regulatory regimes impose detailed and restrictive covenants on the consumption of financial products and services, effectively ruling out whole groups of financial products or at least limiting the consumption of such products while deliberately favouring other kinds of products. Third, to the extent that regulatory systems allow or enable the common consumption of certain types of financial products and services, these systems may nevertheless impose restrictions upon cross-border financial flows effectively balkanizing local markets. The classic comparison to be made is, of course, between the equity and market culture of the Anglo-American world and the banking and bond culture of the Germanic world. The recent EU initiatives designed to facilitate the development of a single market for financial services tackle the second and third implications (Chapter 2).

Taking this point further, consider also the following observations. It seems inevitable that some financial products will never make it to the London market because they are not 'products' rather untraded commercial relationships. At issue, in this context, is the extent to which untraded relationships may be discounted in favour of the market as opposed to institutional intermediation (Boot and Thakor 1997). Some products are so distinctive, reflecting history and geography (path dependence), that they are only reasonably produced at the local and not the global level. Some 'common' products may nevertheless require local management and production because of exacting local reporting requirements that dominate some markets as opposed to the global markets. And some products produced in London draw European and global consumers because they are either not offered locally or if offered locally are done so on the basis of limited experience and expertise. In combination, this accounts for the coexistence of markets and the fact that London and New York offer a broad range of 'global' products and services as well as 'local' products offered for London and European consumers.

But if we are not careful, this logic runs the risk of being overly deterministic: as the past provides an account of differentiation, when pushed into the future to 'explain' persistent difference it may ignore contingency. In fact, we must also be sensitive to forces driving the spatial concentration of the financial services industry. This is especially important when considering London in relation to Europe. Furthermore, the issue of spatial concentration can be seen as a reflection of concomitant forces of competitive change like the increasing concentration in national and international financial industries. Berger *et al.* (1999) provide a comprehensive survey of the causes and consequences of consolidation in the US, European, and international financial service industries. In doing so, they note that the US financial services industry has been comparatively unconcentrated for many years, reflecting no doubt the long-term importance of state-level banking regulations and the barriers imposed on cross-sector consolidation by the Glass-Steagall Act. This topic is widely researched, and as yet unresolved. Here, my argument concerns the interaction between the spatial and industrial consolidation as regards the demand for product type and quality.

I would argue that the importance of London in the European financial services industry is the result of an increasing demand by continental European institutional consumers for financial products based in the London market and often, but not exclusively, provided by the bulge-bracket financial corporations. This suggests there is something special about London as there is something special about the bulge-bracket financial corporations. In summary terms, I would suggest that London provides regulatory systems consistent with the provision of sophisticated financial products, just as the bulge-bracket firms are able to provide management and reporting systems that meet high standards of accountability and the need of many continental institutions for greater transparency in the management process. This does not mean that the systems of regulation, accountability, and transparency are in any sense perfect; rather it is better understood that these systems are superior to continental systems, and are more sensitive to the evolving nature of financial products and services. It is an issue of relative not absolute quality.

To illustrate, let us return to our Swiss pension fund. We have already noted that neither the Zurich market nor for that matter the Frankfurt or Paris markets may be able to provide an adequate choice of vendors and products. The emerging market equity products combine complicated currency hedging with detailed research on far flung markets in non-European regions of the world. Also, the UK regulators have extensive experience in overseeing the flow of such transactions and a mode of regulation quite different from their continental colleagues. This is, perhaps, most easily summarized in a distinction between the (UK) procedural as opposed to the (continental) substantive regulation based upon inherited and statutory conceptions of fiduciary duty (see also Langbein 1997). Furthermore, until very recently continental regulators being centred upon banking and insurance have tended to view hedging and derivative products with great unease. Indeed, continental regulatory systems have imposed strict requirements and closely scrutinized the use and allocation of assets to such products. Of course, going to London does not mean that continental institutions evade local regulators. But it does mean that London based vendors may have far greater experience with the complex nature and regulation of these products compared to their continental based competitors (unless they also locate those functions in London—which is increasingly the case, witness the location decisions of the German, Swiss, and French companies).

There is a further important aspect of the argument. Our pension fund, having relied for many years upon local institutions for financial services, may find London financial institutions more able and willing to provide greater accountability and transparency in the design and execution of their financial services. By breaking away from the close, even personal, relationships that have dominated the Zurich financial centre, our pension fund may be able to redefine desired product quality in relation to local service providers while learning more about the quality of related financial services in international markets. In effect, as London is a market for financial services, it is desired as such by European institutions dominated by long-established relationships. London allows continental European institutions to impose discipline upon their existing networks of product and service providers in their home jurisdictions. Product quality is, consequently, a means by which the relationships between buyers and sellers of financial products may be governed if not formally regulated. Inevitably, the imposition of market price and quality provides a strong weapon driving the observed non-intermediation of European financial industries. The unresolved issue, however, for our pension fund is whether London could or should supplant its long-term local product vendors.

COMPLEMENTARITIES AND CONCENTRATION

So far, we have treated the demand and supply of financial products as a discreet process. Consumers and producers are assumed to enter and leave markets according to product needs and specifications. This has provided a logic whereby the London market dominates European markets by virtue of the combination of separate products offered therein. However, in this section I want to complicate the analysis by suggesting that there are significant complementarities between financial products and services. When our Swiss pension fund purchases an emerging markets equity product they also purchase a variety of complementary financial services either from the immediate provider of the emerging markets product or by providers that can provide services consistent with that type of product. This argument involves at least two related issues: in the first instance, the nature and scope of complementarity and, in the second instance, the organizational structures that can provide the identified complementarities. In developing this analysis, I rely upon the conventional definitions of costs and Richardson's (1990) seminal treatment complementarities.[10]

Let us assume there are three types of costs in the production process. *Variable costs* increase with the volume of output, and as output increases, variable costs increase at a lower rate (increasing returns to scale). *Fixed costs* exist whatever the volume of output. And if output were to cease, fixed costs would be negligible. As output increases, however, producers are able to spread fixed costs across more and more units of output thereby decreasing the per unit costs. There are also *sunk costs*. For simplicity, there are sunk costs at the point of entry into a market and at the point of exit from a market. By definition, sunk costs cannot be recovered. All these costs are the weapons of competitive strategy just as they are burdens upon competitive strategy. To illustrate, as the flow of assets increases more and more people are needed (at a decreasing rate) to manage those assets. Firms must also provide, regardless of the level of output, certain accounting and fiduciary functions that consistently trace the flow of assets in the production process. And firms must have certain capital and technological infrastructures if they are to enter a market and if they are to repel potential competitors (see Armstrong *et al.* 1994 on the interaction between costs and strategy).

Richardson identified a variety of complementarities in the production process. He suggested that '(m)any of the operations taken within one firm are obviously complementary; it is recognized that the cost of obtaining additional output will be less if the level of several operations can be varied and not merely that of one of them' (Richardson 1990: 73). Resources may be switched within the firm to adjust the level of output without changing the overall firm-based level of inputs (TYPE 1). He also noted a second type of complementarity—the result of the unplanned actions of external consumers of inputs. A group of firms may purchase the same inputs thereby increasing returns to scale of the external provider and contributing to the lower costs of production by the purchasers of that product or products (TYPE 2). He also suggested that there might be a close association between the demand for one good, and the demand for other goods (even if he believed this is unusual in advanced economies) (TYPE 3). Finally, he notes 'a further kind of complementarity by which almost all investments are related' (Richardson 1990: 74). Even if there are no close relationships between firms, the multiplier effects of purchasing and producing goods and services will produce income and employment will spread throughout the entire economy adding to the overall flow of demand and supply (assuming the economy is geographically bounded and integrated) (TYPE 4).

I would contend that each and every TYPE of complementarity is present in the global financial services industry, and their existence drives the shared agglomeration or external economies of London as a site of production (relative to its competitors).[11] However, none of these TYPES of complementarities need reside *within* a firm; they may be present and shared *between* firms so that each and every firm could be very small and highly specialized. We also have to account for the coexistence of the bulge-bracket firms with the boutique firms if the analysis is to be entirely relevant to the circumstances of the financial services industry.

To illustrate, let us again return to our Swiss pension fund seeking an emerging markets equity product.[12] In the first instance, the fund will rely upon the expertise of an asset consultant in choosing the product provider. The consultant could be a global consultant, with a branch office in Zurich. Alternatively, the consultant may be 'local' with close London connections. In this way, the client is passed through the consultant into the London market. Assuming a product provider is chosen offering a highly reputable product, it may do so at a low cost by switching resources from within the firm or by sharing the mandate with another, closely related firm. The winning combination of reputation and low cost is made possible by complementarity within and/or between firms (TYPE 1). Also, the firm may be able to offer cost-efficient execution of the product utilizing shared market-clearing electronic infrastructure (TYPE 2). Once the product is 'purchased', a set of related services must also be purchased to transfer assets to and from London. Currency hedging, custodial services, and compliance services are all necessary (TYPE 3). These complementary services may be provided within the firm or on contract from outside the firm. Finally, added together, the purchase of emerging markets equity products by European institutions relies upon competence in London, thereby drawing in talented employees and yet more customers to London (TYPE 4).

Basically, the TYPE 1 complementarity discounts both variable and fixed costs and may do so such that the added mandate is of no added cost (or just a marginal additional cost) to the providing firm. With regard to the TYPE 2 complementarity, the shared market infrastructure may be of double benefit to the providing firm being neither a fixed cost nor for that matter a sunk cost. Indeed, financial services firms may choose London precisely because the infrastructure costs of market execution are already provided and any liability for future costs are borne by third-party institutions. However, the fact that an emerging markets product is actually a product comprised of a set of closely associated products means that the product provider may be able to offer those services from the same set of services offered to other consumers of related products (TYPE 3). It may be able to offer a bundle of associated products at competitive prices relying upon the existing complementaries within the firm or between the firm and its partners (TYPE 1). Of course, if the customer requires some special associated product or service (perhaps related to local regulatory requirements), the diversity and scope of London is such that the product provider can act as a third-party broker sharing its mandate with a firm providing the needed speciality services (TYPE 4).

It would be misleading to imply or suggest that complementarities are so easily resolved in favour of the firm and the customer. For providers, realising the cost advantages of complementarities is an issue of organization (the nature and scope of the firm) and an issue of management (the implementation of desired goals).[13] Both are topics of enormous complexity and significance for the theory and practice of corporate governance. Indeed, as noted above, they reflect a continuing debate about the relative performance of whole systems of national corporate structure and finance. So, for example, whereas the Anglo-American systems combine firms with markets for financial products and services, the German and Japanese systems have tended to internalize the provision of financial products and services within long-term relationships between overlapping institutions (Allen and Gale 2000). Given the global and European financial and capital market integration, the relative performance of rather different mechanisms of organization and management has come into play. Indeed, the move of our Swiss pension fund to London for an emerging-markets product could be interpreted as a move between national systems for financial advantage.

Here, there are two crucial issues. First, the growth of the bulge-bracket financial firms and, second, their functional and spatial concentration in the London real estate market. Like Coase (1988), Richardson (1990: 73) contended that the boundaries of an individual firm are 'in any case, to some extent arbitrary'. This initial point of departure provided Richardson with a rationale for identifying and accounting for the existence of functional complementarities whatever the boundaries of firms. In recent years however, it could be argued that the financial industry has decided that TYPE 1 and TYPE 3 complementarities can be best achieved by increasing the size and scope of firms. This does not mean that the only successful firm need be a large or super-large firm. There is widespread debate about the costs and benefits of mergers and acquisitions in the finance industry (Berger *et al.* 1999). And it is not clear that the strong incentives for senior managers in orchestrating such mergers are realized in the flow of income or in cost savings as represented by extra profits for shareholders. Partnerships and other forms of corporate structure remain important amongst the smaller firms in the Anglo-American finance industry.

As firms have grown larger, as they have brought together complementary functions and products, and as they have sought to integrate marketing and client relationships across related products and markets, they have sought modes of organization that allow and even enhance internal flexibility. One expression of this process of internal coordination and consolidation has been the development of product groups like global fixed income, global equities, advanced derivative products, debt markets and products, etc. Here, the organizational logic has been the integration of overlapping areas and functions across markets and around the world, rather than the continued segmentation of products and markets around star-led personal fiefdoms. Indeed, a related element in this organizational structure has been the creation of hierarchies and management structures aimed at greater internal accountability whatever the location or product. So, for example, the head of global equities may be located in London, drawing together teams of employees based on related products and services from around the world internal to the firm. The management process is daily, weekly, and monthly, and the spatial scope global. This kind of integration has allowed the largest firms the opportunity to discount personality in favour of proclaimed management competence.

It is also apparent that the internalization of complementarities has prompted spatial consolidation. Whereas the old city of London was characterized by networks of similarly located smaller firms, the new model of firm organization and management is one based upon the huge office towers of many thousands of employees. Canary Wharf is a remarkable expression of the search for management solutions to the problem of functional integration. It is not uncommon, amongst the bulge-bracket firms, to bring together on one site 8000 or 10 000 employees co-locating not for interfirm face-to-face synergies (the mantra of the city of London model) but for intra-firm management coherence. In this world, it appears that neither the city of London nor other European markets have the real estate and related infrastructure necessary to sustain such large units of production. In a tangible way, the one-site economies of scale associated with fordist assembly line manufacturing plants have been replicated in the enormous buildings of financial institutions. This is an Anglo-American phenomenon, increasingly mimicked by foreign investment groups locating in London, whether French, German, or Japanese.

LONDON IN EUROPE AND BEYOND

The analysis in previous sections brought together a variety of forces that have contributed to the growth of London in the global economy. By structuring the argument in this way, we have constructed piece-by-piece an economic and geographical logic that explains London's dominance of European financial industries. But the analysis is select-ive: we take from history those forces that have made the success of London seemingly inevitable. For example, on the issue of market size, the history of London as the centre of Empire and trade for more than two centuries suggests that this is an important variable for some, perhaps the most compelling variable (see Bindemann 1999). Likewise, the particular nature of Anglo-American financial regulatory regimes combined with the beneficial consequences of market liberalization in the 1980s can be invoked to 'explain' the contemporary dominance of London over continental European traditions. In effect, path dependence provides the rationale for scale economies and the nature of financial products provides the rationale for agglomeration economies. When these elements are combined with industry competition and corporate strategy, London seems to be the natural place to locate.

However, I am uneasy about this logic on a couple of counts. Implied is an argument of necessity: that history and geography together drive processes of industry competition and corporate strategy. This is a form of structural determinism wherein the agency of firms and competitors depends upon these determining background conditions. Whether this is true or not is actually an empirical question rather than an unassailable fact of life. For example, the large bulge-bracket financial institutions that dominate London have come to London in a very deliberate fashion. Given their financial resources, they have the capacity to choose other locations. For them, history and geography are strategic variables rather than preordained circumstances to which they can only respond. Furthermore, given the enormous flows of revenue through these companies they have significant mobility potential—any investment in a London location could be easily discounted against the flow of future revenue. Sunk costs are rarely a constraint on restructuring; compared to manufacturing enterprises, capital and infrastructure investments are far less significant than the costs of labour. The past is not necessarily the future.

To illustrate, consider the following four disadvantages of London compared to Frankfurt and Paris. *Transport networks*: grid-lock dominates the everyday life of finance industry executives and their employees. London airports are overwhelmed with traffic, the radial road network linking Heathrow in the west with Canary Wharf in the east comes to a standstill during peak hours, and the underground rail system is archaic and subject to widespread disruption. *Canary Wharf*: not withstanding its importance for the bulge-bracket financial institutions, its location on the eastern border of the commercial heart of London makes it an isolated location relative to the residential preferences of employees and domestic corporate headquarters. In fact, accessibility to local finance markets and institutions is obviously not that much better than accessibility to European and international finance markets. *Labour markets*: over the past decade, the UK economy has grown rapidly and employment rates have surged (particularly in the south-east of England). Full employment characterizes the south-east, driving wages and salaries even at the bottom end of skill and occupation. More significantly, interfirm rivalry for the most able finance executives makes London a very expensive location. *Capital markets*: the available evidence suggests that European capital markets are more cost-efficient trading platforms than the London markets. The electronic infrastructures of European markets are more advanced and accessible to securities traders from around the world.

All four issues directly or indirectly affect the costs of producing financial products and services in London relative to Frankfurt and Paris. Whereas we have emphasized the benefits of agglomeration and scale economies accruing to firms located in London, we could also emphasize the costs of agglomeration and the non-economies of scale. Likewise, we could also emphasize the potential significance of electronic transaction and trading systems for the decentralization of the global finance industry. Many products, especially equity and bond products, are easily sold and executed from remote locations or at least other European locations (witness Luxembourg). Distributed electronic networks could replace many of the centralized London-based functions of global financial institutions. Indeed, the development of advanced electronic trading platforms in Frankfurt and Paris has been driven, in part, by very strong Franco-German economic and political interests aimed at discounting the influence of the London and New York financial markets. The advantages of history and geography may be limited to a certain point in time and space.[14]

We should assume that the benefits of a London location (*in situ* scale economies and complementarities) are contingent rather than set in bricks and mortar forever. Even so, I want to suggest that London's capital switching functions will remain important for European financial and pension institutions and may even increase in importance overtime. This is most obvious, at present, in relation to the flow of capital from Europe to the rest of the world (especially the United States of America) and is reflected in the short-term trade in currencies, hedging, and derivatives. Much has been written about the interaction between capital flows, currency exchange rates, and speculation. It is sufficient to observe that the arbitrage process is an industry in its own right. Perhaps less obviously London's switching functions are also vital for those institutions concerned to place European assets in long-term non-European investments, thereby seeking higher rates of return than that which can be achieved in European economies and markets. In doing so, one goal is to 'cover' long-term European pension liabilities with diversified portfolios of industries, regions, and demographies. It is hoped that European institutions will reap stable but higher rates of return so as to make up the difference in slow rates of European economic growth (see Chapter 8). Dutch pension fund institutions have clearly taken advantage of these opportunities (Chapter 6). At the same time, this issue is also important for other larger economies such as France and Germany (Chapters 3, 4, and 5).

I would argue that for European institutions seeking to use market mechanisms to spread demographic and funding risks and to more effectively invest and manage pension assets and liabilities, the London market has two basic virtues. In the first instance, the London market brings together in one place great diversity of market participants and, consequently, great diversity of risk preferences and profiles. The combination of diverse risk profiles and the depth of liquidity apparent in the London market is remarkable (but not without significant competition). Even in the most severe of crises like the recent Asian meltdown (1997), the shocks occasioned by Latin American threats of default, the aftermath of the TMT bubble, and the World Trade Center tragedy, the London market has remained deep enough to accommodate those wishing to buy and those wishing to sell country-specific risks. Being at the centre of capital switching between Asia, Europe, and North America, London remains an essential point of reference in the global economy. Inevitably, as global financial regulatory regimes have sought to smooth interjurisdictional barriers to capital flow, these initiatives have London as a crucial reference point. In this respect, whereas electronic communication networks represent a threat to London, the same networks may simply ease the flow of capital and transactions into and out of London (or a place just like London with its particular location in time and space).

Even so, market diversity and liquidity could be 'electronic' and geographically distributed rather than concentrated in London. However, an essential 'localizing' factor is the talent pool of the London financial industry—something that dominates European markets. This is a complex issue, as we have seen partly driven by the range of financial products and services produced in London as well as the complementarities that draw together the needed diverse sets of skills and expertise. But notice how important the existing talent pool may be in the future: product innovation, the design and execution of products consistent with a wide variety of market players, and the ability to capitalize on complementarities and scale economies all demand highly talented individuals. In this respect, as London has become a vital resource for firms it is also an important income and employment opportunity for talented workers. By contrast, Frankfurt and Paris are not nearly as attractive for talented labour concerned to maximize income and long-term wealth. Whereas the bulge-bracket financial institutions are alarmed at the cost implications of recurrent tournaments for labour, their response has been to increase capital investment and the automation of routine low-skilled functions. It is plausible that these same institutions will use advanced electronic communications to decentralize to Europe the production of routine services. Even so, the competitiveness of financial centres is based less on the costs of routine production and more on the attraction and retention of talent (as in other knowledge-intensive industries; see Florida 2002 and Teece 2000).

The collection of financial capital, the pooling and distribution of risk, and the management of investment are basic functions of any capital market. Historically, in many European countries these functions have been provided internally to partners in overlapping and commonly shared untraded relationships. As we have seen, these relationships are often highly localized and regionalized. The risks of such relationships are also highly localized; witness the research on German capital markets (Clark and Wójcik 2002; Wójcik 2001b). If London is to be geographically spread through Europe, its capital switching and risk pooling functions must be bundled in hyperspace rather than geographical space. The challenge is to build a system of markets that can sustain these functions while avoiding the concentration of risks and the diminution of liquidity and talent inherent in local markets.

CONCLUSIONS

Many studies of the recent history of the city of London document its transformation from a club-like industrial district to a massive conglomeration of one stop financial 'supermarkets' providing diverse products and services. In doing so, studies such as David Kynaston's (2001) bring together the crisis of the early 1980s and the big bang of financial deregulation in 1986 with the demise of indigenous financial institutions. Mergers and acquisitions by the US and other international financial groups have profoundly altered the London financial industry. Being no longer just the city, being the whole region and beyond it is an essential site of production in the international finance industry.

For some, there is genuine regret for the passing of an era. The networks of personal contacts, the emphasis upon custom and convention, and the neighbourly interchange of personalities and institutions has given way to the routine compensation and employment practices of bulge-bracket global financial corporations.[15] In some quarters, but by no means in David Kynaston's book, there is lament for the demise of the city as a national icon. The take over of city institutions has been interpreted as a rejection of national institutions and their leaders. Thus, the rise of London out of the old city can be traced back to the apparent complacency and amateur status of many old city institutions. The city has been replaced by an industry whose 'identity' is self-consciously cosmopolitan, corporate, and international. By contrast, being a British institution the city employed Londoners from the east- and west-end of the city-region but sought to exclude those who did not 'fit in'. My argument in this chapter is that understanding London in the world of finance requires understanding it as an industry, and all that implies in terms of products and services.

In doing so, we have relied heavily on two sets of arguments one having to do with the nature of markets served by London and the other having to do with the complementarities inherent in the provision of financial products and services. On the markets side of the equation, I have argued that scale economies combined with a distinctive regulatory heritage has provided London significant advantages as a central location for the provision of financial analysis services in Europe and around the world. This analysis will be familiar to those economic geographers schooled in the Hotelling-type models of location as well as those familiar with notions of product range and threshold (see for example Berry 1967). As for complementarities, the analysis also provides a production-oriented view of the overlapping and related nature of financial products. Once we recognize the nature and scope of complementarities, we must also recognize the unique interaction between markets and the scope of products produced in London. This much is recognized by the bulge-bracket financial firms that have chosen London as a centre of production. So significant has been this choice of location that the conglomeration of these firms and the centralization of functions within the vast buildings have recreated in concrete an image of the past: factories for the production of financial services and products.

It could be argued, moreover, that whatever the economies of scale and the agglomeration effects of complementarity, London is a necessary feature of the global economy. The global economy requires a centre that brings together diverse risk profiles just as the global economy requires a switching point between Asia, and Europe and North America. In this respect, London is a vital point in time and space for the global financial institutions that manage on a 24-hour basis the flows of capital and transactions around the world. Put slightly differently, if London did not exist its place (in time and space) would have to be invented by the bulge-bracket financial service firms concerned with managing the global risk profiles of their customers and their own accounts. It is no accident that London sits virtually on top of the Greenwich Mean Time, the central reference point for calibrating time and space according to a common and accepted metric around the globe.[16] For financial houses, London's place in time provides them a virtually unique place from which to actively integrate and strategically manage their daily trading books from Tokyo (in the east) to San Francisco (in the west) on any day. Frankfurt and Paris could provide the same geographical function. But they could not match London's market diversity and liquidity or London's depth of talent.

One remarkable aspect of the contemporary debate about London in relation to Europe is the sense in which the national anxieties that accompanied the demise of the old city are being replayed in the leading financial and political centres of Europe. Attempts to develop and protect national financial institutions as competitors with the Anglo-Americans reflect similar UK attitudes of the 1980s. Attempts to fashion EU rules and regulations that can accommodate the competence of Anglo-American financial groups with continental European banking and insurance houses seems, similarly, to be ways of shoring up those houses against the competition. Whether these attempts will be any more successful than the UK last ditch efforts at maintaining the national identity of finance seems doubtful. At the same time, the success of London as an international centre is a profound threat to the international ambitions of Frankfurt and Paris. Indeed, Frankfurt and Paris may be vital cogs in the wheel for mobilizing pension assets and liabilities for trade and transaction through London. By this logic, London never replaces Frankfurt and Paris but uses those centres to organize the continental flow of funds into the world.

NOTES

1. This chapter was written over the summer and fall of 2001. Along the way, the human tragedy apparent in the attack on the World Trade Center in New York caused me to

reflect long and hard on the symbolic character of finance capital. Speculation abounds about the long-term effects of the attack for New York in relation to London (and vice versa). See Martin Dickson in the *Financial Times* (23rd September, 2001: 17) who noted that London is 'now a hub and its own right and should escape the worst. Many of its high value-added functions can only be done with a presence on the ground. And the attack on the World Trade Center has cruelly underscored that there are benefits to geographical diversification'.

2. Compare the comments of Duisenberg (2001) on the supposed hyper-reality of finance with the more careful assessment provided by the Bank of International Settlements (2001: 4–5).

3. Important historical treatments of the topic include the following. Braudel's (1992) assessment of the role and significance of city-states and global finance is very instructive, as is Ferguson's (2001) broad assessment of the interaction between politics and money. The most important source on the city of London is, of course, David Kynaston's multi-volume historical study. The most recent instalment concerns the city of London over the period 1970–2000 (Kynaston 2001). There are many other relevant sources.

4. Recent work on financial centres and the global economy include Houthakker and Williamson (1996) (on economic treatment of the theory and structure of financial markets including reference to 'central trading places') and Warf (2000) (a geographical analysis of the role of the status of Wall Street and New York). Leyshon and Thrift (1997) provide a broad-ranging assessment of the topics relating to the emerging field of financial geography.

5. See the argument of Richardson (1990: 89–90) to the effect that economies of scale are a function of the size of the market, and the rate of growth of the market. He also suggests that economies of scale are factored into short-term decision-making more than long-term decision-making because the latter requires an assessment of, and provision for, the durability of capital as well as the volume of the expected output.

6. Very simply, agglomeration economies can be seen as those benefits that accrue to firms located in the same jurisdiction. In part, they can co-joint location to 'exchange information by face-to-face communications and reduce various kinds of transaction costs between firms' (Tabuchi 1998: 333).

7. This chapter could be seen as yet another attack upon the 'end of geography' thesis. And so it is. We should also recognize that the stickiness of time and space has become a vital ingredient in theorizing the management of institutions as well as theorizing macro-economic integration and stability. See Diamond (1994) for an especially intriguing combination of economics and geography relevant to these issues. Note, however, that there remains a residual belief that the stock markets are different from the neighbourhood commodity markets.

8. There is surprisingly little academic research on the determinants of the prices of financial products. Much of the research takes as given the production process and is concerned with the price efficiency (or otherwise) of financial markets. See, for example, Houthakker and Williamson (1996). Here, I merely assert that the price of a financial product is so determined (based upon my industry interviews).

9. Here, the emerging markets equity products are emphasized because they are so significant for many of the UK and European pension institutions as a means of spreading investments into the global economy outside of the United States of America. This does not mean that the proportion of assets allocated to such investments need be large compared to the apparent 'home bias' and 'asset bias' (which varies also by countries) of these institutions. See, for example, treatment of these issues in Davis (1995) and Clark (2000).

10. While the term 'complimentary' is used to describe the overlaps or interdependence between products and services, I could have invoked the concept of 'scope'. Perhaps

this is more conventional; see Viscusi *et al.* (1995: ch. 11) for more details including reference to original treatments of economies of scope. Even so, Richardson's treatment is more extensive and intriguing.

11. Important complementary financial services include legal services of all kinds. There is considerable evidence supporting the proposition that the US law firms specializing in securities, mergers, and acquisitions, and the market for corporate control in general have come to London to take advantage of its place in relation to Europe. At the same time, the UK law firms have become global, linking Europe through London to the United States of America and beyond. The most significant recent project devoted to the globalization of legal services (bearing upon the finance industry) is that of Beaverstock, Taylor, and Smith (1999) and Beaverstock, Smith, and Taylor (2000).

12. It is also important to acknowledge that emerging markets equity products are very sensitive indeed to the expertise of active investment managers, the flow of information, and its qualitative assessment. As is well appreciated in the industry, these types of products remain the terrain of knowledgeable experts even if passive index products are increasingly dominant in the UK and US investment management community. On the consequences of information for the expertise needed to manage investment products across the world see Clark and O'Connor (1997).

13. For consumers, the existence of complementarities between products may simultaneously offer costs-saving synergies *and* impede the switching of consumption between rival providers. On the consequences of significant switching costs for corporate strategy and price competition see the seminal contribution by Klemperer (1987). At the limit, complementarities combined with significant switching costs may 'trap' consumers within multi-functional firms—the proclaimed difference between financial systems based on markets and those based upon intermediaries may evaporate into a common function but 'different' institutions.

14. See for more details, the study by Schulte and Violi (2001) on the rapidly changing nature and structure of the European Euro-bond futures markets. Whereas just four years ago the London LIFFE market and the EUREX market shared such trading between them, by 2002 the EUREX dominated LIFFE. While a specific instance, rather than a comprehensive pattern across all related products, it is an indication of the powerful forces driving market rivalries and the interest in market consolidation across Europe.

15. The imposition of management systems on 'local' financial firms in London through mergers and acquisitions (and other imperatives) resonates with history. See, for example, Chandler (1977: 415–16) on the early twentieth-century managerial revolution in the US manufacturing enterprises. Therein, he notes that mergers between firms prompted 'top managers' to institute systematic and 'uniform accounting and statistical controls. In hiring and allocating managerial personnel they began to think more systematically about evaluating managerial performance'. The recent history of bulge-bracket firms in the finance industry could be so written.

16. There have been a number of studies published on the creation of Standard Time, drawing together the imperatives of the industrial revolution and its rail transport systems with the need to make systematic according to a common metric the often arbitrary but minor differences in time between places (running east to west). For a US perspective on this issue, emphasizing the role of the railways see Bartky (2000). For a Canadian perspective, referencing an individual and international political economy (among its many other issues) see Blaise (2000). And for a more scholarly and interpretive perspective linking Einstein with almost everything else see Galison (2000).

8

Epilogue: Pension Futures

For those concerned about the future of the European social security systems, global finance appears particularly threatening. It seems as if financial markets have systematically discounted the European national institutions of social income and welfare. Figuratively and symbolically, London and New York are the enemies of social solidarity and continental European political traditions. This is a common refrain of the left-of-centre and right-of-centre political parties, though for different reasons. It is also a complaint of the European governments albeit masked by arguments over the straightjacket imposed by the Stability and Growth Pact. More abstractly, claims made for the nation-state as the proper locus of social justice and welfare are thought to be undercut by the financial processes operating across the world, and through time in ways that are inconsistent with national ideals (compare with Miller 2000). The world is increasingly at odds with tradition even if these traditions are less ancient than presumed and even if those traditions carry with them significant costs set against the past benefits of economic growth and development.

On the other side stand the institutions of global finance. Here, ignorance vies with impatience and resignation as the dominant impulses driving claims that continental Europe is neither sensitive nor responsive to the interests of the future generations of workers and retirees. It is commonplace to suggest that continental Europe is held in a time warp, its future shrouded in a dense fog of inherited relationships. It is a story amenable to exaggeration and to theoretical speculation; witness the applicability of Mancur Olson's (1982) treatise on the rise and decline of nation-states. Ignorance provides financial institutions a convenient cover; it allows the advocates of neo-liberal solutions to the looming European pension liabilities a means of ignoring those who would protect social justice and equitable income distribution. Impatience provides financial institutions a weapon when lobbying of continental governments for 'reform'. Markets will not wait for compromise and negotiation, just as markets will not wait for historians to judge the success or failure of the Euro. And yet, lurking behind the impatience is resignation: a realization amongst some that neo-liberal reforms aimed at promoting private pension arrangements will only succeed if grafted on the skeleton of social solidarity.

In this chapter, I amplify these issues bringing together the threads and themes that have been developed through the book. In doing so my goal is to summarize while opening-up the issues yet to be resolved, rather than prosecute an entirely new argument. So what have we learnt through the project? What do the debates surveyed and the experience of nation-states assessed reveal about the relationship between the European pensions and global finance? To answer these questions requires, in the first instance, a restatement of the lessons learned in each chapter. This is the backdrop for speculation about the evolving relationship between the European pensions and global finance. Whereas much of the debate about the European pensions sets global finance against inherited traditions, there are reasons to suppose that the continental European retirement systems may come to rely upon global finance to sustain social justice. If so, this would be a remarkable change in political sentiments and economic expectations. To imagine that global markets rather than nation-states are now the means of insuring national welfare implies a world thoroughly permeated by finance capital. In this sense, my argument is less conclusive than it is a means of looking forward. No one can be definitive, given the flux of current circumstances and possible events (not least of which is the current and future performance of the Euro).

FINDINGS (CHAPTER BY CHAPTER)

In this section, threads and themes of argument are brought together through a series of findings and related observations. For convenience, these are developed chapter-by-chapter providing a reference point for statements about the tensions between continental Europe and the centres of global finance. So as to remind the reader of their place in the book, findings are enumerated by chapter and according to their place in each chapter. Let us begin with Chapter 1 and its two principal findings.

1.1 The European nation-state is an increasingly fragile entity, under-cut by the reemerging crosscurrents of internal diversity, identity politics, and regionalism (within and between nation-states). This is surely recognized in many works on the welfare state, and is reflected in the changing emphasis of Esping-Andersen's (1990, 1999; Esping-Andersen *et al.* 2001) project. At issue, then, is the locus of social solidarity. For so many years we have assumed it to be co-terminal with the borders of nations. But the reforms of European social security systems are increasingly focused upon the options for individuals and for employer and related affinity groups. Their territorial loyalties may be more or less than the nation (see generally Swyngedouw 2000).

1.2 Likewise, the ideal of a national fiscal sovereignty sounds increas-ingly hollow. The Maastricht Treaty and the Stability and Growth Pact have together imposed limits on the national budgets and expenditures. To spend more on social security now and in the future will require significantly increasing the long-term rate of real economic growth and the flow of revenue to the state and/or shifting budget allocations between competing public goals and organized interests. The mantra of 'sound money' is both an economic goal of the EU and an inexorable political imperative driving the pension reform process in nation-states.

2.1 Demographic trends amongst European nations are viewed by many as alarming with respect to the financial integrity of the nation-state PAYG social security systems. Over the last ten years this issue has come to occupy the very centre of the national and EU policy making, even if the national policy makers attributed initial concerns to the hostile neo-liberal think tanks and the like (e.g. the OECD). In response, however, 'reform' has been more often than not parametric rather than structural, discounting the value of future benefits while slowly removing the incentives for early retirement. Feldstein's (2002) neo-liberal manifesto based on the Anglo-American model is a significant challenge but remains at the margins of debate.[1]

2.2 Higher rates of economic growth (compared to long-term averages) are essential (but not sufficient) if the current and future funding of the PAYG social security is to be maintained with respect to the promised value of retirement benefits (Visco 2001). But the increased rates of growth are, in part, a function of the capital market efficiency, labour productivity, and technical innovation. Therefore 'pension reform' is not just a matter of managing social welfare costs and benefits; it may be also a matter of restructuring the whole economic organization of European nations and the EU at large. For one, Deutschland AG may have to be transformed in a manner consistent with the Anglo-American capital markets if they are to be the willing servants of future retirees' welfare.

3.1 Not withstanding claims to the contrary, the French PAYG social security system will not deliver promised retirement benefits. This is widely recognized amongst French citizens (as it is recognized by many people with respect to their own national pension systems across the EU; see Boeri *et al.* 2001b). Making-up the difference is a crucial issue dominating French politics (Palier 2002). Whereas the institutions of social security have been sites of representation for the social partners, employer groups and industry interests increasingly dispute their role in social security. These groups are committed to private insurance and savings plans as the means of augmenting social security. French citizens are increasingly important consumers of retirement-oriented financial products.

3.2 It seems that some form of pre-funding of the forecast PAYG liabilities will be introduced. By doing so, some policy makers seek higher rates of return than that provided by the current and forecast rates of economic growth. For other policy makers, pre-funding may enhance economy-wide saving in new kinds of financial institutions thereby adding to the available stock of capital for domestic investment in new industries and regional clusters of innovation. In this respect, the Anglo-American world represents both a model of endogenous growth worthy of emulation and a possible destination of European investment capital.

4.1 If the PAYG social security is problematic, what of the role and status of supplementary pensions? In Germany, of course, large manufacturing firms have provided DB or final salary pension benefits for many years. Utilizing book reserve and *pensionskassen* systems of pension financial accounting, most firms have systematically underfunded their liabilities (when compared to similar types of commitments amongst the Anglo-American competitors). Globalization has, however, raised important questions about the financial propriety of such practices, especially with the introduction of the Anglo-American and international accounting rules amongst the largest German firms.

4.2 The adoption of such financial rules can be explained by virtue of the cost advantages of global financial markets as well as the informational needs of those markets. Another explanation of the adoption of these rules could be the advantages due to the corporate management of dispersed ownership (compared to the German practice of closely-held cross-holdings between related firms). There is evidence that the German model is changing quickly, with the market for corporate control assuming increasing importance for managers and shareholders alike (Wójcik 2002). The consequences for book reserve pension systems are all too obvious: they represent an unacceptable financial burden on the estimated value of large German firms.

5.1 The new Riester-style tax-preferred private pension arrangements may not grow in importance over the coming years. As major corporations restructure their supplementary pension systems according to global financial imperatives, social solidarity may be redrawn in favour of firms, unions, and affinity groups. While Riester initiatives open the way for greater decentralization in retirement income planning, national social insurance will remain a core component of retirement income albeit slowly discounted in value in favour of private arrangements. Also implied is a rather different model of German society, one that is less inclusive and more fragmented than hitherto presumed.[2]

5.2 On the other hand, the interest of German corporate managers in reaping the benefits of global financial markets implies a realignment of intra-firm alliances and loyalties. Whereas management and labour were arguably closely aligned with respect to the distribution of current income, the managers and shareholders may be closely aligned in the future as the traded value of the firm comes to dominate corporate decision-making. In this respect, the investment and management of supplementary pension systems is increasingly influenced by the norms and conventions of Anglo-American practice rather than the consensus-seeking practices of the past. Global markets beckon.

6.1 If the German model and its attendant social insurance and supplementary pension systems are changing, one alternative is the Dutch model of corporate governance and co-determination.

For the Dutch, state social security is closely allied with employer-sponsored and funded second pillar private pensions, being a mixture of income streams that provide equitable retirement income benefits. Underpinning the Dutch model, of course, is a system of joint decision-making linking the workplace with financial institutions and financial markets. The high rates of income replacement combined with continental expectations about co-determination have encouraged the development of a distinctive European version of Anglo-American pension fund capitalism (Clark 2000).

6.2 At another level, the Dutch model has become closely attuned to the global market for financial services. Pension investment regimes, management practices and reporting systems have come to match and mimic the Anglo-American practices. As the Dutch government introduced legislation designed to ensure the cost efficiency of pension provision, market imperatives have come to discipline the decision-making of jointly-trusteed pension institutions. In these ways, Dutch pensions are both social and financial institutions drawing from and responding to global financial markets.

7.1 If access to the global financial markets is one solution to the demographic ageing and pensions funding crisis, it is plain that London looms large as an entrée to those markets. It is more than just a trading platform. Indeed, the development of a pan-European electronic trading network would do little to diminish its significance as the world's most important site for the production of international financial services. For Europe, London is the gateway to the global economy and the possibility of augmenting state-sponsored social security with the benefits of finance capital. Also, one crucial aspect of London in relation to Europe is the diversity of its financial services and the depth of talent associated with the provision of those services. Another crucial element in this respect, however, is the extent to which London's place in Europe is the object of national and EU rivalry.

7.2 In this respect, global finance is neither ubiquitous nor undifferentiated place-by-place. It represents the accumulated expertise and financial resources of the Anglo-American capitalism and the world that it has made in its image (Clowes 2000). The challenge for the twenty-first century is to manage global finance on behalf of the interests and needs of nations' citizens—if national solutions to retirement income are to be sustained, global finance must be the servant of national aspirations rather than the weapon used by financial institutions to overturn the past. Informed analysts of global finance such as Soros (2002) and Stiglitz (2002) have serious concerns about the consequences of unregulated global financial markets for the economic and social vitality of many nations outside the 'Washington consensus'.

MODELS OF ECONOMIC GROWTH

One of the lessons of the project is the fragility of the PAYG social security. If a nation's population grows faster than its replacement rate, and if a nation can attract new younger residents with beneficial fertility and birth rates then the PAYG systems appear unproblematic. But as we have seen, the PAYG social security is very sensitive to the demographic balance between generations, current and future rates of employment, and the integrity of social security institutions. This is true of continental Europe, just as it is true of the Anglo-American world (witness the debate over 'reform' of the US social security; see Aaron and Shoven 1999; Munnell 2002). If society must cope with a demographic mismatch between generations, suppressed rates of employment and labour force participation, and 'leakage' of social security reserves from their intended purpose, social solidarity may be just an empty promise (as suggested years ago by Keyfitz 1976 who derided the moral virtues of the PAYG social security).

At any point in time, the cost of social security to a society is the product of two ratios: the benefit to total income ratio and the dependent to active population ratio (as defined in Gillion *et al.* 2000 and illustrated in Chapter 2). Here, I focus on the second ratio before returning to the issue of an equitable and just income policy. As we have seen in the chapter devoted to France, the dependent/active ratio is significantly affected by:

- the volume and relative significance of early retirement,
- the rate of unemployment,
- the rates of labour force participation, notably amongst women, and
- the net out-migration of the employable.

All four elements affecting the ratio of active to total population are themselves a function of the current macroeconomic conditions, particularly the volume of domestic consumption and investment. Given the increasing significance of the European and global markets, these factors are also a function of local and global industrial competitiveness. Over the short term, nation-state economic policy makers may be fortunate or skilled enough to beneficially affect the rate of unemployment (and the other three factors) thereby decreasing the current cost of social security to society. During the last years of the 1990s, the performance of the French economy combined with the positive consequences of the 35-hour week provided a brief respite from the political and economic exigencies of funding social security.

We noted, however, that the EMU and the Stability and Growth Pact have proscribed the fiscal and monetary sovereignty of European nation-states. Consequently, the domestic macroeconomic policy options are fewer and limited in scope. Given the fixed macroeconomic parameters, short-term domestic growth prospects are increasingly reliant upon the relative efficiency of firms and industries in adapting to global competition. By necessity, their adjustment potential is a function of the capital and labour market flexibility. Microeconomics rather than macroeconomics are arguably the crucial driving forces behind the short-term dependency ratio. Over the long term, however, all four factors are determined by the rate of accumulation of national income and the path of national economic development (amongst other factors some of which are surely social and cultural). Furthermore, it is clear that demography (the rate of growth of the domestic population) is an endogenous element of any long-term process of accumulation. French government pessimism about national demographic prospects during the 1930s was overturned by a combination of positive population policy and unanticipated post-war economic growth. I am not convinced that the forecast adverse dependency ratios are inevitable; there is a role for pro-population growth strategies. But any pro-population growth strategy would take years to make a difference and could not be *the* solution.

As for the prospects for microeconomic efficiency-oriented policies, this option may be possible only over the long term. Micro-economic reform has proved to be slow, politically contested, and limited in scope in many continental countries. Even so, microeconomic reform is necessary for long-term growth, just as long-term growth is necessary for employment growth, keeping older people in work, and for increasing the flow of national income. Much has been written about micro-economic reform, its proper logic as well as its European prospects and possibilities. It is the staple diet of think tanks and multi-lateral institutions like the OECD, the IMF, and the World Bank. It is also an essential ingredient in EC commentaries on member states' economic performance and macroeconomic stability. Not surprisingly, greater urgency has been attributed to needed reforms. But we should resist the temptation to imagine that it is the only or the single best solution. Just as the wholesale transformation of European retirement systems to individual retirement accounts linked to securities' markets seems implausible, to imagine that European capital and labour markets will become just like their Anglo-American cousins ignores the real world of social solidarity and the commitment to others' welfare.

There can be no 'solution' to the European demographic ageing and pensions funding crisis without a strong commitment to increasing the long-term real rate of economic growth by perhaps as much as another 1.0 per cent (up to about 3.0 per cent per annum, matching the expected long-term US rate of real economic growth; Jorgenson 2001; Jorgenson and Stiroh 2000). Otherwise, European living standards within and between generations and compared across the developed world must decline in relative terms. Here, though, the issue is at once simple but extraordinary in scope: what model of economic growth could achieve such a result? To my mind there are three important options more or less related but nonetheless with distinct consequences for Europe and its nation-states.

If we take seriously the recent Anglo-American experience, one obvious model is less national and comprehensive in scope than it is regional and highly differentiated in effect. Referencing Silicon Valley, Rt128/495 Boston, and Oxford and Cambridge, this option is one of concentrated growth and development based upon the local clusters of innovation and technology. Its external impacts and linkages may enhance national growth, but may also leapfrog host nations to other corporate entities and regions spread around the world. As we noted in Chapter 2, this model of accumulation relies upon the intellectual capital and systems of reward that are personal rather than social, local rather than national, and wealth- rather than income-oriented (see more generally Teece 2000). While it may be fashionable to dismiss this model in the light of the TMT boom, bubble, and bust, it represents a model of the knowledge economy that is the antithesis of national social solidarity and equitable income distribution. As implied by the Lisbon Declaration, it requires new forms and institutions of financial capital as well as a culture of risk and reward. But it is also a distinct social order that would localize the benefits of growth without necessarily making a substantial difference to national employment growth, labour force participation rates, and the flow of income to national social security reserves.

Another model of long-term economic growth is the national champions model: pan-European and industry-dominant corporations that owe their place in the world to the sponsorship of their nation-states (and the sharing-out of industry-dominant claims between member states of the EU). One can then imagine a certain industrial topography across Europe, combining centres of industry with spatially elongated networks of suppliers and consumers. This model is one that has strong claims in theory (witness the logic of the 'new' economic geography associated with Krugman 1991 and others), and in practice (witness the quiet but persistent efforts of nation-states to build national champions). It is a model that is at once national and European, and it is a model of economic growth that may be resistant to the corrosive forces of globalization. But it is also a model of economic growth that locates social solidarity with the performance of firms rather than nations. As such, the rewards for those within corporate champions may be significant but distinguished from those that flow to the rest of society by privilege rather than equity. As a model of wealth creation, it is more akin to the early twentieth-century monopoly capitalism (as described by Berle and Means 1933) and late twentieth-century shareholder-capitalism (as espoused by Jensen 1998 and others) than mid- to late twentieth-century continental European corporatism.

Equally plausible is economic growth by territorial expansion: EU-enlargement by any other name. The existing national institutions of social security may be paid for by the rate of return due to the colonization of eastern Europe. Larger markets, greater scope for low-cost and higher labour productivity, and population growth may provide the added growth impulses needed to shift overall accumulation to a higher long-term trajectory. Indeed, whereas the knowledge economy of the 1990s provided the United States of America (and to a lesser extent the United Kingdom) a virtuous circle of employment growth, productivity, and wealth creation, territorial expansion may provide the core economies of western Europe the same advantages without the profound microeconomic reform of their labour and capital markets. It may, nevertheless, come at a cost; namely the move of major EU firms into global capital markets so as to take advantage of lower costs of capital. Can such moves to London and New York remain isolated from the mainstream institutions of nation-states? In my view this model, as with the other models, is entirely plausible and already in motion. But none of these models is a comprehensive solution to the problem of insuring income equity within and between the generations in each EU member state.

Here lies the conundrum: the higher rates of economic growth needed to sustain the inherited institutions of nation-state social security carry with them the prospects for greater levels of inequality between working people. My analysis, in this respect, is not that different than that undertaken by Esping-Andersen and others. In effect, my argument is that the European models of economic growth inherited from the second half of the twentieth century cannot pay for the retirement of the baby boom generation without a significant sacrifice by many of the retired, those working, and those not working. Any plausible model of higher rates of growth promises increased social and economic differentiation. Unresolved at present is the extent to which incremental reform via accommodation to neo-liberal imperatives may be more costly to European society than accelerated structural reform in accordance with the Anglo-American model.

There may be a way out. Europe could become a set of rentier societies based upon the rate of return of financial assets invested in countries with prospective higher rates of real economic and population growth. Could global finance manage what seems impossible whatever the chosen European model of economic growth? Could demographic and economic growth in the rest of the world maintain European income equity within and between the generations? This idea has gained increasing acceptance in theory (Shiller 1995, 1999) and practice (Börsch-Supan 2001). But consider the following.

AN UNBOUNDED WORLD?

The idea that diverse demographic futures apparent in the rest of the world could be or should be opportunities to reap higher long-term returns than those available in Europe over the coming 20–30 years has considerable appeal. If continental Europe can mobilize sufficient capital resources, put in place appropriate governance structures, and efficiently funnel those resources through London into the world economy, it may be possible to maintain the current nation-state retirement systems with a modicum of incremental reform. However, this vision of an ageing continental Europe sustained by the beneficial consequences of growth in other markets presupposes a global economy regulated in a manner consistent with the protection of international capital flows. It would be foolhardy to suggest that this is consistent with contemporary circumstances or likely prospects over the next 5–10 years. The ever-present threat of regional economic and financial crisis feeding in and affecting the core economies of the west is reason enough to be cautious of such grandiose visions. Even so, there is little doubt that much effort has been expended in designing a financial architecture for global stability and growth.

The research by La Porta (1997, 1998) and his colleagues have mapped the co-existence of different legal regimes as they affect finance suggesting that even amongst the developed economies of the world there remain significant institutional barriers to capital market integration. Their work shows, of course, that these legal regimes have deep historical roots stretching back to the European countries' experience of international trade since the Middle-Ages and the industrial revolution through the eighteenth and nineteenth centuries. This is hardly the occasion to rehearse the history of law in relation to the stages of economic development. Not only have a number of countries driven the regulation of finance and capital, a handful of countries have also been reference points for the developing world in their own regulatory systems. La Porta *et al.*'s work also shows that the various legal regimes have quite different implications for the size and scope of the nation-state capital markets just as they have significant implications for the efficiency of those capital markets (compared with one another). It would seem, on the basis of their evidence, that the Anglo-American legal system combined with its finance-related regulatory institutions are more consistent with capital market efficiency than other competing regulatory regimes.

We are back at the point of departure for the entire book: we are at the intersection between the nation-state, its history, and its economic and political practices and the imperatives driving global finance. We are also at that point in the argument where continuity with the past as opposed to convergence upon a dominant or hegemonic model of life threatens the integrity of the nation state. Indeed, amongst many European commentators, there is a sense in which this debate is a debate about Anglo-American imperialism as opposed to the evolving institutions of European nation-states and the EU at large (Clark 2001). Most importantly, those that see virtue in the continental European traditions such as the inclusion of stakeholders, worker representatives, and community interests in corporate and financial decision-making are alarmed at the social costs implied by convergence to the Anglo-American model.[3]

By now, it should be apparent that the evidence produced in this book suggests that continuity with the past is a most unlikely outcome. This does not mean that the European systems of finance and retirement income will somehow suddenly collapse or be rearranged in such a comprehensive fashion that convergence becomes the dominant outcome. Perhaps rather meekly, accommodation seems to be the operative strategy. In effect, nation-states and the EU have sought ways of balancing inherited political constituencies and their interests with those that have a strong interest in succeeding according to the terms and conditions that drive the Anglo-American capital markets. Consequently, negotiation over the matching-up of regulatory regimes has gone through a variety of stages over the past 10–15 years. Whereas, a decade ago mutual recognition was a common negotiation strategy, the co-existence of commonality and difference has not been sustainable. Moves towards harmonization have been one response, thereby rationalizing the nation-state differences according to the collective European interests in enhancing global competitiveness. At the limit, at the level of global capital market integration, there has also been convergence upon the Anglo-American standards of reporting and market integration.

Documenting this process of accommodation and its reflection in and through the European systems of pension and retirement income has been the thread integrating the whole book. Here, however, we need to look beyond Europe to the world at large and in particular the prospects for realizing the potential benefits of diverse global demographic futures—as suggested in the Chapter 7. Most importantly, if one solution to the ageing of Europe's baby boom generation is to be found in the outflow of capital to emerging markets we must ask whether or not this is a realistic prospect given the nature and performance of those countries' capital market, legal, and financial systems. To do so, could be a very large project, indeed, one that should properly occupy another book! So at this juncture I simply want to indicate the apparent contemporary constraints on such a strategy referencing research published by the accounting and management consultants PricewaterhouseCoopers (PwC) (2001). Basically, my conclusion is that the effectiveness of a European global investment strategy is conditional upon making the world safe for global finance!

The PwC conducted interviews with respondents familiar with capital market performance and regulation in 35 countries during the second half of 2000. Following the lead provided by the World Bank (2000), countries were grouped according to income thereby distinguishing between the Upper-income (e.g. Greece), Middle upper-income (e.g. Argentina), Middle lower-income (e.g. Columbia), and Lower-income (e.g. China). The full list of countries surveyed is provided in Table 8.1. At issue was the degree to which individual countries could be characterized with respect to 'clear, accurate, formal, easily discernible, and widely accepted practices in the broad arena where business, finance, and government meet' (PwC 2001, p. 3). In essence, the PwC produced an Opacity Index (OI): a means of directly comparing emerging markets according to their perceived riskiness across a set of five different issues or components that affect capital markets. In doing so, contrasts can be drawn between those countries and so-called reference countries characterized by high levels of transparency including the United States of America and the United Kingdom. The reported OI ranges from the lowest score of 36 (US low opacity) to the highest score of 87 (PR China high opacity).

Scoring countries according to the five components perceived to 'affect the cost and availability of capital' was the basis of the OI. These components included reference to the nature and extent of corruption, the degree to which the legal system predictably protects shareholder rights, the perceived capriciousness of government policy, the degree to which accounting practices and disclosure standards are consistent with the fair valuation of traded firms, and the predictability of regulatory policy. By normalizing responses through the common-scaling of each component, the OI allows for a direct comparison between countries' total scores and between countries' individual component scores. While I do not intend to look closely at each country's component scores, it is worth noting that the cross-correlation between component scores suggests that a high score on the perceived corrupt practices would be matched by similarly high scores on other components including, for example, accounting and corporate governance opacity. It can be contended that 'extreme' scores such as that registered for China imply a level of risk far beyond that experienced by institutional investors in the West. Not only should the rate of return be commensurate with perceived risk, the cost of capital in these countries would be far higher than in countries with much lower opacity scores.

Surely there are other ways of comparing markets according to their risk premia.[4] The academic literature is replete with case-studies of corruption in the context of economic development and foreign direct investment.[5] Furthermore, a number of large, multinational investment firms have specialized in this area recognizing the premium western investors are willing to pay for reliable information and judgement

Table 8.1. The projected population (2030), the Opacity Index (OI) score (2000) and risk premium (RP) value by World Bank income group and selected countires

Country	Population (ml)	OI	RP
Low income	3 439	71	912
China	1 477	87	1 316
India	1 398	64	789
Indonesia	285	75	1 010
Kenya	35	69	848
Pakistan	244	62	674
Lower middle income	512	65	750
Columbia	60	60	632
Ecuador	18	68	826
Egypt	92	58	572
Guatemala	19	65	749
Lithuania	4	58	584
Peru	37	58	584
Romania	20	71	915
Russia	129	84	1 225
South Africa	56	60	612
Thailand	77	67	801
Upper middle income	670	60	684
Argentina	48	61	639
Brazil	224	61	645
Chile	20	36	3
Czech Republic	9	71	899
Hungary	9	50	33
Mexico	141	48	308
Poland	38	64	724
South Korea	53	73	967
Taiwan	—	61	640
Turkey	88	74	982
Uruguay	4	53	452
Venezuela	36	45.7	712
High income	576	45	279
Greece	10	57	55
Hong Kong	—	45	233
Israel	9	53	438
Italy	50	48	312
Japan	117	60	629
Singapore	4	29	0
UK	59	38	63
USA	327	36	0

Notes: Where population estimates are not reported, this reflects the political status of those economies at the United Nations. Figures for the World Bank income groups are total projected populations (2030) and current *average* OI and risk premiums for each group of identified countries.

Sources: World Bank (2000) and PricewaterhouseCoopers (2001).

about the true worth of emerging market investment opportunities. It is clear that many of the portfolio investment strategies of the Anglo-American and European investment managers presuppose the availability of relatively reliable information buttressed by consistent and autonomous capital market regulatory regimes (see generally Clark and Wójcik 2002; Portes and Rey 2001). These practices and presumptions do not easily transfer into and across emerging markets characterized by opacity scores of more than 50 (Hungary) (an arbitrary cut off point). Take for example the case of Argentina (OI score of 61). Not withstanding the financial reforms of the past 10 years, the failure to control government spending combined with the default on international loans has brought forth extreme measures such as the expropriation of private pension and savings assets.[6] While perhaps justified by current circumstances, the implications for European investors are obvious and profound—witness the risk premium of 639 basis points.

Here, then, are a number of implications that bear directly upon the prospects of the rest of the world paying for European retirement. In the first instance, there are fewer destinations for European investment than a simple listing of demographic futures would suggest. Indeed, it is clear that a country such as the United States of America characterized by a large and growing population, relatively 'deep' capital markets, and technological innovation (Jorgenson 2001) will remain an attractive destination. In the second instance, expanding the scope of potential destinations for European investment may require concerted intervention by western countries and institutions into many other countries' economic, financial, and political practices. Otherwise, the map of international capital flows will be geographically truncated compared to the map of global demographic futures. This could lead to the development of a closer, asymmetric relationship between Europe and North America, wherein Europe depends upon North America for growth and North America depends upon the rest of the world for markets. Here, the emerging map of prosperity may be a bipolar world with a small developed part characterized as relatively transparent, leaving out of the picture much of the rest of the world whose population grows fast but is starved of capital.[7]

In other words, the European pension futures are also global economic futures. The prospects for global finance alluded to in this section and Table 8.1 are highly geographically differentiated. Furthermore, the risks involved in European investment outside of countries with an OI of more than 50 are substantial. Therefore, managing global finance is not just a matter of managing the possible contagious effects of country-specific currency crises. It is also a matter of managing administrative and regulatory reform in large developing countries with a significant demographic and economic growth potential. This much has been well-appreciated since at least the Asian crisis of the late 1990s. But how are we to accomplish this task? How are we to make the world safe for global finance and the future retirement of Europe's baby boom generation? Here, then, is a most important political implication: whereas we have assessed the European pensions issue in relation to global finance, it could equally be an issue of global political power mediated and controlled by the United States of America as opposed to Europe (along the lines suggested by Nye 2002).

FINAL OBSERVATIONS

Looking back over the project, I am struck by the fact that the tensions between the European pension systems and global finance have only just been realized. So much of the book has been devoted to bringing out into the open the relationship between these forces that we run the risk of supposing the resulting outline sketch exhausts the likely possibilities over the coming decades. In fact, I would suggest here that there are many reasons to suppose that these tensions will continue to dominate the national and EU politics and economics over the coming decades. Accommodation may not, in the end, resolve the matter!

So much of the debate about the integrity of national pension systems is an internal debate to the nations affected. For those who wish to conserve social institutions, 'reform' is best thought to be a matter of keeping to a minimum the incremental changes needed to sustain national social welfare. For others, less comfortable with parametric reform and more concerned to reform the structure of European pension systems, incremental reform is but a first step in the over-haul of European societies according to the Anglo-American model. On the evidence introduced here, accommodation or rather the convergence to Anglo-American practices has been the operative 'solution'. Continuity with the past is increasingly unlikely as 'reform' gathers momentum albeit intertwined with cautious election manifestos and recurrent claims of past privilege. Lurking behind this kind of debate, however, is a realization amongst some that the nature and path of reform may be more than a matter of adapting to an outside world. To the extent that national social security and retirement income are affected by global capital markets, these institutions may become the objects of systemic reform not just accommodation.

At the same time, debate over the future of European pension systems more often than not assumes (or hopes for) a constant relationship between the public institutions and private interests. Listening to the debate, one is often struck by the contested nature of social welfare perhaps *because* its institutions were so important in setting the terms of the post-Second World War political stability. Most observers of European social policy and welfare make this point. Indeed, it is a building block of comparative social policy (witness Esping-Andersen 1990). But the past seems increasingly remote to private interests now seeking their place in an integrated single market and the global economy beyond. Accepted relationships such as those between the social partners and corporations as well as those between corporations and their 'home' countries are under scrutiny. Do they add value? Are they as effective as the rival institutions of the Anglo-American world? Are there, in the end, universally-accepted best-practice institutional forms as suggested by the Anglo-American organization theorists such as Jensen (1998)? Perhaps. Whatever the evidence for and against these questions, when transformed into theoretical propositions they are the weapons used by those seeking room to manoeuvre outside of inherited institutions, social customs, and regulatory frameworks.

Most importantly, it could be argued that Europe has not, as yet, taken seriously the implications of demographic ageing for the welfare of those who will retire over the coming 20–30 years and those who will pay for their retirement. In a number of countries, parametric reforms have made significant changes to the future welfare of many retirees. Often ignored but of considerable importance are the attempts of individual and private institutions to make-up the difference. How will Europe cope, politically and economically, with the increasing inequality of opportunity? Can the European integration project escape being tarnished by emerging gaps in welfare, the decline in comprehensive social welfare, and the separation of some from the ideals and commitments associated with nation-state institutions? Perhaps the answer is twofold. On one hand, the aged will increasingly rely as they have done in the past upon local community commitments and their families. On the other hand, the young will increasingly rely upon the opportunities of enlargement, their place in Europe and the global economy, and their individual trajectories of long-term employment and income. If so, the post-Second World War institutions of national social security and social welfare will be judged to have been relevant for a certain époque but will be slowly replaced as the 'new Europe' responds to the imperatives of global competition.

The alternative appears alarming. Imagine that Europe ignores demographic ageing. Imagine that the Euro fails. Imagine that as a consequence, internal and external barriers to the flow of capital, labour, and innovation are strengthened. And imagine that those who retire over the coming couple of decades hold the balance of power in nation-states. Imagine if you like the past as the future but older. In a world of growing populations and of accelerating economic development and growth in other nations and regions, how will Europe escape being a retirement village with increasingly poor retirees and fewer opportunities for their children? This is surely not the vision of the EC or the elites of its member countries. And yet, it seems to be the vision of those set against systemic reform and those in global capital markets who believe Europe has neither the capacity nor the will to transform the past.

NOTES

1. Throughout the book, I have resisted the temptation to assess the pension arrangements amongst the Anglo-American countries; the focus of the book is on European pensions with the Anglo-American world as a reference point. However, I do suggest at different points along the way that the Anglo-American world is characterized by considerable income inequality and highly uneven patterns of coverage and benefits (see Chapters 1 and 2). Looking to the future, there are reasons to be pessimistic about the levels and extent of income equality amongst the retired in the United States of America and the United Kingdom. See for instance a recent study by the UK Association of Consulting Actuaries (2001) on the consequences of the apparent decline in the DB pension plans and the inadequacy of DC plans.
2. This issue is widely debated in German society, being focused on the joint paper issued by Tony Blair and Gerhard Schröder on the 'Third way'. One element in the debate is the future of solidarity and the notion of 'desolidarisation'—a term translated from the German which refers to the fragmentation of the German model of state and society (see Felhooter and Noppe 2000).
3. See, for example, Dore's (2000) analysis of the changing status of the German and Japanese models of corporate governance in relation to the Anglo-American pension fund capitalism. He is properly alarmed by the rough treatment accorded to the post-war institutions of working class representation and welfare as well as the apparent inequalities accompanying the Anglo-American model.
4. Here the PwC developed their measure of the risk premium based upon the coupon value of sovereign debt (traded bonds). It is, admittedly, a crude measure of risk although it does reveal remarkable differences between countries when compared to the Anglo-American world.
5. For a case in point, see Mauro's (1995) study of corruption and economic development. He used various indices of corruption and political stability to estimate the impact of

investment on economic growth. He also made the following point entirely apt for my own analysis. In part, he said 'I do not necessarily agree with ... consultant's views and subjective indices relating to any individual country' (Mauro 1995: 681). On the other hand, the comparative nature of such indices is such that opinion can be transformed into reality—perceived high levels of corruption for specific countries if shared by many in the investment community can be a limit on the flow of capital to those countries.

6. For a closely argued and detailed analysis of the 'tragedy' of Argentina, including a rather negative assessment of the role of the IMF, see Mussa (2002).

7. It is clear that financial agents in the core markets of the global economy are increasingly wary of peripheral financial markets, adding to existing problems of generating economic growth and maintaining stability in those countries (Stiglitz 2002). So significant are these patterns of discrimination and capital flight that leading authorities on international finance such as George Soros (2002, 127) believe that 'the high cost or unavailability of capital is the new contagion. It manifests itself not only in the lack of foreign investment but also in the flight of domestic capital'. The recent history of Argentina has added concern about these patterns of retreat and the flow of funds to the (relatively) safe havens of the developed world.

Appendix

As indicated, this book has relied upon intensive interviews with many of those involved in European pension and retirement income schemes, investment consultants and managers, government officials, advisors and regulators. The combination of inside information, insight about the issues, and commentaries on related issues juxtaposed one with the other helped enormously to better understand the nature of the relationship between European pensions and global finance. In this Appendix, the methodological issues related to this approach are briefly noted and sources referenced before providing a copy of the summary document and likely questions I used to elicit interviews. A summary list of the formal interviews by name, institution, country, and date is available upon request.

The use of in-depth interviews is a well-recognized and appreciated method of research in the social sciences. While sometimes allied with ethnography and anthropology (see O'Barr and Conley 1992) and sociology (see Abolafia 1996; Lamont 1992), it is a mode of enquiry that has been integrated into the mainstream of economics; witness the National Bureau of Economic Research project on labour productivity (as reported in Feldstein 2000; Helper 2000) and recent developments in economic geography (summarized in Clark 1998; McDowell 1997). At once inductive and constructionist in orientation, it is also a method of enquiry that is inevitably critical of the established theoretical conventions and expectations. Tests of veracity are deeply embedded in 'close dialogue': by successive interviews, the collection of third-party data, and the comparison of responses to common issues and questions a general understanding is built up slowly from successive attempts to represent the world at large. Its operating assumptions are open to scrutiny, and its conclusions are subject to debate. As I mentioned in the Preface and Introduction to the book, my claim to be heard is not one based upon privileged expertise or a presumption of objectivity. Being committed to understanding the world I am also committed to explaining what I have found as if the reader would similarly like to understand the world.

This does not mean that I am neutral, impartial, or hidden from view. Just as my argument has a distinctive flavour, so too have my encounters with respondents provided them with distinctive impressions about me as an academic and as a person. Close dialogue carries with it specific questions of personal motivation, belief, and experience. These issues deserve recognition, and they deserve further reflection and are dealt with in more detail in Clark (1998, 2000). So to better understand how the project developed, and who I discussed these issues with in a formal sense, the following provide the reader with a reference point.

As a first step in establishing contact with the person I wished to interview, a letter, email, or FAX was sent to the target. Enclosed with the letter was (often) reference to some one who had recommended them as a potential interviewee. In the Preface, I identify a number of people who provided me gateways into whole networks, countries, and institutions. As part of the letter, I also enclosed the following summary of the project (see the Enclosure) plus a one-page biography of myself. The biography is not included here because it seems to me so obvious ... but if any reader would wish to look at that as well, I would be pleased to provide it upon application via email. Having established contact, I then set about making an appointment. Very few people refused an interview. Indeed, I am amazed at the access and welcome afforded the project. For all their enthusiasm, I am very grateful for their cooperation.

Detailed notes were taken at every interview. From those notes, a more general commentary was produced locating the firm, the respondent, and the answers to the questions in a standard template. Rarely did I take down direct quotations. And as indicated above, none of the respondents expected to be directly quoted and cited. While some social science researchers believe direct quotations sustain and substantiate an argument, in the main I used the answers to the questions for intelligence gathering purposes. In many cases, answers to questions were the basis for further questions of a broader or narrower nature depending upon the insight or issues triggered by response and conversation. It should also be noted that I rarely cited others views back to industry respondents. When asked about others views on similar issues, I tended to associate those views with companies rather than people, and with situations rather than the positions of other respondents. Basically, I am very cautious about attributing views to particular respondents. In part, this is because their livelihoods should not be my responsibility. Also, given the rapidly changing European and global circumstances plus possible changes in their own positions and employers, they might have changed their opinions. It would be invidious to hold them hostage to fortune.

Finally, on the issue of respondent opinion and argument I should also indicate that I rarely argued against the views expressed by respondents. Given my limited time with each respondent (up to an hour with most), I sought their advice, their insight, and their knowledge. To make an argument in the book against a named person would effectively take advantage of my position as the author. All being well, I would likely win the argument. And they could hardly react or respond if the argument is conducted in the pages of the book.

Enclosure: 'The Single Market and European Pensions'
Professor Gordon L Clark
University of Oxford, Oxford, UK

Overview

With the advent of the Euro, European pension fund asset allocation formula are being reviewed—equities are now on the agenda, sectoral allocations are being reviewed, and new benchmarks established relevant to cross-border European investments. In this context, there will be increased competition between existing financial service providers and new market entrants for the provision of advanced risk management, custodial and investment management services. *An important issue for this project is to better understand the changing demand for financial services among European retirement and insurance plans and their sponsors.*

At the same time, there are increasing pressures on European governments to bring national regulation of their pensions and insurance sectors in line with the new realities of the Euro, while accommodating EC (DGIV and DG XV) initiatives for a single market for financial services. Competition policy, pension policy, and insurance regulation are increasingly converging. *A second important issue is the understanding of the process of policy harmonisation, involving different regulatory institutions affecting pan-European competition in the financial services industry.*

The prospect of a single European market for financial services has prompted retirement and related benefit plans (inside and outside of the Euro) to re-think their benefit arrangements and investment strategies. Harmonisation could result in cross-national consumption of retirement products, and may require pan-European firms to integrate the design and provision of retirement benefits to plan beneficiaries previously treated very differently behind national borders. *A third issue studied in this project is the extent to which large plan sponsors have sought to integrate their pensions investment and management across Europe.*

Focus of Research

To begin, we have conducted a programme of interviews with different sets of agents. *The study has focused on large European plan sponsors*, especially pan-European corporations and the extent to which changing conditions have been adjusted to with respect to the demand and supply of related financial services. *The second group interviewed have been the asset and related financial service consultants*—the advisors to plan sponsors in the UK and continental Europe. *The third group have been the representatives of pension plans*, including UK and continental European lobby groups like the NAPF, the Dutch sector funds organisation, the German ABA, and their Brussels associates. *The fourth group to be interviewed are the regulators*—DGIV, DGV, and DGXV, the OECD, and country competition, pensions and insurance regulators.

Collaboration

The project is sponsored by the University of Oxford, and the UK government social science research agency—the ESRC (with Professor Adam Tickell). Accomplishing this research project also relies upon the cooperation of market agents like firms, pensions and insurance sponsors as well as non-market organisations like governments and regulatory agencies. The project is assisted by the cooperation of the financial industry and the support of AIGfpc (London).

Interview Questions

The following questions represent in a broad manner the types of issues that underpin the project. Note comments and answers to questions will not be attributed and communicated to other organisations interviewed as part of this project.

1. [If a pension plan] what benefits are currently offered plan benefici-
    aries? Do you anticipate this changing in the near future? How?

2. [If a pension plan] how do you manage cross-border pension benefits
    among your beneficiaries? Will this change in the near future? How?

3. [If a pension plan] do you currently rely upon external service
    providers for plan management? What financial products and services
    do they provide?

4. [If a plan sponsor] how geographically extensive are your operations?
    Will the single market make a difference to the organisation of your
    firm?

5. [If a plan sponsor] are financial matters currently decentralised or
    centralised? Is there a difference between your pension plans and other
    financial operations?

6. [If a plan sponsor] are you concerned about liability with regard to the
    equal treatment of firm employees re pension entitlements (whatever
    their 'home')?

7. [If an asset consultant] what range of advice do you offer? To whom?
    Has this changed over the past few years?

8. [If an asset consultant] are you independent? Are you linked to an
    existing financial service provider? Anglo-America or continental
    European?

9. [If an asset consultant] as the single market emerges, what kind of
    retirement products are likely to be required?

10. [If an asset manager] what are your company's principal types of
    financial products? Are these products complimented by other related
    services?

11. [If an asset manager] how is the market for financial products changing
    in response to the single market? What kinds of new products are now
    important?

12. [If an asset manager] have new competitors entered the your market(s)
    for retirement products? What are their advantages and disadvantages?

13. [If a regulator] what have been the important 'forces' driving the
    harmonisation of financial services? What have been the impediments
    to harmonisation?

14. [If a regulator] what are the benefits of harmonisation for the provision
    of retirement products? Is financial innovation a desirable goal of
    harmonisation?

15. [If a regulator] what are the limits of harmonisation re the country-by-
    country provision of pension benefits?

BIBLIOGRAPHY

Aaron, H. (1966). 'The social insurance paradox', *Canadian Journal of Economics and Political Science*, 33: 371–74.

—— and Shoven, J. (eds) (1999). *Should the United States Privatise Social Security?* Cambridge MA: MIT Press.

Abolafia, M. (1996). *Making Markets: Opportunism and Restraint on Wall Street.* Cambridge MA: Harvard University Press.

Admati, A. and Pfleiderer, P. (1998). 'Forcing firms to talk: financial disclosure regulation and externalities', *Working Paper* 1470R, Graduate School of Business, Stanford University.

Aggarwal, R. and Samwick, A. (1999). 'Executive compensation, strategic competition, and relative performance evaluation: theory and evidence', *Journal of Finance*, 54: 1999–2044.

Aglietta, M. (2000). 'Shareholder value and corporate governance: some tricky questions', *Economy and Society*, 29: 146–59.

—— and de Boissieu, C. (1997). 'Problèmes prudentiels', in *Coordination Européenne des Politiques Économiques* (pp. 63–70). Conseil d'Analyse Economique Paris: La Documentation Française.

Allen, F. and Gale, D. (1994). 'A welfare comparison of the German and US financial systems', *Working Paper* 12–94, Wharton School, University of Pennsylvania, Philadelphia.

—— —— (1995). 'Universal banking, inter-temporal risk smoothing, and European financial integration', *Working Paper* 95–6, Economic Research Division, Federal Reserve Bank of Philadelphia, Philadelphia.

—— —— (2000). *Comparing Financial Systems.* Cambridge MA: MIT Press.

Ambachtsheer, K. and Ezra, D. (1998). *Pension Fund Excellence: Creating Value for Stakeholders.* New York: Wiley.

Amin, A. and Thrift, N. (1992). 'Neo-marshallian nodes in global networks', *International Journal of Urban and Regional Research*, 16: 571–87.

Andre, T. J. (1998). 'Cultural hegemony: the exportation of Anglo-Saxon corporate governance ideologies to Germany', *Tulane Law Review*, 73: 69–171.

Aranda-Hassel, C. and Duval-Kieffer, C. (2001). 'Labour mobility: a challenge for EMU', in *Global Demographics Report: 2001 Europe.* London: Credit Suisse First Boston Corporation.

Armstrong, M., Cowan, S., and Vickers, J. (1994). *Regulatory Reform: Economic Analysis and British Experience*. Cambridge MA: MIT Press.

Arrow, K. J. [1965] (1984). 'Insurance, risk, and resource allocation', in *Collected Economic Papers Volume 4: The Economics of Information* (pp. 77–86). Cambridge MA: Harvard University Press.

Arthur, W.B. (1992). *Increasing Returns and Path Dependence in the Economy*. Ann Arbor MI: University of Michigan Press.

Association of Consulting Actuaries (2001). *Occupational Pensions: The End of an Era?* London.

Auerbach, A. K., Kotlikoff L. J., and Leibfritz, W. (eds) (1999). *Generational Accounting Around the World*. Chicago: University of Chicago Press.

Bagehot, W. [1873] (1999). *Lombard Street: A Description of the Money Market* (Foreword by Peter Bernstein). New York: Wiley.

Balassone, F. and Franco, D. (2000). 'Public investment, the stability pact and the "golden rule" ', *Fiscal Studies*, 21: 207–29.

Barber, T. (2001). 'A wager on Europe', *The Financial Times*, 2 February: 20.

Barker, T. (2001). 'EC fudges the pension issue', *International Tax Review*, 12: 49–53.

Barr, N. (2002). 'The pension puzzle: prerequisites and policy choices in pension design'. *Economic Issues* 29. Washington DC: International Monetary Fund.

Bartky, I.R. (2000). *Selling Time: Nineteenth-Century Timekeeping in America*. Stanford: Stanford University Press.

Basu, S., Fernald, J. G., and Shapiro, M. D. (2001). 'Productivity growth in the 1990s: technology, utilization, or adjustment', *Working Paper Series* WP-01-04, Federal Reserve Bank of Chicago.

Baumol, W. (2002). *The Free Market Innovation Machine: Analyzing the Growth Miracle of Capitalism*. Princeton: Princeton University Press.

Beaverstock, J. V., Smith, R. G., and Taylor, P. J. (2000). 'Geographies of globalization: US law firms in world cities', *Urban Geography*, 21: 95–100.

Beaverstock, J., Hoyler, M., Pain, K., and Taylor, P. J. (2001). *Comparing London and Frankfurt as World Cities: A Relational Study of Contemporary Urban Change*. London: Anglo-German Foundation.

—— Taylor, P. J., and Smith, R. G. (1999). 'The long arm of the law: London's law firms in the globalising world economy', *Environment and Planning A*, 31: 1857–76.

Bebchuk, L. and Roe, M. (1999). 'A theory of path dependence in corporate governance and ownership', *Stanford Law Review*, 52: 127–70.

Beetsma, R. and Uhlig, H. (1999). 'An analysis of the stability and growth pact', *Economic Journal*, 109: 546–71.

Béland, D. (2001). 'Does labor matter? Institutions, labor unions and pension reform in France and the United States', *Journal of Public Policy*, 21: 153–72.

Bennett, P. (2000a). 'Anti-trust? European competition law and mutual environmental insurance', *Economic Geography*, 76: 5–67.

—— (2000b). 'Mutuality at a distance: risk and regulation in marine insurance clubs', *Environment and Planning A*, 32: 147–63.

Benston, G. J. (1990). *The Separation of Commercial and Investment Banking: The Glass-Steagall Act Revisited and Reconsidered*. New York: Oxford University Press.

Berentsen, W. (1999). 'Socio-economic development of eastern Germany, 1989–1998: A comparative perspective', *Post-Soviet Geography and Economics*, 40: 27–43.

Berger, A. N., Demsetz, R. S., and Strahan, P. E. (1999). 'The consolidation of the financial services industry: causes, consequences, and implications for the future', *Journal of Banking and Finance*, 23: 135–94.

Berle, A. and Means, G. (1933). *The Modern Corporation and Private Property*. New York: Macmillan.

Berlinski, M. R. and Western, S. R. A. (1998). 'Perspectives on the US asset management business', in H. Blommenstein and N. Funke (eds), *Institutional Investors in the New Financial Landscape* (pp. 109–30). Paris: OECD.

Berndt, C. (1998a). 'Ruhr firms between dynamic change and structural persistence–globalization, the "German Model" and regional place-dependence', *Transactions, Institute of British Geographers*, NS 23: 331–52.

—— (1998b). 'Corporate Germany at the crossroads? Americanization, competitiveness and place dependence', *Working Paper* 98, ESRC Centre for Business Research, Cambridge.

—— (2001). 'Americanization? Cultural constructions of institutional change in Germany', *Mimeo*, Department of Geography, Katholische Universitat Eichstatt, Eichstatt.

Berndt, E. (2002). 'Productivity', *NBER Reporter* (Spring): 1–6.

Berry, B. J. L. (1967). *The Geography of Retailing and Distribution*. Englewood Cliffs: Prentice-Hall.

Bindemann, K. (1999). *The Future of European Financial Centres*. London: Routledge.

Bismans, F. and Docquier, F. (1996). 'Consummation, épargne et accumulation dans la transition démographique', *Revue Economique*, 3: 667–76.

Blaise, C. (2000). *Time Lord: Sir Sandford Fleming and the Creation of Standard Time*. London: Phoenix.

Blake, D. (1995). *Pension Schemes and Pension Funds in the United Kingdom*. Oxford: Oxford University Press.

—— (1998). 'Pension schemes as options on pension fund assets: implications for pension fund management', *Insurance: Mathematics and Economics*, 23: 263–86.

—— Lehmann, B. N., and Timmermann, A. (1999). 'Asset allocation and pension fund performance', *Journal of Business*, 72: 429–61.

Blanchet, D. and Pelé, L.-P. (1999). 'Social security and retirement in France', in J. Gruber and D. Wise (eds), *Social Security Programs Around the World* (pp. 101–33). Chicago: University of Chicago Press.

Bliss, M. and Flannery, M. J. (2000). 'Market discipline in the governance of US bank holding companies: monitoring vs. influencing', *WP-00-03*, Research Department, Federal Reserve Bank of Chicago, Chicago.

Blomsma, M. and Jansweijer, R. (1997). 'The Netherlands: growing importance of private sector arrangements', in M. Rein and E. Wadensjö (eds), *Enterprise and the Welfare State* (pp. 220–65). Cheltenham: Edward Elgar.

Bloomer, C. (ed.) (1999). *The IASC-US Comparison Project: A Report on the Similarities and Differences between IASC Standards and US GAAP*. Norwalk: FASB.

Bodie, Z. and Shoven, J. B. (eds) (1983). *Financial Aspects of the United States Pension System*. Chicago: University of Chicago Press.

Boeri, T., Borsch-Supan, A., Brugiavini, A., Disney, R., and Peracchi, F. (eds) (2001a). *Pensions: More Information, Less Ideology*. Dordrecht: Kluwer Publishers.

——Borsch-Supan, A. and Tabellini, G. (2001b). 'Would you like to shrink the welfare state? The opinions of European citizens', *Economic Policy*, 16: 7–50.

Boldrin, M., Dolado, J. J., Jimeno, J. F., and Peracchi, F. (1999). 'The future of pensions in Europe', *Economic Policy*, 14: 289–321.

Bolkestein, F. (2000). Integration of financial markets in Europe, 23 September, Prague. Available at http://europa.eu.int/comm/internal_market/en/speeches

Bonin, H. (2001). 'Will it last? An assessment of the 2001 German pension reform', *Geneva Papers on Risk and Insurance*, 26: 547–64.

Bonoli, G. (2000). *The Politics of Pension Reform: Institutions and Policy Change in Western Europe*. Cambridge: Cambridge University Press.

——George, V., and Taylor-Gooby, P. (2000). *European Welfare Futures: Towards a Theory of Retrenchment*. Oxford: Polity Press.

——and Palier, B. (2001). 'Pension reform and the expansion of private pensions in Europe', *Jahrbuch fuer Europaeische Verwaltungsgeschichte*, 12: 1–22.

Boot, A. W. and Thakor, A. V. (1997). 'Financial system architecture', *Review of Financial Studies*, 10: 693–733.

Borsch-Supan, A. (2000a). 'A model under siege: a case study of the German retirement insurance system', *Economic Journal*, 110: F24–F45.

——(2000b). 'A blue print for Germany's pension reform'. Department of Economics, University of Mannheim, Mannheim.

——(2000c). 'Discussion', *Working Paper* 4/2000, Center for Research on Pensions and Welfare Policies, Turin.

——(2001). *Pension Reform in Six Countries. What Can We Learn From Each Other?* Berlin: Springer.

Bouthevillain, C. *et al.* (2001). 'Cyclically adjusted budget balances: an alternative approach', *Working Paper* 77, European Central Bank, Frankfurt.

Boyer, R. (1996). 'Why does employment differ in the course of time and across nations? An institutional answer in the light of the "regulation" theory', *Metroeconomica*, 48: 1–35.

Brahs, S. J. (2001). 'Public policy implications of the world's ageing populations', *Geneva Papers on Risk and Insurance*, 26: 105–13.

Braithwaite, J. and Drahos, P. (2000). *Global Business Regulation*. Cambridge: Cambridge University Press.

Braudel, F. (1992). *The Perspective of the World. Volume* 3, Civilization and Capitalism 15th–18th Century (Translated from the French by S. Reynolds). Berkeley: University of California Press.

Brealey, R. A., Cooper, I. A., and Kaplanis, E. (1999). 'What is the international dimension of international finance?' *European Finance Review* 3: 103–19.

Brennan, J. J., Driscoll, D.-M., Haaga, P. G., Johnson, M. H., Lyons W. M., and McDonough, G. C. (1999). *Enhancing a Culture of Independence and Effectiveness: Report of the Advisory Group on Best Practices for Fund Directors*. Washington DC: Investment Company Institute.

Breyer, F. (2001). 'Why funding is not a solution to the "Social Security Crisis"', *Discussion Paper No.* 254, University of Konstanz and DIW Berlin, Berlin.

Brydon, D. (ed.) (2000). *'Prudent Man' and European Pensions: A Collection of Essays*. London: European Asset Management Association.

Budd, A. and Campbell, N. (1998). 'The roles of the public and private sectors in the UK pension system', in M. Feldstein (ed.), *Privatizing Social Security* (pp. 99–134). Chicago: University of Chicago Press.

Bundesregierung Deutschland (2001). Bericht der Unabhängigen Kommission 'Zuwanderung'. Bundesminterium des Innern, Bundesregierung Deutschland, Berlin: 04/07/01. Available at http://www.bmi.bund.de/top/dokumente/Artikel/ix_46876.htm.

Byrne, J. and Davis, E. P. (2002). 'A comparison of balance sheet structures in major EU countries', *National Institute Economic Review*, 180: 83–94.

Camerer, C. and Weber, M. (1992). 'Recent developments in modelling preferences: uncertainty and ambiguity', *Journal of Risk and Uncertainty* 5: 325–70.

Carlin, W. and Mayer, C. (1999). 'How do financial systems affect economic performance?' *Working Paper* 1999-FE-08, Said Business School, University of Oxford, Oxford.

Chandler, A. D. (1977). *The Visible Hand: The Managerial Revolution in American Business*. Cambridge MA: Harvard University Press.

Charpin, M. (1999). *L'Avenir de nos Retraites*. Paris: La Documentation Française.

Chemillier-Gendreau, D. (2000). 'Prudent man rule', in D. Brydon (ed.), *'Prudent Man' and European Pensions* (pp. 11–13). London: European Asset Managers Association.

Chirinko, B., Van Ees, H., Garretsen, H., and Sterken, E. (1999). 'Firm performance, financial institutions and corporate governance in The Netherlands', *Working Paper* 210, CESifo, Munich.

Choi, J., Laibson, D., Madrian, B., and Metrick, A. (2001). 'The path of least resistance in 401(k) plans', *Working Paper* 8651. National Bureau of Economic Research, Cambridge MA.

Christopherson, S. (1993). 'Market rules and territorial outcomes: the case of the United States', *International Journal of Urban and Regional Research*, 17: 274–88.

—— (2002). 'Why do national labour market practices continue to diverge in a global economy: the "missing link" of investment rules', *Economic Geography*, 78: 1–20.

Clark, G. L. (1993a). 'Costs and prices, corporate competitive strategies and regions', *Environment and Planning A*, 25: 5–26.

—— (1993b). *Pensions and Corporate Restructuring in American Industry: A Crisis of Regulation*. Baltimore: Johns Hopkins University Press.

—— (1998). 'Stylised facts and close dialogue: methodology in economic geography', *Annals, Association of American Geographers*, 88: 54–78.

—— (2000). *Pension Fund Capitalism*. Oxford: Oxford University Press.

—— (2001). 'The vocabulary of Europe: code words for the new millennium', *Environment and Planning D: Society and Space*, 19: 697–717.

—— (2002). 'Pension systems: a comparative perspective', in M. Warner (ed.), *The International Encyclopedia of Business and Management: IEBM Handbook of Economics* (2nd Edition, pp. 5194–204). London: Thompson.

—— and Dear, M. (1984). *State Apparatus*. Boston: Allen & Unwin.

—— Feldman, M., and Gertler, M. (eds) (2000). *Oxford Handbook of Economic Geography*. Oxford: Oxford University Press.

—— and O'Connor, K. (1997). 'The informational content of financial products and the spatial structure of the global finance industry', in K. Cox (ed.), *Spaces of Globalization: Reasserting the Power of the Local* (pp. 89–114). New York: Guilford.

——Tracey, P., and Lawton Smith, H. (2001). 'Rethinking comparative studies', *Working Paper* 01-01, School of Geography and the Environment, University of Oxford, Oxford.

——and Wójcik, D. (2002). 'How and where should we invest in Europe? An economic geography of global finance'. *Working Paper* 02–09, School of Geography and the Environment, University of Oxford, Oxford.

Clasen, J. (ed.) (1999). *Comparative Social Policy: Concepts, Theories, and Methods*. London: Routledge.

Claus, J. and Thomas, J. (2001). 'Equity premia as low as three percent? Evidence from analysts' earnings forecasts for domestic and international stock markets', *Journal of Finance*, 56: 1629–66.

Clout, H. (1994). 'Demographic and social change', in H. Clout, M. Blacksell, R. King, and D. Pinder (eds), *Western Europe: Geographical Perspectives* (3rd edn, pp. 23–42) London: Longman Scientific and Technical.

Clowes, M. J. (2000). *The Money Flood: How Pension Funds Revolutionalized Investing*, New York: Wiley.

Coase, R. H. (1988). *The Firm, the Market, and the Law*. Chicago: University of Chicago Press.

Cohen, T. (1994). 'The regulation of foreign securities: a proposal to amend the reconciliation requirement and increase the strength of domestic markets', *Annual Survey of American Law*, 491–550.

Coleman, D. (ed.) (1996). *Europe's Population in the* 1990s. Oxford: Oxford University Press.

Coleman, J. L. (1992). *Risks and Wrongs*. Cambridge: Cambridge University Press.

Coleman, J. S. (1990). *Foundations of Social Theory*. Cambridge MA: Harvard University Press.

Conard, A. F. (1991). 'The European alternative to uniformity in corporation laws', *Michigan Law Review*, 89: 2150–200.

Cooke, P. and Morgan, K. (1998). *The Associational Economy: Firms, Regions and Innovation*. Oxford: Oxford University Press.

Crouch, C. (1999). *Social Change in Western Europe*. Oxford: Oxford University Press.

——and Streeck, W. (1997). 'Introduction: the future of capitalist diversity', in C. Crouch and W. Streeck (eds.), *Political Economy of Modern Capitalism* (pp. 1–18). London: Sage.

Davis, E. P. (1995). *Pension Funds: Retirement Income Security and Capital Markets. An International Perspective*. Oxford: Oxford University Press.

——(1996). 'International experience of pension fund reform and its applicability to The Netherlands', *Working Paper* 11, Birkbeck College, University of London, London.

——and Steil, B. (2001). *Institutional Investors*. Cambridge MA: MIT Press.

de Burca, G. (1999). 'Re-appraising subsidiarity's significance after Amsterdam', *Jean Monnet WP* 7/99, Harvard Law School, Harvard, Cambridge.

De Ryck, K. (1999). *Rebuilding Pensions: Security, Efficiency, Affordability. Recommendations for a European Code of Best Practice for Second Pillar Pension Funds*. Brussels: European Commission.

Deakin, S., Lane, C., and Wilkinson, F. (1997). 'Contract law, trust relations, and incentives for co-operation: a comparative study', in S. Deakin and J. Michie (eds), *Contracts, Co-operation, and Competition: Studies in Economics, Management, and Law* (pp. 105–39). Oxford: Oxford University Press.

Deutsche Bank (1996). 'From pension reserves to pension funds: an opportunity for the German financial market', *Special Study*, Frankfurt am Main: DB Research Management.

—— (1999). 'Pension funds for Europe', *Special Study*, Frankfurt am Main: DB Research Management.

Deutsche Bundesbank (2001). 'Company pension schemes in Germany', *Monthly Report* (March): 43–58.

DeYoung, R. and Hunter, W. (2001). 'Deregulation, the internet, and competitive viability of large banks and community banks', *Working Paper* 01–11, Research Department, Federal Reserve Bank of Chicago, Chicago.

—— Spong, K., and Sullivan, R. J. (1999). 'Who's minding the store? Motivating and monitoring hired managers at small, closely held firms: the case of commercial banks', *WP-99-17*, Research Department, Federal Reserve Bank of Chicago, Chicago.

Diamantopoulou, A. (2000). 'Sustainable pensions: Commission launches plan to modernise pensions in Europe'. http://europa.eu.int/comm/employment_social/soc-prot/schemes/news/pension2000_en.htm

Diamantopoulou, A. (2001). 'Forward by the Commissioner', in *Employment in Europe 2001: Recent trends and prospects*, July 2001 DG Employment and Social Affairs, Unit A.1 Employment Analysis, European Commission, Brussels. http://europa.eu.int/comm/employment_social/empl&esf/docs/emple-urope2001_en.pdf.

Diamond, P. A. (1977). 'A framework for social security analysis', *Journal of Public Finance*, 8: 275–98.

—— (1994). *On Time: Lectures on Models of Equilibrium*. Cambridge: Cambridge University Press.

—— (2000). 'Towards an optimal social security design', *Working Paper* 4/2000, Center for Research on Pensions and Welfare Policies, Turin.

Dickie, J. (1996). 'Imagined Italies', in D. Forgacs and R. Lumley (eds), *Italian Cultural Studies: An Introduction* (pp. 19–33). Oxford: Oxford University Press.

Dimson, E., Marsh, P., and Staunton, M. (2002). *Triumph of the Optimists: 101 Years of Global Investment Returns*. Princeton: Princeton University Press.

Disney, R. (1996). *Can We Afford to Grow Older?* Cambridge MA: MIT Press.

—— (2000). 'Crises in public pension programmes in OECD: what are the reform options?' *Economic Journal*, 110: F1–F23.

Dore, R. (2000). *Stock Market Capitalism: Welfare Capitalism. Japan and Germany versus the Anglo-Saxons*. Oxford: Oxford University Press.

Dufey, G. (1998). 'The changing role of financial intermediation in Europe', *International Journal of Business*, 3: 49–67.

Duisenberg, W. (2001). 'Developments in international financial markets'. Frankfurt: European Central Bank [available at www.ecb.int].

Dupont, G. and Sterdyniak, H. (2000). *Quel Avenir Pour Nos Retraites?* Paris: La Découverte.

Durkheim, E. (1984). *The Division of Labour in Society* (with an Introduction by L. Coser; translated by W. D. Halls). London: Macmillan.

Dyson, K. and Featherstone, K. (1999). *The Road to Maastricht: Negotiating Economic and Monetary Union.* Oxford: Oxford University Press.

Edey, M. and Simon, J. (1998). 'Australia's retirement income system' in M. Feldstein (ed.), *Privatising Social Security* (pp. 63–97). Chicago: University of Chicago Press.

Edwards, J. and Fischer, K. (1994). *Banks, Finance and Investment in Germany.* Cambridge: Cambridge University Press.

Edwards, J. and Weichenrieder, A.J. (1999). 'Ownership concentration and share valuation: evidence from Germany', *Working Paper* 193, CESifo, Munich.

Eggertson, T. (1990). *Economic Behaviour and Institutions.* Cambridge: Cambridge University Press.

Eichengreen, B. (1997). *European Monetary Unification: Theory, Practice, and Analysis.* Cambridge MA: MIT Press.

Ellis, C. (1998). *Winning the Loser's Game* (3rd edn). New York: Wiley.

Engelen, E. (2002). 'Financialization, pension restructuring, and the logic of funding', *Mimeo*, Amsterdam: Department of Geography and Planning, University of Amsterdam.

Ermisch, J. (1995). 'Demographic developments and European labour markets', *Scottish Journal of Political Economy*, 42: 331–46.

Ernst and Whinney (1986). *Employers' Accounting for Pensions: Understanding and Implementing FASB Statement No. 87,* New York.

Esping-Andersen, G. (1990). *The Three Worlds of Welfare Capitalism.* Oxford: Polity Press.

——(1999). *Social Foundations of Postindustrial Economies.* Oxford: Oxford University Press.

——Gallie, D., Hemerijck, A., and Myles, J. (2001). 'New Welfare Architecture for Europe'? Report to the Belgium Presidency of the European Union, Brussels.

European Central Bank (2001). *Monthly Bulletin*, September, Frankfurt.

European Commission (2000a). 'EU Financial Reporting Strategy: The Way Forward', COM (2000) 359 Final, Brussels. Available at http://europa.eu.int/eurlex/en/com/cnc/2000/com2000_0359en01.pdf.

——(2000b). 'Proposal for a directive of the European Parliament and of the Council on the co-ordination of laws, regulations and administrative provisions relating to institutions for occupational retirement provisions', 507 provisional, 11 October, Brussels. Available at http://europa.eu.int/comm/internal_market/en/finances/pensions/com507en.pdf.

——(2000c). Communication from the Commission to the Council, to the European Parliament and to the Economic and Social Committee. The future evolution of social protection from a long-term point of view: safe and sustainable pensions, 17 October, Brussels. Available at http://europa.eu.int/eurlex/en/com/cnc/2001/com2001_0362en01.pdf.

——(2000d). Progress report to the Ecofin Council on the impact of ageing populations on public pension systems, EPC/ECFIN/581/00-EN-Rev.1, 6 November, Brussels. Available at http://europa.eu.int/comm/economy_finance/epc/epc-ageing-report_en.pdf.

——(2001a). Report on the Implementation of the 2000 BEPG. Brussels: Economic and Financial Affairs.

—— (2001b). 'Recommendation for the 2001 Broad Guidelines of the Economic Policies of the Member States and the Community', COM(2001)224 final, Brussels.

—— (2001c). 'Employment in Europe 2001: Recent Trends and Prospects. July 2001'. Brussels: DG Employment and Social Affairs, Unit A.1 Employment Analysis. Available at http://europa.eu.int/comm/employment_social/.

—— (2001d). 'Budgetary challenges posed by ageing populations', EPC/ECFIN/655/01-EN final, Brussels.

European Federation for Retirement Provision (2000). *A European Institution for Occupational Retirement Provision*, Brussels.

Evans, A. (1998). *A Textbook on European Union Law*. Oxford: Hart Publishing.

Fama, E. and French, K. R. (2002). 'The equity premium', *Journal of Finance*, 57: 637–59.

Fassman, H. and Munz, R. (1992). 'Patterns and trends of international migration in western Europe', *Population and Development Review*, 18: 457–80.

Faull, J. and Nikpay, A. (eds) (1999). *The EC Law of Competition*. Oxford: Oxford University Press.

Featherstone, K., Kazamias, G., and Papadimitriou, D. (2001). 'The limits of external empowerment: EMU, technocracy, and reform of the Greek pension system', *Political Studies*, 49: 462–80.

Feldman, M. P. (2000). 'Location and innovation: new economic geography of innovation, spillovers, and agglomeration', in G. L. Clark, M. P. Feldman, and M. Gertler (eds), *Oxford Handbook of Economic Geography* (pp. 373–94). Oxford: Oxford University Press.

Feldstein, M. (1998). 'Introduction', in M. Feldstein (ed.), *Privatizing Social Security* (pp. 1–29). Chicago: University of Chicago Press.

—— (2000). *The NBER-Sloan project on productivity change*. Cambridge MA: National Bureau of Economic Research.

Feldstein, M. (2002). 'Europe's pensions', *Working Paper*, National Bureau of Economic Research, Cambridge.

—— and Horioka, C. (1980). 'Domestic savings and international capital flows', *Economic Journal*, 90: 361–8.

—— and Leibman, J. (2002). 'Social security', in A. J. Auerbach and M. Feldstein (eds), *Handbook of Public Economics*, Amsterdam: North-Holland (forthcoming).

—— and Morck, R. (1983). 'Pension funding decisions, interest rate assumptions, and share prices', in Z. Bodie and J. B. Shoven (eds), *Financial Aspects of the United States Pension System* (pp. 177–210). Chicago: University of Chicago Press.

Felhoolter, G. and Noppe, R. (2000). 'Germany after the millennium: discourses and strategies of restructuring and redefining the role of the state', *Tijdscrift voor Economische en Sociale Geografie*, 91: 237–47.

Fenge, R. (2002). 'On the efficiency of unfunded pension schemes', *Mimeo*, Munich: IFO Institute for Economic Research.

Ferguson, N. (2001). *The Cash Nexus: Money and Power in the Modern World*, 1700–2000. New York: Basic Books.

Financial Accounting Standards Board (1998). *International Accounting Standard Setting: A Vision for the Future*, Norwalk.

Fishman, M. J. and Hagerty, K. (1997). 'Mandatory vs. voluntary disclosure in markets with informed and uniformed customers', *Working Paper* 2333, Kellogg School of Management, Northwestern University, Evanston.

Florida, R. (2002). 'Bohemia and economic geography', *Journal of Economic Geography*, 2: 55–71.

Flutter, C. (2001). 'France's regional unemployment problem and the 35-hour week', *Working Paper* 01–07, School of Geography and the Environment, University of Oxford, Oxford.

Ford, M. J. (1994). 'Broken promises: implementation of Financial Accounting Standards Board rule 106, ERISA, and legal challenges to modification and termination of post-retirement health care benefit plans', *St. John's Law Review*, 68: 427–58.

Forder, J. (2001). 'Image and illusion in the design of the EMU' in A. Menon and V. Wright (eds), *From the Nation State to Europe? Essays in Honour of Jack Hayward* (pp. 158–74). Oxford: Oxford University Press.

Franks, J. and Mayer, C. (1998). 'Bank control, takeovers, and corporate governance', in K. J. Hopt, H. Kanda, M. J. Roe, E. Wymeersch, and S. Prigge (eds), *Comparative Corporate Governance: The State of the Art and Emerging Research* (pp. 641–58). Oxford: Oxford University Press.

Friedman, B. (1983). 'Pension funding, pension asset allocation and corporate finance: evidence from individual company data', in Z. Bodie and J. B. Shoven (eds), *Financial Aspects of the United States Pension System* (pp. 107–52). Chicago: University of Chicago Press.

Friot, B. (1999). *Et La Cotisation Sociale Creera L'Emploi*. Paris: La-Dispute.

Galison, P. (2000). 'Einstein's clocks: the place of time', *Critical Inquiry* 26: 355–89.

Gardiner, K. (1999). *De-Fusing the demographic bomb* (Special Economic Study). London: Morgan Stanley Dean Witter.

Gertler, M. (2001). 'Best practice? Geography, learning and the institutional limits to strong convergence', *Journal of Economic Geography* 1: 5–26.

Gigerenzer, G. and Todd, R. (1999). *Simple Heuristics that Make Us Smart*. Oxford: Oxford University Press.

Gillion, C., Turner, J., Bailey, C., and Latulippe, D. (eds) (2000). *Social Security Pensions: Development and Reform*. Geneva: International Labour Office.

Goffee, R. and Jones, G. (1998). *The Character of a Corporation*. New York: HarperCollins.

Goodin, R., Headey, B., Muffels, R., and Dirven, H-J. (1999). *The Real Worlds of Welfare Capitalism*. Cambridge: Cambridge University Press.

Gorton, G. and Schmid, F. (2000). Class struggle inside the firm: a case study of German co-determination, *Working Paper*, Wharton School, University of Pennsylvania, Philadelphia.

Greenspan, A. (2000). 'Globalisation'. Washington DC: Federal Reserve Board.

Greenwich Associates (1999). *Investment Management in The Netherlands: Market Dynamics Tables*, 8 Greenwich Office Park, Greenwich, CT.

Gruber, J. and Wise, D. 1999. 'Introduction and summary', in J. Gruber and D. Wise (eds), *Social Security and Retirement Around the World* (pp. 1–35). Chicago: University of Chicago Press.

Guerrieri, P. (1999). 'Patterns of national specialisation in the global competitive environment', in D. Archibugi, J. Howells, and J. Michie (eds), *Innovation*

Policy in a Global Economy. Cambridge: Cambridge University Press, 139.

Hall, P. and Soskice, D. (eds) (2001). *The Varieties of Capitalism: The Institutional Foundations of Comparative Advantage*. Oxford: Oxford University Press.

Hancher, L. and Moran, M. (1989). 'Organising regulatory space', in L. Hancher and M. Moran (eds), *Capitalism, Culture, and Economic Regulation* (pp. 271–99). Oxford: Clarendon Press.

Hannah, L. (1986). *Inventing Retirement: The Development of Occupational Pensions in Britain*. Cambridge: Cambridge University Press.

Hassler, J. and Lindbeck, A. (1998). Intergenerational risk sharing, stability and optimality of alternative pension systems, *Working Paper*, Institute for International Economic Studies, University of Stockholm, Stockholm.

Hawley, J. and Williams, A. (2000). *The Rise of Fiduciary Capitalism: How Institutional Investors Can Make America More Democratic*. Philadelphia: University of Pennsylvania Press.

Hay, D. (1993). 'The assessment: competition policy', *Oxford Review of Economic Policy*, 9: 1–26.

Heikensten, L. and Ernhagen, T. (2000). 'Economic policy coordination in the EU/euro area', *Economic Review*, 1: 5–21.

Helm, D. and Jenkinson, T. (1997). 'The assessment: introducing competition into regulated industries', *Oxford Review of Economic Policy*, 13: 1–14.

Helper, S. (2000). 'Economists and field research: "you can observe a lot just by watching"', *American Economic Review*, 90 (2): 228–32.

Hine, D. (2001). 'Constitutional form and Treaty reform in Europe', in A. Menon and V. Wright (eds), *From the Nation State to Europe? Essays in honour of Jack Hayward* (pp. 118–38). Oxford: Oxford University Press.

Hokenson, R., Keating, G., Larosa, C., and Roy, A. (2001). 'European demographics' 2001 edn, in *Global Demographics Report*: 2001 Europe. London: Credit Suisse First Boston Corporation.

Holderness, C. G., Kroszner, R. S., and Sheehan, D. P. (1999). 'Were the good old days that good? Changes in managerial stock ownership since the great depression', *Journal of Finance*, 54: 435–70.

Hollingsworth, J. R. and Boyer, R. (eds) (1997). *Contemporary Capitalism: The Embeddedness of Institutions*. Cambridge: Cambridge University Press.

Hopt, K. J., Kanda, H., Roe, M. J., Wymeersch, E., and Prigge, S. (eds) (1999). *Comparative Corporate Governance: The State of the Art and Emerging Research*. Oxford: Oxford University Press.

Hotelling, H. (1929). 'Stability in competition', *Economic Journal*, 39: 41–57.

House of Commons (1996). *Unfunded Pension Liabilities in the European Union*, First Report, Social Security Committee. London: Stationary Office.

Houthakker, H. S. and Williamson, P. J. (1996). *The Economics of Financial Markets*. Oxford: Oxford University Press.

Huebeck, K. and Baum, G. (1998). 'New types of pension fund in Germany', *Benefits and Compensation International*, November: 2–6. Or see www.ggy.bris.ac.vu/staff/information/ggatt/german_model.pdf

Hutton, W. (1995). *The State We Are In*. London: Jonathon Cape.

—— (2002). *The World We Are In*. London: Little Brown.

IASC (2000). *International Accounting Standards* 2000, London.

International Bank of Settlements (2001). 'The changing shape of fixed income markets', *BIS Papers* 5: 1–43, Basel.

International Financial Services London (2001). *International Financial Markets in the UK* (April), London.

International Monetary Fund (2000). 'Germany: Selected Issues', *Country Report* 00/142, Washington DC.

——(2001). France: 2001 Article IV consultation concluding statement of the mission, 11 July 2001. IMF: Washington DC. Available at http://www.imf.org/external/np/ms/2001/071101.htm.

Jenkinson, T. and Ljungqvist, A. (1999). 'The role of hostile stakes in German corporate governance', *Working Paper* 99-FE-02, Said Business School, University of Oxford, Oxford.

Jensen, M. C. (1993). 'The modern industrial revolution, exit, and the failure of internal control systems', *Journal of Finance*, 48: 831–80.

——(1998). *Foundations of Organizational Strategy*. Cambridge MA: Harvard University Press.

Johnson, R. (2000). 'The effect of old-age insurance on male retirement: evidence from historical cross-country data', *RWP00-09*, Research Division, Federal Reserve Bank of Kansas City, Kansas City.

Jones, R. A. (1999). *The Development of Durkheim's Social Realism*. Cambridge: Cambridge University Press.

Jorgenson, D. (2001). 'Information technology and the US economy', *American Economic Review*, 91: 1–32.

Jorgenson, D. and Stiroh, K. J. (2000). 'US economic growth at the industry level', *American Economic Review*, 90 (2): 161–7.

Kaen, F. R. (1995). *Corporate Finance: Concepts and Policies*. Cambridge MA: Blackwell.

Kamlah, K. (1996). 'The new German insolvency act: *Insolvenzordnung*', *American Bankruptcy Law Journal*, 70: 417–35.

Keyfitz, N. (1976). 'Discussion', in A Munnell (ed), *Funding Pensions: Issues and Implications for Financial Markets* (pp. 67–79). Boston: Federal Reserve Bank of Boston.

Klemperer, P. D. (1987). 'Markets with customer switching costs', *Quarterly Journal of Economics*, 102: 375–94.

Kluth, M. F. and Andersen, J. (1999). 'Globalisation and financial diversity: the making of venture capital markets in France, Germany and UK' in D. Archibugi, J. Howells and J. Michie (eds.), *Innovation Policy in a Global Economy* (pp. 120–38). Cambridge: Cambridge University Press.

Koenig, P. and Mahnert, S. (2001). 'German pension reform: survival of the fittest?' *Global Pensions Quarterly*, March: 28–38.

——and van der Lende, E. (1999). 'The pension system of "Germany PLC"', *Global Pensions Quarterly*, October/November: 1–14.

Krueger, A. B. (2000). 'From Bismarck to Maastricht: the march to European Union and the labor compact', *Labor Economics*, 7: 117–34.

Krugman, P. (1991). *Geography and Trade*. Cambridge MA: MIT Press.

Kynaston, D. (2001). *The City of London, Volume 4. A Club No More: 1945–2000*. London: Chatto and Windus.

La Porta, R., Lopez-De-Silanes, F., Shleifer, A., and Vishny, R. W. (1997). 'Legal determinants of external finance', *Journal of Finance*, 52: 1131–50.

————————(1998). 'Law and finance', *Journal of Political Economy*, 106: 1113–55.

Laing, J. N. and Sharpe, S. (1999). 'Share repurchases and employee stock options and their implications for S&P 500 share retirements and expected returns', *Mimeo* 1999–59, Washington DC: Division of Research and Statistics, Federal Reserve Board.

Lamont, M. (1992). *Money, Morals, and Manners: The Culture of the French and the American Upper-Middle Class*. Chicago: University of Chicago Press.

Langbein, J. H. (1995). 'The contractarian basis of the law of trusts', *Yale Law Journal*, 105: 625–75.

—— (1997). 'The secret life of the trust: the trust as an instrument of commerce', *Yale Law Journal*, 107: 165–89.

Langer, R. and Lev, B. (1993). 'The FASB's policy of extended adoption for new standards: an examination of FAS No. 87', *The Accounting Review*, 68: 515–33.

Lannoo, K. (1996). 'The draft pension fund directive and the financing of pensions in the EU', *Geneva Papers on Risk and Insurance*, 20: 67–79.

Lascelles, D., MacDougall, D., and Minford, P. (2001). *The Economic Case Against the Euro*. London: The New Europe Research Trust.

Laulajainen, R. (2001). 'End of geography at exchanges', *Zeitschrift für Wirtschaftsgeographie*, 45: 1–14.

League of Nations (1931, 1935). *International Statistical Yearbook*. Geneva.

Leibfritz, W., Roseveare, D., Fore, D., and Wurzel, E. (1995). 'Ageing populations, pension systems and government budgets: how do they affect savings'? *Working Paper* 156, Economics Department, OECD, Paris.

Leinert, J. and Esche, A. (2000). *Advance Funding of Pensions*. Gütersloh: Bertelsmann Foundation Publishers.

Levy, J. and Dore, O. (1999). 'Generational accounting for France', in A. J. Auerbach, L. J. Kotlikoff, and W. Leibfritz (eds), *Generational Accounting Around the World* (pp. 239–76). Chicago: University of Chicago Press.

Leyshon, A. and Thrift, N. (1993). 'Restructuring in the UK financial services industry in the 1990s: a reversal of fortune'? *Journal of Rural Studies*, 9: 223–41.

—— —— (1997a). 'Spatial financial flows and the growth of the modern city', *International Social Science Journal*, 15: 41–53.

Leyshon, A. and Thrift N. (1997b). *Money/Space: Geographies of Monetary Transformation*. London: Routledge.

Licht, A. (1997). 'Games commissions play: 2×2 games of international securities regulation', *Discussion Paper* 11/97, Harvard Law School, Harvard University, Cambridge.

Liebtag, B. (1984). 'Controversy livens FASB hearings on pension accounting', *Journal of Accountancy*, 157: 55–60.

Lindbeck, A. (2000). Pensions and contemporary socioeconomic change, *Working Paper*, Institute for International Economic Studies, University of Stockholm, Stockholm.

Logue, D. E. and Rader, J. S. (1997). *Managing Pension Funds: A Comprehensive Guide to Improving Fund Performance*. Boston: Harvard Business School Press.

Lowenstein, L. (1996). 'Financial transparency and corporate governance: you manage what you measure', *Columbia Law Review*, 96: 1335–62.

Luhmann, N. (1995). *Social Systems* (Translated by J. Bednarz with D. Baecker). Stanford: Stanford University Press.

Lynes, T. (1967). *French Pensions*. London: Bell.

—— (1985). *Paying for Pensions: The French Experience.* London: Suntory-Toyota International Centre for Economics and Related Disciplines, London School of Economics.

Maarek, G. (2000). 'Le rôle des facteurs financiers dans la nouvelle economie Américaine', in *Nouvelle Economie* (pp. 149–62), Conseil d'Analyse Economique. Paris: La Documentation Française.

Mantel, J. (2000). *Demographics and the Funded Pensions System: Ageing Populations, Mature Pension Funds and Negative Cash-Flow.* London: Merrill Lynch.

—— (2001a). 'The impact of ageing population on the economy, a European perspective: from baby boom to baby bust', *Geneva Papers on Risk and Insurance*, 26: 529–46.

—— (2001b). 'Progress report: European pension reforms'. London: Merrill Lynch.

—— and Bergheim, S. (2000). 'German pension reform'. London: Merrill Lynch.

—— and Bowers, D. (1999). 'European pension reforms'. London: Merrill Lynch.

—— and Thomsen, M. (2000). 'Pension Reform in France'. London: Merrill Lynch.

March, J. (1994). *A Primer on Decision Making: How Decisions Happen.* New York: Free Press.

Martin, R. L. (2000). 'Local labour markets: their nature, performance and regulation', in G. L. Clark, M. P. Feldman, and M. Gertler (eds), *Oxford Handbook of Economic Geography* (pp. 455–76). Oxford: Oxford University Press.

—— (2001). 'EMU versus the regions? Regional convergence and divergence in Euroland', *Journal of Economic Geography*, 1: 51–80.

—— and Minns, R. (1995). 'Undermining the financial bases of regions: The spatial structure and implications of the UK pension fund system', *Regional Studies*, 29: 125–44.

Mauro, P. (1995). 'Corruption and growth', *Quarterly Journal of Economics*, 90: 681–712.

Mayer, M. C. J. and Whittington, R. (1999). 'Strategy, structure and "systemness": national institutions and corporate change in France, Germany and the UK, 1950–1993', *Organization Studies*, 20: 933–59.

McConnell, P., Pegg, J., and Zion, D. (1999). *Accounting Issues: Retirement Benefits Impact Operating Income.* New York: Bear Stearns.

—— —— —— (2001a). *Accounting Issues: Pension and Other Retirement Benefits I: A Historical Perspective.* New York: Bear Stearns.

—— —— —— (2001b). *Accounting Issues: Pension and Other Retirement Benefits II: Forecasting 2002 Cost (income).* New York: Bear Stearns.

McDowell, L. (1997). *Capital Culture: Gender at Work in the City.* Oxford: Blackwell Publishers.

McLeay, S., Ordelheide, D., and Young, S. (2000). 'Constituent lobbying and its impact on the development of financial reporting regulations: evidence from Germany', *Accounting, Organizations, and Society*, 25: 79–98.

Miller, D. (2000). *Citizenship and National Identity.* Cambridge: Polity Press.

Miller, P. B. (1987). 'The new pension accounting. Part I', *Journal of Accountancy*, 163: 98–108.

Mitchell, O. S. (1998). 'Administrative costs in public and private retirement systems', in M. Feldstein (ed.), *Privatizing Social Security* (pp. 403–52). Chicago: University of Chicago Press.

—— and Utkus, S. P. (2002). 'Company stock and retirement plan diversification', *PRC WP* 2002–4, Pension Research Council, Wharton School, University of Pennsylvania, Philadelphia.

Mittelstaedt, H. F. and Warshawsky, M. J. (1993). 'The impact of liabilities for retiree health benefits on share prices', *Journal of Risk and Insurance*, 60: 13–35.

Modigliani, F., Ceprini, M., and Muralidhar, A.S. (2001). 'A better solution in the social security crisis: funding with a common portfolio', *Mimeo* 1-01, Cambridge MA: MIT, Sloan School of Management.

Moss, D., Dias, A., and Stephann, B.O. (1997). 'The French pension system: on the verge of retirement', *Case N*9-798-032, Boston: Harvard Business School Publishing.

Munnell, A. (2002). 'Restructuring pensions for the 21st century: the United States debate', *Mimeo*, Chestnut Hill MA: Boston College Carroll School of Management.

Murray, R. (1976). 'Discussion', in *Funding Pensions: Issues and Implications for Financial Markets* (pp. 152–5) (Conference Series No. 16). Boston: Federal Reserve Bank of Boston.

Mussa, M. (2002). 'Argentina and the fund: from triumph to tragedy', *Mimeo*, Washington DC: Institute for International Economics.

Neven, D., Papandropoulas, P., and Seabright, P. (1998). *Trawling for Minnows: European Competition Policy and Agreement Between Firms*. London: Centre for Economic Policy Research.

Nöcker, R. (2000). 'The recent proposals for individual funded pensions in Germany—repeating the UK experience'? London: Centre for Pensions and Social Insurance, Birkbeck College, University of London.

Novak, S. B. (1998). 'A step towards globalization: the move for international accounting standards', *Indiana International and Comparative Law Review*, 1: 203–24.

Nussbaum, W. (1999). *Das System der beruflichen Vorsorge in den USA*. Berne: Haupt.

Nye, J. (2002). *The Paradox of American Power: Why the World's Only Superpower Can't Go It Alone*. New York: Oxford University Press.

O'Barr, W. and Conley, J. M. (1992). *Fortune and Folly*. Homewood IL: Business One Irwin.

O'Neill, P. (2001). 'Financial narratives of the modern corporation', *Journal of Economic Geography*, 1: 181–200.

O'Sullivan, M. (2000). *Contests for Corporate Control; Corporate Governance Economic Performance in the United States and Germany*. Oxford: Oxford University Press.

OECD (1997). *Ageing in OECD Countries: A Critical Policy Challenge*. Paris.

OECD (1998a). *Maintaining Prosperity in an Ageing Society*, Paris.

—— (1998b). *OECD Economic Survey* 1997–1998: Netherlands, Paris.

—— (1999a). *OECD Economic Surveys: France*, Paris.

—— (1999b). *OECD Economic Surveys: Germany*, Paris.

—— (1999c). *OECD in Figures: Statistics on Member Countries*, Paris.

—— (2000). *Reforms for an Ageing Society: Social Issues*, Paris.

Oguchi, N. and Hatta, T. (2001). 'Switching the Japanese social security system from pay-as-you-go to actuarially fair: a simulation analysis'. London: Centre for Economic Policy Research.

Olson, M. (1965). *The Logic of Collective Action*. Cambridge MA: Harvard University Press.

—— (1982). *The Rise and Decline of Nations*. New Haven: Yale University Press.

Orszag, P. E. and Stiglitz, J. E. (1999). 'Rethinking pension reform: ten myths about social security', *Mimeo*, Washington DC: World Bank.

Orszag, P. (2002). 'House "Enron" pension legislation includes troubling provisions that could harm rank-and-file workers', *Mimeo*. Washington DC: Brookings Institution.

Ottaviano, G. I. P. and Thisse, J-F. (2001). 'On economic geography in economic theory: increasing returns and pecuniary externalities', *Journal of Economic Geography*, 1: 153–80.

Palier, B. (2000). '"Defrosting" the French welfare state', *West European Politics*, 23: 113–36.

—— (2002). 'Facing the pension crisis in France', *Mimeo*, Oxford: School of Geography and the Environment, University of Oxford.

Pastor, L. and Stambaugh, R. F. (2001). 'The equity premium and structural breaks', *Journal of Finance*, 56: 1207–39.

Peck, J. (2000). 'Doing regulation', in G. L. Clark, M. P. Feldman, and M. Gertler (eds), *Oxford Handbook of Economic Geography* (pp. 61–80). Oxford: Oxford University Press.

—— and Tickell, A. (2001). 'Neoliberalizing space: the free economy and the penal state', *Mimeo*, Bristol: School of Geographical Sciences, University of Bristol.

Pesando, J. E. (2000). 'The containment of bankruptcy risk in private pension plans', in *Private Pension Systems and Policy Issues No. 1* (pp. 337–70). Paris: OECD.

—— (1992). 'The economic effects of private pensions', in *Private Pensions and Public Policy* (pp. 115–33). Paris: OECD.

Petrone, K. (1999). 'Comparative analysis of IAS 19 (1998) and US GAAP including FASB Statements No. 87 and No. 106', in C. Bloomer (ed.), *The IASC-US Comparison Project: A Report on the Similarities and Differences between IASC Standards and US GAAP* (pp. 231–61). Norwalk: FASB.

Pistor, K. (1999). 'Co-determination in Germany: a socio-political model with governance externalities', in M. Roe and M. Blair (eds), *Employees and Corporate Governance* (pp. 87–103). Washington DC: Brookings Institutions.

Ploug, N. and Kvist, J. (1996). *Social Security in Europe: Development or Dismantlement?* The Hague: Kluwer Law International.

Portes, R. (2001). 'A monetary vision in motion: the European experience', *Discussion Paper* 2954, London: Centre for Economic Policy Research.

—— and Rey, H. (2001). 'The determinants of cross-border equity flows', *Working Paper*, London Business School, London.

Power, M. (1998). 'The audit implosion: regulating risk from the inside'. London: Department of Accounting and Finance, London School of Economics.

Pratt, J. and Zeckhauser, R. (eds) (1985). *Principals and Agents*. Boston: Harvard Business School Press.

PriceWaterhouseCoopers (2001). *The Opacity Index*, New York.

Prigge, S. (1998). 'A survey of German corporate governance', in K. J. Hopt, H. Handa, M. J. Roe, E. Wymeersch, and S. Prigge (eds), *Comparative*

Corporate Governance: The State of the Art and Emerging Research (pp. 943–1043). Oxford: Oxford University Press.

Prins, F. (1999). 'Introduction to the Dutch pension system'. Rijswijk: Vereniging van Bedrijfspensioenfondesn (VB).

Queisser, M. (1996). 'Pensions in Germany', *Mimeo*, Washington DC: World Bank.

—— (1998). 'Pension reform: lessons from Latin America', *Policy Brief* 15, Paris: OECD Development Centre.

Rawls, J. (1971). *A Theory of Justice*. Cambridge MA: Harvard University Press.

Rees, P.H. and Kupiszewski, M. (1999). *Internal Migration and Regional Population Dynamics in Europe: A Synthesis*, Population Studies 32, Strasbourg: Council of Europe Publishing.

Rees, R. (1993). 'Tacit collusion', *Oxford Review of Economic Policy*, 9: 27–40.

—— and Kessner, E. (1999). 'Regulation and efficiency in European insurance markets', *Economic Policy*, 29: 365–99.

Rein, M. and Wadensjo, E. (eds) (1997). *Enterprise and the Welfare State*. Cheltenham: Edward Elgar.

Reynaud, E. (2000). 'Introduction and summary', in E. Reynaud (ed.), *Social Dialogue and Pension Reform* (pp. 1–10). Geneva: International Labor Organisation.

Rhodes, M. (1998). 'Capital unbound? The transformation of European corporate governance', *Journal of European Public Policy*, 5: 406–27.

Rhodes, M. and van Apeldoorn, B. (1998). 'Capital unbound? The transformation of European corporate governance', *Journal of European Public Policy*, 5: 406–27

Richardson, G. (1990). *Information and Investment: A Study of the Working of the Competitive Economy*. Oxford: Clarendon Press.

Roe, M. J. (1994). *Strong Managers, Weak Owners: The Political Roots of American Corporate Finance*. Princeton: Princeton University Press.

—— (1998a). 'German Securities Markets and German Codetermination', in K. J. Hopt, H. Kanda, M. J. Roe, E. Wymeersch, and S. Prigge (eds), *Comparative Corporate Governance: The State of the Art and Emerging Research* (pp. 361–72). Oxford: Oxford University Press.

—— (1998b). 'German codetermination and German securities markets', *Columbia Business Law Review*, 1: 167–83.

Ross, S. (2001). 'Financial regulation in the new millennium', *Geneva Papers on Risk and Insurance*, 26: 8–16.

Salminen, K. (1993). *Pension Schemes in the Making: A Comparative Study of Scandinavian Countries*. Helsinki: Central Pension Security Institute.

Samuelson, P. (1958). 'An exact consumption-loan model of interest with or without the social contrivance of money', *Journal of Political Economy*, 66: 467–82.

Sapir, A., Buigues, P., and Jacquemin, A. (1993). 'European competition policy in manufacturing and services: a two-speed approach'? *Oxford Review of Economic Policy*, 9: 113–32.

Sass, S. (1997). *The Promise of Pensions*. Cambridge MA: Harvard University Press.

Saxenian, A. (1994). *Regional Advantage: Culture and Competition in Silicon Valley and Route* 128. Cambridge MA: Harvard University Press.

Scargill, D. I. (1985). 'The population of France', *Research Paper* 34, Oxford: School of Geography, University of Oxford.

Schama, S. (1996). *Landscape and Memory*. New York: Knopf.

Schaub, A. (1998). 'Competition policy objectives', in C. D. Ehlermann and L. L. Laudati (eds), *European Competition Law Annual* 1997: Objectives of Competition Policy (pp. 119–28). Oxford: Hart Publishing.

Scheiber, S., Hewitt, P., Tuljapurkar, S., Li, N., and Anderson, M. (2000). 'Demographic risk in industrial societies', *World Economics*, 1 (4): 27–72.

Schoenberger, E. (2001). 'Corporate autobiographies: the narrative strategies of corporate strategists', *Journal of Economic Geography*, 1: 277–98.

Schulte, W. and Violi, R. (2001). 'Interactions between cash and derivatives bond markets: some evidence for the euro area', *BIS Papers* 5, Basel: Bank of International Settlements.

Sharpe, W. and Alexander, G.J. (1995). *Investments* (5th edn). Englewood Cliffs: Prentice-Hall.

Shaw, J. (2000). 'The paradox of the "European polity"', in M. G. Cowles and M. Smith (eds), *State of the European Union* 5: *Risks, Reform, Resistance and Revival* (pp. 64–88). Oxford: Oxford University Press.

Shiller, R. (1995). 'Aggregate income risks and hedging mechanisms', *Quarterly Review of Economics and Finance*, 35: 119–52

—— (1999). 'Social security and institutions for intergenerational, intragenerational, and international risk-sharing', *Carnegie-Rochester Conference Series on Public Policy*, 50: 165–204

—— (2000). *Irrational Exuberance*. Princeton: Princeton University Press.

Shleifer, A. (1985). 'A theory of yardstick competition', *Rand Journal of Economics*, 16: 319–27.

Siegel, S. (1996). 'The coming revolution in accounting: the emergence of fair value as the fundamental principle of GAAP', *Wayne Law Review*, 42: 1839–62.

Simon, H. (1956). 'Rational choice and the structure of the environment', *Psychological Review*, 63: 129–18.

Sinn, H-W. (1999). 'The crisis of Germany's pension insurance system and how it can be resolved', *Working Paper* 2175, Centre for Economic Policy Research, London.

Smalhout, J. H. (1996). *The Uncertain Retirement: Securing Pension Promises in a World of Risk*. Chicago: Irwin.

Smith, R. C. and Walter, I. (1997). *Global Banking*. New York: Oxford University Press.

Soros, G. (2002). *On Globalization*. Oxford: Publicaffairs Ltd.

Steinberg, M. I., Arner, D., and Olive, C. D. (1999). 'The development of internationally acceptable accounting standards: a universal language for finance in the 21st century'? *Securities Regulation Law Journal*, 27: 324–65.

Stiglitz, J. (2002). *Globalization and its Discontents.* New York: Norton.

Stone, D. (1999). 'Learning lessons and transferring policy across time, space and disciplines', *Politics*, 19: 51–9.

Story, J. and Walter, I. (1997). *Political Economy of Financial Integration in Europe. The Battle of Systems*. Manchester: Manchester University Press.

Streeck, W. (1997). 'German capitalism: does it exist? Can it survive?' in C. Crouch and W. Streeck (eds), *Political Economy of Modern Capitalism* (pp. 33–54). London: Sage.

Sullerot, E. (1978). *La Demographie de la France: Bilan et Perspectives*, Counseil Economique et Social. Paris: La Documentation Francaise.

Supiot, A. (2001). *Beyond Employment: Changes in Work and the Future of Labour Law in Europe*. Oxford: Oxford University Press.

Swaan, A. (1998). *In Care of the State: Health Care, Education, and Welfare in Europe and the USA in the Modern Era*. Oxford: Polity Press.

Swaine, E. T. (2000). 'Subsiduarity and self-interest: federalism at the European Court of Justice', *Harvard International Law Journal*, 41: 1–128.

Swyngedouw, E. (2000). 'Elite power, global forces, and the political economy of "glocal" development', in G. L. Clark, M. P. Feldman, and M. Gertler (eds), *Oxford Handbook of Economic Geography* (pp. 541–58). Oxford: Oxford University Press.

Szasz, A. (1999). *The Road to European Monetary Union*. Basingstoke: Macmillan.

Tabuchi, T. (1998). 'Urban agglomeration and dispersion: a synthesis of Alonso and Krugman', *Journal of Urban Economics*, 44: 333–51.

Taverne, D. (2000). *Can Europe Pay for its Pensions?* London: Federal Trust.

Taylor-Gooby, P. (1999). 'Policy change at a time of retrenchment: recent pension reform in France, Germany, Italy and the UK', *Social Policy and Administration*, 33: 1–19.

Teece, D. (2000). *Managing Intellectual Capital*. Oxford: Oxford University Press.

Thaler, R. (1992). *The Winner's Curse: Paradoxes and Anomalies in Economic Life*. New York: Free Press.

Thomson, M. (1999). 'French public opinion on pensions'. London: Global Securities Research & Economics Group, Merrill Lynch.

Thrift, N. (2001). '"It's the romance, not the finance, that makes the business worth pursuing": disclosing a new market culture'. Bristol: School of Geographical Sciences, University of Bristol.

Tickell, A. (2000). 'Finance and localities', in G.L. Clark, M. Feldman, and M.S. Gertler (eds), *Oxford Handbook of Economic Geography* (pp. 230–51). Oxford: Oxford University Press.

Towers Perrin (2000). 'Another Year of Big Gains for Pension Plans', New York (available at http://www.towers.com).

UNICE (1998). *Benchmarking Europe's Competitiveness: From Analysis to Action*. Brussels: Union of Industrial and Employer's Confederations of Europe.

United Nations (various years). *Year Book*. New York.

US Board of Trustees (2002). *The Annual Report of the Board of Trustees of the Federal Old-Age and Survivors Insurance and Disability Insurance Trust Funds*, Washington DC.

US Government (2001). *Private Pensions: Issues of Coverage and Increasing Contribution Limits for Defined Contribution Plans*. GAO-01-846. Washington DC: General Accounting Office.

Valdes-Prieto, S. (ed.) (1997). *The Economics of Pensions*. Cambridge: Cambridge University Press.

van Amersfoort, H. (1999). 'International migration and civil rights: the dilemmas of migration control in an age of globalization' in E. Guild (ed.), *The Legal Framework and Social Consequences of Free Movement of Persons in the European Union* (pp. 73–88). London: Kluwer Publishers.

Verzekeringskamer (1999). *Financiele Gegevens Pensioenfondsen*. Apeldoorn.

Vickers, J. (1997). 'Regulation, competition and the structure of prices', *Oxford Review of Economic Policy*, 13: 15–26.

Visco, I. (2001). 'Paying for pensions: how important is economic growth'? *Banca Nazionale del Lavoro Quarterly Review*, 216: 73–102.

Viscusi, W. K., Vernon, J. M., and Harrington, J. E. (1995). *Economics of Regulation and Antitrust* (2nd edn). Cambridge MA: MIT Press.

Waddington, J. and Hoffman, R. (eds) (2001). *Trade Unions in Europe: Facing Challenges and Searching for Solutions*. Brussels: European Trade Union Institute.

Wang, Z. (2001). 'Discussion', *Journal of Finance*, 56: 1240–45.

Warf, B. (2000). 'New York: the Big Apple in the 1990s', *Geoforum*, 31: 487–99.

Warshawsky, M. J., Mittelstaedt, H. F., and Cristea, C. (1993). 'Recognising retiree health benefits: the effects of SFAS 106', *Financial Management* (Summer): 188–99.

Waterson, M. (1984). *Economic Theory of the Industry*. Cambridge: Cambridge University Press.

Watson Wyatt (1998). Executive Summary: The World's Major Savings Markets. Reigate.

—— (2000). Pension income: here today, here tomorrow. Available at http://www.watsonwyatt.com/homepage/us/new/insider/new/2000/2000_0503.asp.

Weiler, J. H. H. (2000). 'Cain and Abel—convergence and divergence in international trade law' in J. H. H. Weiler (ed.), *The EU, the WTO, and the NAFTA: Towards a Common Law of International Trade* (pp. 1–4). Oxford: Oxford University Press.

Weiner, J. (1999). *Globalization and the Harmonization of Law*. London: Pinter.

Weiss, M. (1995). *Labour Law and Industrial Relations in Germany*. Deventer: Kluwer Publishers.

Weiss, R. (1976). 'Private pensions: the impact of ERISA on the growth of retirement funds' in *Funding Pensions: Issues and Implications for Financial Markets* (pp. 137–51). Conference Series No. 16. Boston: Federal Reserve Bank of Boston.

Whitehouse, E. (2000). 'Paying for pensions: An international comparison of administrative charges in funded retirement-income systems', *Occasional Paper* 13, London: Financial Services Authority.

Whiteside, N. (2000). 'From full employment to flexibility: Britain and France in comparison, 1960–2000', in *After Full Employment: European Discourses on Work and Flexibility* (pp. 107–33). Oxford: PIE-Peter Lang.

Whitley, R. (1999). *Divergent Capitalism: The Social Structuring and Change of Business Systems*. Oxford: Oxford University Press.

Winchester, H. (1993). *Contemporary France*. Harlow: Longman.

Wójcik, D. (2001a). 'Cross-border corporate ownership in Europe is not consistent with an integrated capital market: evidence from portfolio and industrial holdings', *Working Paper* 01–06, School of Geography and the Environment, University of Oxford, Oxford.

—— (2001b). 'Regions are the building blocks of the German capital market', *Working Paper* 01–12, School of Geography and the Environment, Oxford University, Oxford.

—— (2002). 'The emerging capital market in Germany: a geographical perspective on cross-holding', *Working Paper* 02-01, School of Geography and the Environment, Oxford University, Oxford.

Wolf, M. (2000). 'The lure of the American way', *The Financial Times*, 1 November: 25.

World Bank (1994). *Averting the Old Age Crisis*, Washington DC.

World Bank (2000). *Population Projections*, Washington DC.

Zanni, G. (2001). 'Euro area special: re-centering the debate on pensions.' London: Economic Research, Credit Suisse First Boston.

CITATION INDEX

INDEX